Trial of Translation

Trial of Translation

An Examination of 1 Corinthians 6:9 in the
Vernacular Bibles of the Early Modern Period

Adam L. Wirrig

PICKWICK *Publications* · Eugene, Oregon

TRIAL OF TRANSLATION
An Examination of 1 Corinthians 6:9 in the Vernacular Bibles
of the Early Modern Period

Pickwick Publications
An Imprint of Wipf and Stock Publishers
199 W. 8th Ave., Suite 3
Eugene, OR 97401

www.wipfandstock.com

PAPERBACK ISBN: 978-1-7252-7756-4
HARDCOVER ISBN: 978-1-7252-7754-0
EBOOK ISBN: 978-1-7252-7755-7

Cataloguing-in-Publication data:

Names: Wirrig, Adam L., author.

Title: Trial of translation : an examination of 1 Corinthians 6:9 in the vernacular Bibles of the early modern period / by Adam L. Wirrig.

Description: Eugene, OR: Pickwick Publications, 2022 | Includes bibliographical references.

Identifiers: ISBN 978-1-7252-7756-4 (paperback) | ISBN 978-1-7252-7754-0 (hardcover) | ISBN 978-1-7252-7755-7 (ebook)

Subjects: LCSH: Bible—Versions—History. | Bible—Corinthians, 1st, VI, 9—Criticism, interpretation, etc.—Europe—History—16th century. | Bible—Corinthians, 1st, VI, 9—Criticism, interpretation, etc.—Europe—History—17th century.

Classification: BS450 W57 2022 (print) | BS450 (ebook)

03/11/22

To Dave, who taught me the love of exegetical study.

David, who kindled my love of history.

Bill and Jane, who never gave up on an occasionally
exasperating doctoral student.

Contents

Introduction: Historical Significance and Difficulty | 1

CHAPTER ONE
Germany: Reformation, Reticence, and Indictments | 11

CHAPTER TWO
France: Malignment and Alignment across a Broad Reformation | 40

CHAPTER THREE
England: Twists, Turns, Plots and Problems | 79

CHAPTER FOUR
Italy: Hotbed of Sodomy, or. . . not? | 114

Conclusion | 147

Bibliography | 157

Introduction: Historical Significance
and Difficulty

I nterpreting the text of the Bible has vexed many people for almost two millennia. In biblical texts, one finds a juxtaposition of infinite faith and finite human enterprise, history, and the present day. For translators and interpreters, this means that matters of philology, lexicography and palaeography mingle with matters of soul, self and eternity. Moreover, questions of confessional allegiance and identity require both readers and translators to understand and, consequently, to translate, passages in specific ways, further confusing this already difficult venture. Such a milieu has thus created a process that has spawned the interpretation and re-interpretation of texts on an on-going historical basis. Far from invalidating textual understanding, with "old" yielding to "new," this process of interpretation and re-interpretation has, in a historical sense, provided excellent opportunities to understand what a particular text did or did not mean within given societies at times.

The sixteenth and seventeenth centuries constituted a significant era of production for vernacular versions of the Bible.[1] Critical to these productions was the desire of Protestant reformers to translate the Bible into languages that could be representative of orthodoxy and lead to orthopraxy for the laity.[2] To accomplish this, the reformers adopted the humanist initia-

---

1. One cannot deny that there were a few versions of the Bible produced prior to the sixteenth century. While some of these Bibles, such as Wycliffe's, could be seen as forerunners of the Bibles produced during both the Protestant Reformation and the wider enlightenment, they were mainly versions of Jerome's Vulgate. The simplification of printing methods and, as discussed below, the *ad fontes* initiative of both humanism and the Protestant reformers resulted in a deluge of publications.

2. This engagement, largely begun by both the Lutheran and the Calvinist streams of the reformation, developed in vastly different ways. Inevitably, personal reading and interpretations created the distinct possibility of incorrect interpretations and the promulgation of heterodoxy. In response, the Lutherans eventually dissuaded personal reading of the Bible by individuals who were outside of the church or who did not

tive of returning *ad fontes*, or to the sources, of biblical writings.[3] *Ad fontes* scholarship was not solely a construct of Reformation ideology, but was instead a wider humanist initiative that sought to return classical understanding to early modern life, above and beyond the "dark" of medieval thought.[4] For the Protestant reformers, who were seeking to substantiate their break with the Roman church, such an engagement focused on their encountering the text in a "trilingual" manner incorporating Latin, Koine Greek and ancient Hebrew.[5] Though nouveau in particular application, this *ad fontes* approach to scholarship should not be seen as being entirely different from the preceding tradition.

Although the *ad fontes* initiatives of Luther, Calvin, Tyndale, and others received considerable attention and importance within the Protestant Reformation, they were not entirely out of line with previous medieval standards. The four-fold method of interpretation, perhaps best described by Gregory the Great and later by Nicholas of Lyra, emphasized several elements that subsequent Protestant reformers would adopt in their translations of biblical texts.[6] This method emphasized that the biblical texts should be encountered and explained in terms of four conceptual realities, namely literal, allegorical, topological, and anagogical. The reformers in the sixteenth and seventeenth centuries, in their *ad fontes* initiative, might thus be seen as descendants of Medieval biblical interpretation, and not necessarily as the inventors of a completely new system of hermeneutics.[7]

---

have theological learning. Instead, the text of the Bible was engaged with by individuals through the homilies of the priest and the learning of the catechism. Calvinism, on the other hand, continued to advocate individual reading of and engagement with the biblical text. To encourage the proper translation and interpretation of the text, the Genevan reformers created a textual apparatus that amplified, cross-referenced, and corroborated the biblical text. See O'Sullivan, "Introduction," 2–3 and Higman, "Without Great Effort and With Pleasure," 115, 120.

3. See Rummel, "Renaissance Humanists," 281.

4. As Tracy has pointed out, the humanists saw the medieval Thomistic understanding of Scripture as excessively rationalistic and presumptuous regarding the importance of human law and reason. See Tracy, "Ad Fontes," 252.

5. Griffiths, "Introduction," 2.

6. See Muller, "View from the Middle Ages," 9. Luther's exegetical strategies were largely a product of the methodologies previously found in late medieval thought, particularly those of Jean Gerson, as will be seen later in this study. The primary difference between these two approaches is Gerson's historical emphasis and Luther's focus on grammar and what has been called the *sensus literalis*. See Burrows, "Jean Gerson on the 'Traditional Sense' of Scripture as an Argument for an Ecclesial Hermeneutic," 154, 159.

7. Certainly, some authors, such as Luther, would argue at times that theirs was a new advent and a return to the original meanings of the texts. All the same, in wider context, even Luther would be hard pressed to refer to the reformers as anything

New system or not, scholars such as Erasmus, LeFevre, and Pagnini led a movement that, at least on paper, was concerned with wresting textual interpretation from the scholastic doctors of the church and returning it to the languages in which it originated.[8] The fruits of these labours culminated in multiple, so-called improved/corrected re-issuings of the Latin Vulgate Bible, together with humanist editions of the Greek and Hebrew texts. These Greek, Hebrew and novi-Latin texts served as the basis of and framework for others, such as Luther and the later Tyndale, moving the biblical text into popular language.[9] This act of moving the Bible from Latin into its original languages and then to the language of common society was, at its core, rooted in the Protestant doctrine of *sola scriptura*.[10] This doctrine of "scripture alone" required potential, although not unmitigated, access to the Bible in popular languages for the wider populace. In addition to such access, to authenticate originality, these new vernaculars required a compilation of supporting documents, lexicons, commentaries and other writings, which both grounded and amplified the humanist venture.[11] Overall, these actions created the first systematic attempt, both in commentary and presentation, to return to the "original meaning" and to present that to the "vulgar masses" since the time of Saint Jerome.[12]

However, this appetite for vernacular translation should not be taken to imply that the action was always simple. As with any new idea or venture, there were proponents and opponents of the processof vernacular translations. Some scholars, perhaps most famously Thomas More, opined that the Protestant vernacular machine was simply a means to co-opt the Bible into

other than renaissance evolutions of their medieval predecessors. See O'Sullivan, "Introduction," 2.

8. See Griffiths, "Introduction," 1–3. Reformers, such as Urbanus Rhegius, were adamant in their insistence that not to engage with biblical texts in their original languages rendered the reader as a foreigner to the texts. Thus, primacy was placed upon learning and applying original languages, particularly Hebrew and Greek. See Hendrix, "Use of Scripture in Establishing Protestantism," 38.

9. The most prominent examples of these texts are The Complutensian Polyglot of 1514 and Desiderius Erasmus' *Novum Instrumentum Omne* published in 1516. See *Biblia Polyglotta*, and Erasmus, *Novum Instrumentum Omne*.

10. See O'Sullivan, "Introduction," 1.

11. These lexical aids stand, in this study, as something of a contextual wildcard. Often lacking their own historiography, these texts, while providing critical information, are not easily probed for author bias or interpretive methods as vernacular Bibles might be.

12. Again, this is not to say that no Bibles were being issued prior to the Protestant reformation. These were, however, the first systematic attempts to create a text that returned to the original meaning and was not a continuance or development of the Latin Vulgate. See Tracy, "Ad Fontes," 254.

a social and political venture that re-translated the ancient sacred text for modern gain.[13] Without doubt, discrepancies about difficult translations, such as the somewhat convoluted debate about "priests" or "elders," seem to point towards both a text and an interpretive method that were hotly contested and fiercely important.[14] What seems apparent in a number of these situations is that the debate in this early modern world of the sixteenth and seventeenth centuries tended to descend into confessional rigour and polemic in short order. Moreover, the biblical text itself was not always, if ever, an easy discussion even amongst Protestants. One need not look too far into any of the Protestant histories to find instances of differing interpretations impacting on differing theological viewpoints.[15] In summary, when examining the concepts of "who, how, what, or why," reformers' translations of difficult or sensitive passages within the biblical text is a venture often fraught with confessional bias, political machinations, and perhaps more than a little personal interference.

Taking all of this into consideration, one might be tempted to view the sixteenth and seventeenth centuries as times of both great progress and production, and yet also as a period of utmost contention regarding the biblical text. Instead of producing texts that brought both the laity and the learned closer to original meaning, one might assume that the Protestant venture instead deeply confessionalized and largely personalized the Bible through the act of vernacular translation. To validate or castigate this thought

13. More was a classic example of someone who adopted a hermeneutic of suspicion regarding Protestant biblical production, with good reason. As will be seen in a later chapter of this study, the act and art of biblical interpretation, particularly in sixteenth and seventeenth century England, was one that often, at least on the surface, seemed quite a political enterprise. More's ire was particularly pointed around the vernacular translation of William Tyndale, whom he viewed as not translating from one book to another, but instead producing a new work for his own interests. See Duerden, "Equivalence or Power? Authority and Reformation Bible Translation," 9–13.

14. This discrepancy centered on the Koine Greek term πρεσβυτερος, which was previously rendered as "priest" within the Latin Vulgate and later rendered as "elder" within several Protestant texts. Whether the word was translated to original meaning or was co-opted to be a not-so-subtle jibe at the hierarchy of the Roman church made up a considerable amount of debate between Tyndale and opponents. See Moynahan, *William Tyndale*, 72.

15. This difference might again be highlighted through the discrepancies centered around πρεσβυτερος within the Protestant reformation. The Church of England was keen to keep the term defined as "priest" within both the Thirty-Nine Articles and also within the Book of Common Prayer. See Buchanan *A to Z of Anglicanism*, 154. One might also look to the disagreeements between Luther and Zwingli within the Colloquy of Marburg as strong evidence that, even amongst the titans of the Protestant reformation, there was considerable difference in thought over biblical translation and understanding.

further, one must seek out and engage with a sample text within the world of this vernacular translation. This sample text must be both lexically difficult, requiring considerable philological resources from *ad fontes* translators, and theologically important enough to occasion some form of commentary from the leading thinkers of the day. Such a passage is 1 Corinthians 6:9, as it is at once difficult to interpret due to complex historicity and problematic neologisms, and yet holds direct cultural, social, and personal applications for both translators and readers. Whereas debates about "priests" and "elders" were important to the life and work of the church within the sixteenth and seventeenth centuries, in 1st Corinthians 6:9, one finds a debate on just who might inherit eternity.

Encountered in its Koine Greek rendering, 1 Corinthians 6:9 provides a detailed list of "those who will not inherit the "Kingdom of Heaven," and reads: ἢ οὐκ οἴδατε ὅτι ἄδικοι θεοῦ βασιλείαν οὐ κληρονομήσουσιν; μὴ πλαν ᾶσθε: οὔτε πόρνοι οὔτε εἰδωλολάτραι οὔτεμοιχοὶ οὔτε μαλακοὶ οὔτε ἀρσενοκ οῖται.[16] While most of the malefactors to be excluded from heaven are easily identified in this text, the clause οὔτε μαλακοὶ οὔτε ἀρσενοκοῖται is decidedly ambiguous.[17] In this clause, the apostle Paul presents two words, one of which is vague and has various definitions in Koine, while the other is a neologism of the apostle's making.[18] Thus, these two terms, one blandly vague and the

16. Aland et al., *Greek New Testament 4th ed.*, 578.

17. Paul is thought to have derived these from common lists of forbidden excesses, perhaps from those put forward by the Stoics. See Wibbing, "Die Dualistische Struktur der Paulinischen Teugend und Lasterkataloge," 108–14. Nissinen pointed out that there is considerable debate regarding whether Ἄρσεν can be considered the subject or object of κοιτε. This is quite significant. Thus, it is unclear whether the term implies "one who lies with men" or "a male who lies." Nissinen also noted that the term could have appeared, as Robin Scroggs suggested, as a Greek approximation of the Hebrew prohibitions in Lev 18:22 and 20:10. See Nissinen, *Homoeroticism in the Biblical World*, 113–14, 116. See also Scroggs, *New Testament and Homosexuality*, 83. It is worth noting that Boswell did argue that the term should be understood as subject and not object. See Boswell, *Christianity, Homosexuality, and Social Tolerance*, 350–52.

18. This neologism is particularly vexing, as terms such as χινεαδυς were available in the first century. The term is thought to be, in terms of its root, a combination of the Koine words αρσεν (man) and κοιτες (bed). The Didache does echo some of 1 Cor 6:9 but leaves out οὔτε μαλακοὶ οὔτε ἀρσενοκοῖται. Whether this is intentional or not is difficult to say. Nonetheless, this simply serves to underscore the scant employment of the term throughout antiquity. See ΔΙΔΑΧΗ ΤΩΝ ΔΩΔΕΚΑ ΑΠΟΣΤΟΛΩΝ: *The Teaching of the Twelve Apostoles*, 5:1–2. Nissinen also noted that the term does not appear in any of the church fathers' works, particularly not in the writings Clement of Alexandria and John of Chrysostom who discussed same-sex acts much more frequently than did their contemporaries. See Nissinen, *Homoeroticism*, 115. For a further study on the lexical evolution and understanding ofοὔτε μαλακοὶ οὔτε ἀρσενοκοῖται, please see Liddell et al., *Greek-English Lexicon*, 1076–77; Liddell and Scott, *Greek-English Lexicon American Edition*, 881; Bauer, *Griechisch-deutsches Worterbuchzu den Schriften des neuen*

other hyper-specialized represent a passage in which great lexical care and consideration must have been required by the Protestant reformers. Again, the overall context of 1 Corinthians 6:9 highlights the gravity and necessity of diligently trying to define οὔτε μαλακοὶ οὔτε ἀρσενοκοῖται, particularly within its original context. The apostle Paul included these characters in a list of those who would not inherit the Kingdom of Heaven. At worst, failing to understand Paul could result in eternal damnation. At the very least, ignorance could lead concerned individuals—and societies/states—to fail to control and prevent such activities, perhaps facing subsequent social disorder and discord. That these words have, for a vast portion of the history of Christianity as seen below, been thought to reference sex and sexuality, themes that were in considerable flux for much of the Reformation, makes this text even more intriguing.

The Reformation represents a significant disruption in the theology and practice of the previous millennia. Sexuality, particularly the reconstitution of sex and sexual function, was a critical aspect of the Protestant movement. Defining who and what was sexually licit exercised the Reformers, who were reacting against the perceived failures of Catholic celibacy, greatly. Most notably, the venerated sexuality of the celibate priest was denounced as an abomination.[19] Instead, sexuality and sexual function were to be embraced by all men including, and perhaps most specifically, the clergy.[20] As 1 Corinthians 6:9 seems to imply actions of illicit sex, a type so serious it could exclude one from the Kingdom of Heaven, this might only have amplified its importance and the difficulty for reformers.[21]

In addition to this question of sexual licitness, there is also a significant question of gender in οὔτε μαλακοὶ οὔτε ἀρσενοκοῖται. Defining which

---

Testaments und der ubrigenurchristlichen Literatur, 172, 767; Alexander Souter, *Pocket Lexicon to the Greek New Testament*, 38, 151; Thayer, *Greek English Lexicon of the New Testament*, 75, 387; and Bauer et al., *Greek English Lexicon of the New Testament and other Early Christian Literature*, 135, 613.

19. John Bale saw all Papists as potential sodomites; the celibacy of Catholic priests and religious orders was equivalent to sexual disorder. See Betteridge, "Sodomy in and Out of the Chronicle," 12–13.

20. See Harrington, *Reordering Marriage and Society in Reformation Germany*, 61; Parish, *Clerical Celibacy in the West C. 1100–1700*, 123–25; and Stephenson, *Performing the Reformation*, 72–73.

21. Such an importance has been thoroughly summed up in the writings of Diarmaid MacCulloch and his tome concerning the reformation. In several chapters, MacCulloch notes the gravity of sexual reformation as being central to both the Protestant and Counter Reformations and as being of societal importance due to the humanist recovery of classical literature that was often more open to differences of sexual expression than late medieval writings might have been. See MacCulloch, *Reformation*, 599–607, 620–29.

men, the type of men, or even whether the referents were only men, is an important element for understanding *οὔτε μαλακοὶ οὔτε ἀρσενοκοῖται*. The world of the Protestant Reformation, in addition to providing biblical translations that attempted to relay original meaning and social structures that redressed sexual propriety, was also greatly concerned with defining—or re-defining—the "proper" male. Authors such as Scott Hendrix and Raymond Mentzer have detailed that Protestant reforms greatly changed the ways in which men—from across Europe—could and should respond to their own masculinity.[22] During the Reformation, the words of the Bible and the men who heard them were new and changing creatures, both seeking to return to their original biblical meaning and "godly purpose." Were *οὔτε μαλακοὶ οὔτε ἀρσενοκοῖται* meant to deal with the portrayal and implementation of masculinity, together with the determinants for eternal salvation, its importance for the Reformation, with its desire to recast masculinity and enable salvific reality, would seem paramount. Thus, understanding what Paul meant must have been both a difficult and a critically necessary exercise for the early modern period; thus, one would expect to find it studied in some detail by the Reformers.[23]

In what follows, it will become clear that the Protestant Reformation engaged with these concerns, in some places providing a detailed analysis of just what *οὔτε μαλακοὶ οὔτε ἀρσενοκοῖται* meant, although not always explicitly, via the vernacular biblical text. In examining this tension, the study will review an effort that both complimented and criticized the *ad fontes* initiative. Ultimately, as will be presented, the writings of the reformers detailed *ουτεοὔτε μαλακοὶ οὔτε ἀρσενοκοῖται* as a phrase that vacillated

---

22. While the Protestant Reformation did not change the overall state of men and women, it certainly altered the societal perceptions of how each should behave in terms of propriety. That is, men and women were still men and women according to the Protestant ideology. However, they were expected and allowed differing options and paths to engage their countenances. This is covered succinctly in Hendrix, "Masculinity and Patriarchy in Reformation Germany," 71–89, and Mentzer, "Masculinity and the Reformed Tradition in France," 120–39.

23. In fact, one might well expect this passage to create a considerable amount of confessional polarization, with the Genevans possibly taking stricter view than the English, and so on. As the study below will show, although this passage received attention from and treatment by several leading reformers, it did not generate the confessional debate that other complicated texts did. The reason for such reticence is debatable. On one hand, the passage may not have been considered important by the reformers, with any implication of sexuality being sufficiently encompassed within the Levitical code. On the other hand, it might have been that the passage was sufficiently lexically difficult for them to hedge their bets and say as little as possible to avoid putting their foot in it. Furthermore, it might be that the passage, by virtue of the gravity attributed to its subject matter, was a hushed dialogue.

between vexation and validation, involving both a functional definition and a great number of caveats as well. As such, 1 Corinthians 6:9, particularly the phrase οὔτε μαλακοὶ οὔτε ἀρσενοκοῖται, will present a unique opportunity to examine a philologically challenging, extremely important passage to understand exactly what the reformers meant with their interpretations. Such an engagement will then enable the study to detail whether, and to what degree, the vernacular enterprise of the Protestant movement was bound to political and confessional considerations. This, in turn, will allow the study to demonstrate whether a clear meaning of Scripture can truly be discerned in the sixteenth and seventeenth century Protestant reformations, or whether it was, in fact, a muddled and murky venture.

To accomplish this project, the study will need to engage with several items in various ways. Firstly, the study will seek to place the text within the vernacular biblical translations of leading Protestant reformers of the sixteenth and seventeenth centuries. Where critical reformers, such as John Calvin, failed to issue personal vernaculars, the study will use their prime commentary works to support other vernacular translations.

Upon stating its findings regarding vernacular translation, the study will then contextualize the translations with lexical backgrounds. This lexical contextualisation will be created using the lexicons and dictionaries that were prominent in the world of the Protestant reformers. In this process, the study will, admittedly, preface lexicons and lexical functions as contextual aids. The rationale for this choice centres on the fact that these lexicons and dictionaries were works in which the words of vernacular translation were so often succinctly placed with the definitions and understandings that made them so powerful within society. This lexical contextualisation will therefore provide an explicit understanding of how the words of the Protestant translators might have been understood within their wider societies. Moreover, the study will work to develop this contextualisation in a historical sense, engaging with works in successive historical senses and creating a history of the word in the sixteenth and seventeenth centuries. In prefacing lexical works, the study will largely choose not to engage with sermons, lectures and other texts that, although prominent within the Protestant Reformation, were subject to great personalisation and confessionalisation by their writers and which, when dealing with sexual matters, were notoriously circumspect or even obtuse.[24] The goal of this exclusion will be to create a

---

24. A study of the selected text could, with little doubt, lead to a substantial study on sexual theory in the early modern period. This study, as useful as it might be for robust contextualization, would be sizeable to the point of detraction from the current study. Moreover, the study can succinctly define οὔτε μαλακοὶ οὔτε ἀρσενοκοῖται in lexical and social contexts. Sexual theory would, again, amplify these findings, but is

"clean" understanding of textual interpretation that relies little, if at all, upon the theological proclivities of those performing the act of translation.[25] The study will, however, seek to take its lexical understandings and further contextualize them through a search for persons and societal instances that referenced or echoed such understandings. Specifically, the study will focus on legal cases and standing, as these were situations in which words, definitions and understanding worked together to illustrate a societal understanding of many "who would not inherit the Kingdom of Heaven" in a very real sense, often from the words that were ascribed to a person or persons. Based on these findings, the study will examine whether the vernacular translations of the reformers were reflective of genuine textual originality, or if their translations were driven by confessional and socio-political biases. Such results, in addition to defining a problematic phrase, should speak to both the efficacy of the translational task the reformers undertook and the subsequent criticism it engendered.

---

not necessarily critical to level them outright.

25. Admittedly, there is an element of theological inclination that will never truly be separated from the words of the translators. Again, there is an inescapable reality that, to some extent, confessional attitudes and political exigency drove some elements of biblical interpretation. Nonetheless, while certainly acknowledging this, the study will try not to base its understandings of the offered words on confessional extrapolations that were often found within sermons, lectures, and general addresses. See Duerden, "Equivalence," 9.

CHAPTER ONE

Germany: Reformation, Reticence, and Indictment

Any examination of vernacular Bibles from the early modern period must begin with Martin Luther's 1522 *Neuen Testament*. Luther's vernacular testament was the first testament translated into German that did not rely on the Vulgate, but was instead an attempt to return *ad fontes*, to the sources, using the most scholarly editions of the original Greek and Hebrew texts. Moreover, while other vernacular Bibles appeared in Reformation Germany, most were largely based on Luther's translation, thus giving Luther's work predominance.[1] Luther, as previously touched upon in the introduction, was interested in garnering a literal understanding of the biblical text but was also not outside the bounds of previous medieval methodology. Largely following the four-fold method of interpretation, Luther often simply amplified the literal and tropological senses rather than the anagogical or allegorical ones.[2] Thus, one might posit that Luther was interested in creating a biblical interpretation that was both historically accurate and, at least in some respect, historically based on acceptable modes of translation. Ultimately, Luther's goal was to convert the text into readable and understandable German, a German that could include both vernacular and colloquial renderings.[3] This task, admirable though it might have been, brought about some considerable issues in the translation of problematic verses such as 1 Corinthians 6:9.

1. Flood, "Martin Luther's Bible in its German and European Context," 57. Luther's translation is later echoed by Emser, even in his 1551 translation of the New Testament, which was quite anti-Lutheran. See Emser et al., *Das Naw Testament nach lawt der Christliche kirchen bewerte text, corrigirt, vu widerumb zu recht gebracht*, Vii^v; and Emser, *Das new Testament, so durch den hochgelerten Hieronymum Emser seligen verteutscht, etc*, 259.

2. As Gritsch noted, Luther was a well-schooled adherent of Lyra's methodology. See Gritsch, "Luther's Humor as a Tool for Interpreting Scripture," 196.

3. Flood, "Luther," 63–65 and O'Sullivan, "Introduction," 2.

From the fourteenth century, at the very least, one of the common interpretative practices for problematic texts, particularly those that spoke of sexual sin, was to cloak interpretation or exegesis in obscurity, thus rendering them only transparent to the learned.[4] This culture of secrecy, particularly regarding sex, derived from medieval German exegetes such as Berthold of Regensburg, Ulrich of Pottenstein, and Nikolaus of Dinkelsbuhl.[5] All of these commentators advocated silence or reticence when discussing sexual deviancy or sins that were *contra naturam* (i.e., sodomy). In place of any direct dialogue concerning sexual sins, particularly those concerning the *sodomitch*, or sodomite, there were creative and colourful euphemisms. Generic terms from the Middle Ages, such as *kezzer* (heretic) or *verwazenketzerie* (damned heresy) were employed to discuss actions of sodomy and sins *contra naturam*.[6] These terms did not refer to a specific person or action, but instead alluded to a nebular conceptualisation of construct. Luther's translation both continued and departed from this previous practice, listing on one hand a nebulous type of person and, on the other, a new and very narrow understanding. Moreover, Luther's translation, while incorporating *ad fontes* elements, was also less than explicit regarding how the reader might understand 1 Corinthians 6:9.[7]

With reference to 1 Corinthians 6:9, Luther translated οὔτε μαλακοὶ οὔτεἀρσενοκοῖται as *nocht die weichling und nocht die knabenschender*.[8] In this translation, Luther seems to have been painfully true to the apostle Paul, using both an equivalently imprecise word to translate the μαλακοὶand a neologism all his own for the ἀρσενοκοῖται. Taken at its most literal, the *weiche* was that which was soft, weak, or foolish. As with the original Koine term for the μαλακοὶ, the noun *weiche* could refer to physical, emotional, animate, or inanimate objects.[9] While there were many options for defining the *weiche*, the *knabenschender* was another story entirely. The word *knabenschender* was a combination of the terms for "boy," particularly a young boy, and "shame, abuse, the genitals, and

---

4. Puff, *Sodomy in Reformation Germany and Switzerland*, 23–25.

5. Puff, *Sodomy*, 55–67.

6. Spreitzer, *Die stumme Stunde*, 119–20.

7. Whether Luther intended his readers to be lay people or clerics is open to debate. Lutheranism began by encouraging individual reading of the Bible, but quickly turned to discouraging unlearned readings in favor of the catechism and weekly homily. See O'Sullivan, "Introduction," 3.

8. Luther, *Das Gantz Neüw Testamet Recht Grüntlich Teutscht*. I am using a later version than Luther's original Wittenberg copy. This is mainly due to issues of location, not translation.

9. Grim and Grimm, *Deutsches Worterbuch*, 11:1311–23.

stigma."[10] This compound neologism, by virtue of its root words, conjures up images of sex and sexuality, particularly pederasty, within the reader. Nonetheless, defining how, or if, Luther understood the term to imply a specific sort of sexual misconduct is problematic.

Contextualising Luther's vernacular translation is a difficult enterprise. Although Luther seemed dedicated to providing a translation that was meaningful, applicable, and powerful, he was somewhat coy about exactly what he intended *weiche* and *knabenschender* to imply. The two terms, again, indicated those who would not inherit the Kingdom of Heaven; those who could, as it were, never be brought to salvation. Thus, one might expect Luther, as a pastorally minded reformer, to elucidate exactly what he understood these terms to mean for the average German. This, however, was simply not the case. Luther never discussed the *weiche* or the *knabenschender* directly within his entire corpus of writings. Thus, understanding who or what Luther himself meant his terms to mean is virtually impossible.

It is possible; perhaps even likely, that Luther was anticipating his audience to decipher his words via contextual and cultural clues. It is also equally probable that the text was not particularly important to Luther, as the Holiness Code of Leviticus provided ample fodder for sexual regulation for the reformers.[11] Nonetheless, in the context of this study, Luther was frustratingly obscurantist about precisely who or what he intended the *weichling,* and particularly the *knabenschender,* to describe. Thus, one should note two things: firstly, Luther's vernacular gave names to the malefactors in 1 Corinthians 6:9 and therefore adhered to the Protestant and humanist concept of *ad fontes* vernacular translation. Luther was again painfully true to the Pauline text by substituting neologism for neologism. Nonetheless, Luther seemed tacitly to follow previous conventions

10. Lexer, *Mittlehoch deutsches Handworterbuch,* 2:655–56.

11. Luther does use the term *knaben* in another part of the sodomy proscriptions of Lev 18:22, where he uses *knaben* to say *du sollst nicht beim Knaben liegen wie beim Weibe.* Thus, in 1 Cor 6:9, one might be tempted to see Luther as extrapolating or continuing his prohibition from Lev 18:22, with *knabenschender* being a logical extension of *knaben.* This, however, is problematic as it presupposes that the singular *knaben* and the compound *knabenschender* meant the same thing. *Knaben,* while most often used to describe a "boy" could also be used to qualify the "knave," or one who was unscrupulous. Understood in such a way, the usage makes sense as "lying with an unscrupulous man in the same manner as a woman" while the insertion of "boy" for *knaben* only obscures the passage. Certainly, this opens the option that Luther could have understood *knabenschender* to mean "those who abuse the unscrupulous or knaves," but this ignores the consistent lexical attributions for *knabenschender* as pederast and pederasty. Undoubtedly, Luther would have seen pederasty as like or a part of sodomy, to say that he saw the *knabenschender* of 1 Corinthians and the *knaben* of Lev 18 as extensions of one another, however, is quite problematic. See Lexer, *Worterbuch,* Bd. 1 Sp. 1641.

concerning certain sexual incontinence by never actually illustrating or detailing the terms in his vernacular.[12]

While Luther was somewhat reticent about the purpose of his translations, the two terms did find lexical expression within wider early modern German culture. The *weichling* was defined by Dasypodius as the consummate effeminate male.[13] This definition of the "un-masculine male" was largely echoed in the 1541 lexicon of Maaler.[14] Fries, writing in 1596, summarized the *weichling* as the "conceding, weak, or yielding" within society.[15] These definitions were all ultimately in keeping with the *Mittle-hochdeutsch* rendering of the root word, *weiche*. The *weiche* was a piece of curled or tangled yarn; it was bent, twisted and pliable. In some instances, it was compared to the tail of a pig or the mucus in the back of the mouth.[16] These evocative definitions implied that a *weicheling* was "twisted" because of some inherent pliability. It was bent in comparison with society at large, and referred to pliable, easily moved, and mouldable characters.

German lexicons of the period also linked *weicheling* to the Latin *mollis*. Thus, to obtain an even deeper understanding of what might have been understand by Luther's translation, it is worth approaching the word from this direction as well. Placum's 1536 lexicon described the *mollis* as "lascivious, drunk, *cinaedus* and catamite," and required that such individuals and their actions should be suppressed and not discussed lest others be tempted to commit similar acts. In this way, Placum echoed previous sentiments that writing or speaking explicitly about certain sexual acts did more harm than good.[17] Placum's last two synonyms (*cinaedus* and catamite) are particularly

12. In this, one sees some of the tensions in early modern translation, its attempts to "return to the sources" and the problem with deflecting the criticism of creating something new and entirely self-serving.

13. Dasypodius, *Dictionarium Latino-Germanicum*, E21ᵛ.

14. Maaler, *Die Teutsch Spraach*, 488.

15. Fries, *Novum Latinogermanicum et Germanicum latinum Lexicon*, 878. Fries was primarily a Zurich-based theologian but, as will be presented later, there was little if any difference between the translations from Zurich and those in the wider German-speaking world. As a notable early modern lexicographer, his writing is essential. See Kettler, "Johannes Fries—'Günstling' Zwinglis, Lexikograph und Pädagoge," 207–12.

16. Lexer, *Mittelhochdeutsches Handwörterbuch*, Bd. 3, Sp. 737 *bis* 738 and Benecke et al., *Mittelhochdeutsches Wörterbuch*, Bd. 4, Sp. 617b *bis* 618b.

17. Placum, *Lexicon Biblicum Sacrae*, 455. Placum, writing from Cologne in the sixteenth century, is also notable for linking sexual incontinence to being drunk or having a lack of self-control. Compare the cases of Herren Boudin and Krafft, examined later in this chapter, in which alcohol acted as a disinhibitor. That Placum was writing from Cologne, which was staunchly imperial and Catholic, seems to describe that, regardless of affiliation, theologians in early modern Germany were unanimous about what constituted made a *weiche*, though perhaps not "who" was one.

useful for understanding the *weicheling* in the early modern German world. The catamite was often the personally beloved but societally despised pet of a pederast, but the term could also mean the man who kept a "pet" boy for pederasty.[18] The *cinaedus* was widely seen as the embodiment of shame, a wanton, someone who incited lust in others, and, in particular, a practitioner of a vice of the ancient Greeks.[19] Pareus' seventeenth-century lexicon, expanding upon the word of preceding authors, defined the *cinaedus* as:

> *cinaedus: dicitursultator, velpantomimus*
> *cinaeduscalamistratus: de pueris mollibus et impudicis*[20]

> cinaedus: meaning a dancer, or pantomime[21]
> cinaedus calamistratus: about weak/soft/effeminate and shameless boys.[22]

The lexicons of Garth and Frisius provide further clarification of *cinaedus*. According to these authors, a *cinaedus* was a dancer.[23] A dancer, within the sixteenth and seventeenth centuries, mainly referred to an erotic dancer or the performer of a dance that, at the very least, inspired erotic behaviour.[24] The dancer was a person who drew the attention of others to themselves and enticed them to mental or physical desires.[25] This connotation with the *cinaedus* seems even more plausible when one considers how the term

18. Bergomatis, *Dictionarium Latinae Linguae*, L3ʳ; Pasor, *Lexicon Graeco-Latinum*, (Herborn, 1619), 403. Frustratingly, *mollis* is not found in earlier lexicons such as those of Dasypodius, Maaler, or Serranus.

19. Cholinus, *Dictionarium Latino-Germanicum*, 191; Ambrosii, *Dictionarium*, M5v.; Garth, *Theologogicum Lexicon Latino-Germanicum*, 907; and Reyheri, *Thesaurus Latinitatis Universae Reherianus Recognitus et auctos*, 406. Reyher was a seventeenth-century academic from staunchly Protestant Leipzig.

20. For a better understanding of this, see Deacy and Pierce, *Rape in Antiquity*; and Skinner, *Sexuality in Greek and Roman Culture*.

21. This is arguably a reference to professional actors flaunting their bodies in public or for display to others.

22. Pareus, *Lexicon Plautinum*, 67, 75. Pareus was a seventeenth-century Latinist who received schooling both in Germany and neighbouring Switzerland. See Zedler: *Grosses vollständiges Universal-Lexicon Aller Wissenschafften und Künste*, Band 26, Leipzig 1740, Spalte 854 f. "Calimastratus" is equivalent to artificially curled hair, an epithet that we will see used again in Henri III's France.

23. See Garth, *M. Balthasaris Garthiitheologi Lexicon Latinograecum*, 106. For more information on Garth, see "Garth Balthasar," 372; and Frisius, *Novum Latino-Germanicum et Germanico Latinum Lexicon*, 106.

24. See Karant-Nunn, *Reformation of Ritual*, 28. This assumed eroticism is why many reformers were staunchly against dancing and dancers.

25. See Roper, *Holy Household*, 146–47.

was further defined as πορνος and παιδορος, the latter being a derivative of παιδεραστής.[26] Frisius, in particular, seems to have been acutely sensitive to the dangers of discussing the *cinaedus*, cloaking his definition within the safe ambiguity of Koine Greek. Nonetheless, it is apparent that the author intended the *cinaedus* to be understood as being "pornographic" and/or as a "pederast."[27]

These definitions provide parameters for the meanings of *cinaedus* or catamite as a subset or possible translation of the wider *mollis* or *weichling*. A catamite was a sexual callboy of sorts, while the *cinaedus* encouraged shameful and uncontrollable passions within society. The *cinaedi* were wanton, vain, and un-masculine. Overly concerned with personal appearance, they flaunted their bodies. They lacked self-restraint, and they expressed their sensuality publicly, not in decent privacy. They were the opposite of everything that society demanded of men.[28]

One should note that, while these lexicons include helpful details in their definitions of the *weiche*, the *cinaedus* and others, they did not limit the description of these terms to a specific group of sexual actors. In general, although the *cinaedi* were effeminate, there is no specific mention of their actions being related to sodomy.[29] While it is clear that, sodomy was among the potential misdeeds of the *cinaedi*, it is equally plausible that "hetero-sexual" actions, in modern usage, could also be performed by a *cinaedus*. Overall, the *weichling* or *mollis* was a character who could be defined by many actions: he might be a drunkard, a person of lax morals, one given to sexual intrigue and wantonness, a sexually provocative dancer orperhaps even a passive male prostitute.[30] This potential variation in the identification of the *weiche/mollis* was illustrated in Niels Hemmingsen's

---

26. Liddell, *Greek-English Lexicon*, 1286, 1450.

27. Πορνος, in the sixteenth century, was understood to be "*scortum masculum, cinaedus, qui corpore quaestum facit, idem quaestuarius nam haec vox communis cuinis corpori meritorio*" (Male prostitutes, catamites, those who profit from bodily performance, the same ones who also hire their bodies in public). Παιδεραστής was understood as "*amator puerorum, paedico*" (Lover of boys, pederast). See *Lexicon sive dictionarium graecolatinum*, III3[R], Sss3[R]. Although this work was published in Geneva, Melanchthon's contribution to it would have guaranteed it a place in German society.

28. Roper, *Oedipus and the Devil*, 57.

29. This may, in fact, have been one of the things an audience of the time would simply have assumed. This understanding—un-masculinity as inherently implying sodomy—is an assumption that has been passed down throughout centuries in translations. See McNeill, *Church and the Homosexual*, 247n28.

30. The use of the masculine pronoun in this is no accident, as there is no record of any of these terms ever applying to the female gender.

late sixteenth-century writings from Strasbourg. Regarding 1 Corinthians 6:9, Hemmingsen noted:

> But how is this denunciation to be understood? The following prayer of Paul shows, and the overall meaning of the passage reveals this: that such persons are excluded from the inheritance of the kingdom of God, unless they perform penance ... The soft, to Paul, are those who betray their profligacy with meretricious speeches, effeminate gestures and clothing and other indulgences.[31]

For Hemmingsen, the defining characteristic of the *mollis/weicheling* was a mental one, which was readily displayed in betraying features such as effeminate gestures and clothing choices. Thus, for Hemmingsen, the external characteristics of a man were indicative of his internal characteristics. Disorder in one's outward set of actions would therefore reflect the disorder of one's inward actions. Men were men only in so far as they displayed their masculinity. Salvation was mutually acknowledged only if it were publicly visible. The *mollis* was "afflicted" with a mental condition or outlook. To be a *mollis* was to engage, as one might term it today, in a lifestyle of sorts, albeit one brought about by personal disorder. While these definitions provide an impression of the *weiche* in early modern Germany, Luther's *knabenschender* remains undefined and problematic. The first problem is the German word itself. *Knabenschender* was a neologism combining "boy" and "abuse," just as ἀρσενοκοῖται almost certainly combined the Koine terms for "men" and "bed." Consequently, the term is not listed within early lexicons such as those of Dasypodius, Maaler, or Serranus.[32] Moreover, that Luther himself did not use the word descriptively elsewhere prevents this study from contextualising the neologism within the writings of the one who invented it. The word is found, undoubtedly

---

31. Hemmingsen, *Commentaria in omnes Epistolas Apostolorum,* 181. Hemmingsen's original stated: *Quomodo autem haec denunciatio intelligenda sit sequens oratio Pauli ostendit, et summa sententiae huc redit, quod tales excludantur a regni Dei haereditate, nisi egerint poenitentiam: ... Molles Paulo sunt, qui verborum lenociniis effoeminato gestu et vestitu alijsqui delitijs, impudicitiam suam produnt.*

32. Dasypodius does, however, provide definitions for *Cinaedi* and *Pederastes* that hint at the compound word *knabenschender*. See Dasypodius, *Dictionarium et vice versa Germanico-Latinum*, E3^r, Vv1^v. Puff indicates that a derivative of the word was in use during at least one late medieval trial, thus perhaps positioning the term as a colloquialism. Nonetheless, the term is absent in foundational German lexicons of the early sixteenth century. See Puff, *Sodomy*, 47.

because of the widespread influence of Luther's Bible, in several lexicons in the latter part of the early modern period.[33]

Lexicons of the late sixteenth and seventeenth centuries defined the *knabenschender* as being synonymous both with the Latin word for pederast and with *contra naturam*.[34] These definitions seem to fit rather fluidly with the root terms of Luther's neologism. That pederasty should be the ultimate meaning of a neologism that combined "boy" and "abuse" seems quite logical. For such actions to be considered *contra naturam* is also logical. Defining the *knabenschender* as a pederast, based on the seventeenth century understanding of the term, however, also creates its share of problems. The *knabenschender* is missing from sources for nearly two generations after Luther, and there is no explicit support for this link with pederasty before the seventeenth century.[35] Thus, it is perhaps easiest and more accurate to say what *knabenschender* was *not* instead of attempting to define what it was.

To begin, it is difficult to say that the *knabenschender* was intended simply as a substitute term for sodomites in early modern Germany. Sodomy, as defined in early modern Germany, was a complex and intricate classification, not simply one singular action or defining act. The *Constitutio Criminalis Carolina*, the first legal code in the Holy Roman Empire and subsequently in early modern Germany, described sodomy as follows:

> *Constitutio Criminalis Carolina Artikel 116*
> *Item so Mensch mit Thier, Man mit Man, Weib mit Weib,*
> *Unkeusch treiben, die haben das Leben verwirken und sollen der*
> *gemeinen Gewohnheit nach mit dem Feuer vom Leben zum Tode*
> *gerichtet werden*

---

33. It is again entirely possible that, prior to the end of the Reformation, the term was readily understood in colloquial dialect and was only added to later lexicons and dictionaries to codify its place as an official, although previously colloquial, term.

34. Frisius, *Novum Latino-Germanicum et Germanico-Latinum Lexicon*, 455. Frisius, writing at the end of the sixteenth and beginning of the seventeenth centuries, seems to be the first actually to employ the term. Later lexicons, such as Grimm's *Worterbuch*, would link the *knabenschender* to pederasty almost entirely based on Frisius' reference. See Grimm, *Worterbuch*, Bd11, Sp. 1325. Passor, *Lexicon Graeco-Latinum, in Novum . . . Testamentum . . . Editio quarta, prioribus plenior*, 403. Passor was a Hessian linguist of the late sixteenth and early seventeenth centuries. His lexicon was one of the first to appear in Herborn where he was largely influenced by Reformed ideology. See Ulrich, "Georg Pasor," Bd. 17, Sp. 1055–59.

35. Again, Dasypodius seemed to hint at this union, but no other sixteenth-century lexicographer connects the two terms.

> Item: re: Human with Animal, Man with Man, Woman with Woman Unchaste lust/desire, which forfeits life and, according to the common custom, requires execution by burning.[36]

The *Carolina* suggested that early modern German society had a clear view of what constituted sodomy, which was synonymous with the entire spectrum of non-procreative sexuality. Sodomy, per the *Carolina*, was not just one sinful act, but a potential host of acts. Johann Altensteig offered further details of this:

> Sodomy: is dishonour made upon a male, as it is said [reference-given to unidentified source.] And, according to [the] B[lessed] Tho[masAquinas] 2.2, sodomy, that is, intercourse of males is a variety of lust against nature: and interpreted as a silent Zodoma. And therefore, he is accustomed to throw the silent, who have not confessed, into a lake of burning sulphur, of which the smoke of the tormented rises for eternity (says Jean Gerson in a sermon he gave at Konstanz on the Feast of St Anthony. . .). This vice is far worse and more flagrant than others. Lactantius-Firmianus complains of the sodomites in book 6 chapter 23 of [his] *Divine Institutes*: "It is not possible (he says) to discuss this matter on account of the greatness of the offence. I can call them nothing more than impious men and parricides, for whom the gender given them by God does not suffice, so that they play with their own gender profanely and wantonly, etc." He says many things in other places about the vice of sodomy and those most vicious and worst of men, and we have noted a few things about the triumph of Venus in book 5.[37]

36. The *Constitutio Criminalis Bamberg* says virtually the same thing as the *Carolina*, save that the former is in *Mittelhochdeutsche*. *Constitutio Criminalis Bamberg* 141: "*straff der unkeusch / so wider die natur geschicht. So ein mensch mit einem uihe / man mit man / weyb mit weyb / vnkeusch treyben / Die haben auch das leben verwürckt / vnd man sol sie dergemeinen gewonheyt nach mit dem fewr vom leben zum todt richten.*" See Constitutio Criminalis Carolina, *Dess aller durchleuchtigsten*, 116 and Constitutio Criminalis Bambergis, *Bambergische peinliche Halszgerichts-Ordnung*, 141.

37. Altensteig, *Lexicon theologicvm*, 857–58. Altensteig's original stated Sodomia: *Sodomia: est turpitudo in masculum facta ut habetur 32.q.2.ca.Vsus. & secundum B.Tho.2.2 Sodomia, id est coitus masculorum, est species luxuriae contra naturam: et Zodoma muta interpretatur, et ideo quia mutos sine confessione consuevit praecipitare in stagnum sulphuris ardentis, cuius fumus tormentorum ascendit in secula (inquit Gers. p. 1 sermone facto Constantiae in die sancto Antonii.).Vitium hoc caeteris longe peius et flagitiosius. In Sodomitas invehitur Lactantius Firmianus lib. 6. ca. 23. di. instit. Non potest (inquit) haec res pro magnitudine sceleris enarrari. Nihil amplius istos appellare possum quam impios et parricidas, quibus non sufficit sexus a Deo datus nisi et suum sexum prophane ac petulanter illudant, &c. Alias multa de sodomiae vitio et vitiosis et pessimis illis hominibus dicitur, et in triumpho Veneris pauca annotauimus*

Sodomy, in Altensteig's understanding, was a category in which all sins that involved same-sex or same-gendered sexual action might be included, including pederasty. Obviously, sodomy and pederasty are not the same. A pederast is a sodomite, but a sodomite might not necessarily be a pederast. However, they were placed in the same grouping of cognates and related words and deeds. What they shared and where they overlapped was in an association with (male) same-sex activities. The difference was that pederasty was intergenerational, involved an adolescent (*eink naben*), and there was usually a difference in station/status. Sodomy, on the other hand, could occur generically between any two males without any implied further qualification, and could include acts between men and women, animals, or even singular individuals in masturbation. Thus, pederasts were sodomites, but not all sodomites were pederasts; they were united simply by their *contra naturam*s but defined by their individual practices. Altensteig, drawing largely from the medieval work of Jean Gerson, further defined this specification:

> The sin against nature: generally, the sins against nature are assigned to four types or modes. The first is when, without having sex with anyone, but for pleasure, sexual pollution is procured, and this is properly called softness [masturbation], and this belongs to the sin of venereal or self-indulgent filthiness. The second kind is if one uses as a sex-partner something not of one's own species, and this is properly called bestiality. The third kind is if one uses as a sex-partner someone of the same species, but not of the proper gender, for example, of a man with a man, or a woman with a woman. And this is properly called sodomitical. The fourth kind is if one uses as a sexual partner someone of the same species and the proper gender, but it is not done in the appropriate orifice, or in other ways, some monstrous unnaturalness is performed, or filthiness in the ways of having sex.[38]

lib. 5. This is a late printing of Altensteig, who died as Luther's Reformation was just hitting its stride. Altensteig was frustratingly quiet about both sodomy and pederasty in his other writings, most famously his "Vocabularum" dating from the early sixteenth century. Whether this later exposition is due to a change of heart or simply a verbose editor is not entirely clear. Nonetheless, such a descriptive definition attests to a late medieval/early modern awareness, at least amongst theologians, of the acts and actions of sodomites. See Stegemann, "Altensteig, John," 215.

38. Altensteig, *Lexicon*, 670–71. The original text stated *Peccatum contra naturam: et communiter peccati contra naturam quatuor species seu modi assignantur. Primus est quando absq; omni concubitu causa delectationis venereae pollutio procuratur, et vocatur proprie mollities, pertinetque ad peccatum immunditiae venere seu lubricosae. Secundus modus est si fiat per concubitum ad rem non eiusdem speciei et vocatur proprie bestialitas. Tertius modus est si fiat concubitus ad rem eiusdem speciei, sed non ad debitum sexum,*

Altensteig's definitions provide a clear understanding of "unnatural" sexual deviancy in early modern Germany. Sexual deviance, as a sin, was not a singular action or set of actors. It was, instead, a quartet of actions, namely: masturbation (or self-weakness), bestiality, same-gendered sex and non-procreative acts (such as oral or anal sex) between a man and a woman.[39] What one might glean from this was that sexual propriety, in Altensteig's mind at least, was largely concerned with potentially procreative copulation. Certainly, the *knabenschender*, by its seventeenth-century definition, would have fit into this category of *contra naturam* sin. It would not however, have been indicative of all things *contra naturam*, nor even of all things related to sodomy. Thus, it is possible to say that the *knabenschender*, at least by the later part of the early modern period, was indicative of pederasty and was involved in the wider taxonomies of both sodomy and *contra naturam* sexuality. Still difficult to qualify, however, is whether Luther ever intended the term to be used in this way.

Luther was, again, entirely silent concerning his precise definitionof the *knabenschender*, creating, and employing the term, but never elucidating just to whom or what it should be understood to refer. Nonetheless, were Luther meaning 1 Corinthians 6:9 to define general sodomy, it would have been far more useful and socially applicable to have used *sodomitischensundt*. Moreover, early modern Germany had words such as *florenzed* or *geflorentzed* that indicated simple anal penetration.[40] In other instances, terms such as *bubenketzer* and *ketzerie* were used in early modern German legal cases to describe sodomites.[41] That Luther did not use any of these and employed the neologism of *knabenschender* instead makes a connection with the concept of adult sodomy (in its wider meanings) problematic.

---

ut puta, masculi ad masculum, vel foeminae ad foeminam. et vocatur proprie sodomiticum. Quartus modus est si fiat concubitus ad rem eiusdem speciei et debiti sexus, sed non fiat in debito instrumento, vel alias fiat monstrosa quaedam deordinatio et vilitas in modis concubendi. That Altensteig was quoting the much earlier Gerson seems, as has been described previously, to point towards a thought process in which reformation ideology, while different from the overall statements of the Roman church, was not something new, but was instead a harkening back to the historical underpinnings that had previously been associated with the church. It may also show that several reformers were quite conscious of the criticisms being levelled at them by More and others.

39. This is something of an interesting attitude for Altensteig to have taken. His opinions seem to include strong influence from both Aquinas and as will be seen in the next chapter, Nicolaus of Lyra, particularly with his association of masturbation and the *molles*.

40. Dierauer, *Chronik der Stadt Zurich*, 244.

41. Puff, *Sodomy*, 134.

While Luther was silent about his intent with regard to οὔτε μαλακοὶ οὔτε ἀρσενοκοῖται, particularly the *knabenschender*, his writings do provide some tacit possibilities concerning whom or what he might have meant. A survey of Luther's writing from the *Tischreden* to his commentaries and letters, provides interesting aspects to consider. Luther's writings were replete with discussions of sexual incontinence, sins *contra naturam* and general sexual deviancy, particularly when he discussed Italian and/or Roman Catholic practices.

To understand the level of opposition Luther and other Protestant leaders felt towards Roman clergy, one needs to understand the economy of marriage within the Reformation. Marriage, for Luther and others, was not simply the sacramental matter it once had been. Instead, marriage was very much both a spiritual reality and a social and civic building block; it was the cornerstone of the Protestant social and spiritual agenda. Marriage was the ideal state for male and female members of society; men of the day were expected to create idyllic mini kingdoms, the mutual support of which was for the betterment of the wider society.

Certainly, one must admit that the Protestant Reformation did little to change the prevailing social constructions of masculinity or femininity.[42] Men remained men and women remained women, one group the dominant actor in social situations, the other the dominated.[43] What changed with the Protestant Reformation was that sexual actions were re-imagined, transforming their realities into ones that should be embraced as socially dignified and personally enjoyable activities within the conjugal household. Obviously, there were families (conjugal households) before the Reformation. The sexual aspects of these households, however, were, if not "necessary evils," certainly not celebrated as a healthy and vibrant part of interpersonal, marital relationships due to the long-established trend in Christian thought that privileged virginity over marriage.[44] With the rise of Luther's Reformation came a profound alteration of ideas about sex that provided the general populace with an opportunity to express their sexuality with grace

42. This sounds more sensational than it really is. The Protestant Reformation did as little to change masculine and feminine understandings as it did to change the employment of those understandings; in other words, men and women were still men and women in Protestant ideology; however, they were expected and allowed differing options and paths to engage their countenances. Scott Hendrix covers this succinctly. See Hendrix, *Masculinity*, 71–89.

43. See Salisbury, *Sex and the Middle Ages*, 3, 29. Luther saw women's lust as not necessarily being as potent as men's; however, women were extremely capable of manipulating and tempting men via lust. See Wiesner-Hanks, "Lustful Luther," 209.

44. For more information about how Luther's new approach would celebrate sexuality, see Karant-Nunn and Wiesner-Hanks, *Luther on Women*, 137–39.

and dignity within the confines of marriage. No longer was sexual action something to be predominantly defined by procreation but, instead, it was to be a celebrated and vibrant part of the early modern German household although, as will be seen, only potentially procreative sexuality was fully celebrated.[45] While this certainly had an impact on the lives of husbands and wives, the reordering of the sexual hierarchy had its greatest impact on the clergy with the effective demotion and devaluing of clerical celibacy.[46]

Undisputedly, there were sexually active clergy, even sexually active cardinals and popes, prior to the Protestant Reformation.[47] Such actions, however, were never seen as dignified, nor were they encouraged. They were, instead, a barely tolerated reminder of the baseness of humanity and its failings before that, which was Holy. The Lutheran Reformation presented, for the first time, the opportunity for those of clerical vocation to engage their own sexuality and sexual function in a dignified, socially open, and accepted manner. Men, clerical or lay, were no longer simply to employ sex as a procreative function. Nor were they, in the case of the cleric, to see sexual engagement as a sign of frailty and insufficient holiness. Instead, men were to channel their sex and sexuality into their homes.[48] They were to create a vibrant life there, where sex with their spouses was to be joyous and healthy.[49] Although the open toleration of brothels was ended, with obvious consequences for single men, married men need no longer look to prostitutes for "fun" sex—this was now an acceptable aspect of their relationships with their wives. In fact, the man was to be both the sexual and physical caretaker of his wife's needs and of the their household. He was to be the provider and progenitor of all things.[50] He was to provide order and structure, safety, security, and regularity. His wife, at the same time, was to be caretaker, both of her husband and of their household. She was to be the domestic guide and enabler, the one who would take provisions from her

45. WATR 3:3508.

46. Luther envisioned a re-imagining of the whole of human sexuality. Procreation and the desire to multiply were to be naturally designed and ordained. However, the sinful fall of humanity had corrupted such things and brought about the concept and drive of lust. The only effective way to counteract lust, for Luther, was to be harmoniously joined in a procreative relationship or household. See LW 1:10; WA 42:79. See also WATR 3:129.

47. See Haliczer, *Sexuality in the Confessional,* 122, 137.

48. This is not to suggest that sexuality had always been confined to the procreative act prior to the Protestant Reformation. Instead, ideal sexual interaction was to be confined to the marriage bed in most cases.

49. WATR 3:3182a.

50. This was, in many ways, exhibited in the *Hausvater* concept of early modern Germany. See Hendrix, *Masculinity,* 71.

provider, be they sexual or physical, and make something wonderful and new out of them, whether creating a meal, weaving a garment, or growing a child within the womb.[51] The conjugal household presented both men and women, for the first time, with an approved and celebrated outlet for their innate sexual desires and functions in a companionable relationship. Being a spouse was a godly vocation in all its aspects including—and perhaps most importantly—the sexual.

Thus, with marriage, the conjugal household, and ordered but joyful sexuality being so central to the Protestant movement, one might grasp the Protestant disdain for Roman Catholic celibacy and its constraint of sexuality. The Roman cleric, who not only promoted pious chastity and virginity but also and not particularly secretly flouted those ideals, was therefore utter anathema to the Protestant movement.

This association of Italy and sexual disorder, simple though it might seem, was more than mere rhetoric or slanderous propaganda. Roman Catholic sexual mores were widely seen as lax in Germany, and Luther would most likely have been brought up to accept this general stereotype which, as with most stereotypes, had some basis. In late 1519, Luther received a letter from the German humanist Johannes Rubeanus about the latter's travels through Italy and the deplorable state of sexual deviancy he found there. Rubeanus told Luther that the Pope's following was composed of "unchaste women and young male prostitutes."[52] In addition, Rubeanus accused the Roman Curia of supporting *scorta ac cynaedos* with their *palliis, indulgentiis, bullis, nugis, and gerris*.[53] This later declaration associated the money-raising schemes of the Roman church with the keeping of escorts and male prostitutes by leading church figures. The letter seemingly had a profound impact on Luther and its timing coincided with Leo X's condemnation.[54] One should thus not be surprised that, after receiving Rubeanus' letter, Luther described the Roman Curia, the Italian city-states and the Papal States as the seat and epitome of sexual deviancy, particularly of sins *contra naturam*. For Luther, the *contra naturam* sexuality of those in Rome was so debauched that "so great is their wickedness that no one is able to believe it unless they witness it with their eyes and ears"; furthermore, "but it is not a sin to Rome, but instead a great honour to the Italians and Romans."[55] These

51. See Roper, *Oedipus*, 37–40.

52. In the original: *impudicae mulieres ac prostituti pueri*

53. "*Crotus Rubeanus and Luther*," in WABR, 1:542.

54. See Leonis, *Contra Errores Martini Lutheri et Sequacium.*

55. *Nemo potest persuaderi tantam esse malitiam, nisi adhibeat testes oculos, aures et experientiam* in WATR, 5:468 and *Aber es ist kein sunde zu Rom, sondern grosse ehre gegen der Welsschen und Romisschen keuscheit!* In WA, 54:213.

statements suggest Luther's ire and horror; since he states that the Catholic clergy were so debauched that they gloried in that which was unthinkable elsewhere, and their sin was so great that only "seeing would be believing." Luther, perhaps speaking to an audience more worthy of detailed analysis, outlined the sexual sins of the Roman church by stating:

> The chastity of popes and cardinals is, in Italian, called peder-
> asty, namely, the chastity of Sodom and Gomorrah . . . in Italy,
> bishops and cardinals did this (sodomy) with joy and impunity.[56]

In this passage, Luther provides a tacit link, as did Altensteig, between sodomy and pederasty, while still differentiating between the two. The reference to pederasty seems potentially to provide a critical designation of just whom the early modern *knabenschender* might have been intended to reference. This association was taken further when, in his *Predigiten Jahres 1538*, Luther, with reference to pederasty, insisted: "Amongst us Germans this occurs not in glory and honour, but in shame, so that they might be regarded as a rascal (buben)."[57] Within this passage, there is a critical word that potentially adds clarity to Luther's previous vernacular translation and his demeaning of all things Italian: *buben*.

　　Buben was a term that, at its most basic, described a boy or youth.[58] This, however, was not the only meaning of the term. Colloquially, in early modern Germany, the term implied wantonness, youthful sexual indiscretion, and pederasty.[59] Moreover, by the eighteenth century, the term was linked lexically with *knabenschender* as being indicative of pederasty.[60] Luther, while silent about the *knabenschender* in his writings, did employ

　　56. Luther, *Warnung*, 303; Martin Luther, "*Predigten des Jahres 1538*," in WA. 46:216. The original stating: *die Papstlichen und Cardinalisschen keuschheit und heisst auf welsch pueronen, nemlich die Sodomitische und Gomorrische keuschheit . . . ut in Italia impune et Bischofe und Cardinale thuns mit freuden*

　　Pueronen is a most curious choice here. It is most likely that Luther is referring to the instance of "propter puerum," which was the common way of notating pederasty in late fifteenth-century Germany and Switzerland. It seems Luther is using a colloquialism, based on both Latin and German, to describe the loving of boys which he sees as integral to the Roman curia. Puff, *Sodomy*, 37; Albert, *Der gemeine Mann von dem geistlichen Richter*, 193–95.

　　57. *Apud nos germanos tamen non fit mit rhum und ehre, sed mit schanden, quod wird einer angesehen fur ein buben!* In Luther, *Predigten*, 217. This statement shows that it is interesting that Luther would comment upon the situation at all.

　　58. Dasypodius, *Dictionarium*, L1r.

　　59. Frisius, *Lexicon*, 665. Evidence of this is also attributed to Luther, noting the term as indicating *scortari paedicare,* although with an unclear source, in Grimm and Grimm, *Worterbuch*. Bd.2, Sp. 462.

　　60. Grimm, *Worterbuch*, Bd. 11, Sp. 1325.

buben. Although never directly equating the *buben* with pederasty, or even with sodomy, Luther employed the term to indicate those of a destructive spiritual nature, specifically those who meant to teardown proper spirituality and/or hinder the gospel and salvation; those who were decidedly not of the kingdom of God.[61] This association only seems more plausible the further one extrapolates upon it. The malefactors described in Luther's writings were those who revelled in and enjoyed their sins. They corrupted their sexuality and employed or enticed others to do the same, all while preserving the ruse of clerical piety. With sexuality, as surmised within the conjugal household, holding such a central place within Protestant writings, it would not seem a particular stretch to conclude that those who practiced sexuality *contra naturam*, the *buben* or *knabenschender*, might fit the description of those who might be excluded from the kingdom of God. Thus, while Luther was frustratingly silent on just what he intended the terms in his vernacular Bible to mean, there seems, at the very least, to be a possible link among the actions of the *buben*, the *knabenschender,* and the Roman clergy.[62]

The connection of the *buben*, the *knabenschender* and the Roman clergy might further help to understand Luther's choice for his vernacular, particularly the omission of such terms within his other writings. According to Luther, the sins attributed to the Italians were occasions for shame and social grief in early modern Germany; they were never celebrated or encouraged. Such people were, according to Luther's reasoning, entirely "un-German." They were the absolute outsiders and the social "other." Therefore, one might speculate that Luther failed to expand upon his translation of 1 Corinthians 6:9 because there was no need to expand upon these creatures; Germans were already aware of just who and what they might be. Luther potentially underlined the "otherness" of these people, such as the *weiche* and the *knabenschender*, by writing:

> Italian Marriages. In the course of the conversation, he then spoke about Italian marriages. These exceed by far all the lewdness and the adulteries of the Germans. The sins of the latter are nevertheless human, but the filthiness of the former [the

---

61. Luther, *Martini Lutheri piae ac doctae operationes, in XXII. Psalmos priores. Iam tertio recognitae*, 291; *Enarrationes In Primum Librum Mose,* 509, and *Annotationes In Aliquot Capita Matthei*, 3, 49, 60; all within Luther, *Opera omnia Domini Martini Lutheri.*

62. In some ways, this would seem to validate the later critique of the Englishman, More. While Luther seemed quite wedded to creating an *ad fontes* interpretation, he might not have been above making the commentary to that text serve other exigencies.

Italians] is Satanic. God protect us from this devil. By God's grace, no German dialect even had a word for this heinous offense.[63]

In Luther's Germany, "Italian marriages" was a coded way of saying "pederasty" or "pederastic relationships" and efficiently stated by whom and where such actions originated and flourished.[64] German sexual sins, such as those evidenced later in this chapter, were bad, but they were secretive and frowned upon, thus making them "human." The sexual sins of the Italians were *contra naturam*, encouraged at the highest levels, practiced without shame, and were therefore definitively non-German. As such, these words and actions merited mention, but not discussion within early modern Germany. Luther thus potentially employed a neologism in his translation of 1 Corinthians 6:9 not to impose modesty or impose penance upon the German populace, but to mark a new and distinct adversary, the Roman church, in a succinct way.[65] This association of the *weicheling* and the *knabenschender* as being indicative of the Italian/Roman "other" seems to find support by examining instances, both in Luther's work and in wider early modern Germany, where the terms might have otherwise been employed, but instead remained absent or were applied only to foreigners.

In May 1598, Ludwig Boudin was brought to trial in the city of Frankfurt for the act of sodomy.[66] The impetus for legal proceedings against

63. WATR: 631:3807. The original states: *Nuptiae Italicae. Deinde in Curru dicebat de nuptuiis Italicis, quae longe excellerent omnem impudicitiam et adulteria Germanorum quae tamen essent humana peccata, illorum immunditiae essent Sathanicae: Gott behut uns fur diesem tueffel! Nulla lingua in Germanicum de illo scelere Dei gratia aliquid novit.* We might note the linguistic switch by Luther. This would ensure that, regardless of their ability in Latin, those reading his text would understand that whatever it was he was saying—and they would most likely have understood *Italicae*—it was so bad it was not appropriate for the vernacular (and ears of young men, females, domestics, et al., who might be nearby).

64. We can deduce that Luther's reference was to sodomitical action or sexual deviancy due to his need to differentiate between Italian and "normal" marriages and the state of Italian lands at the time. Helmut Puff has provided an in-depth look at this concept. See Puff, *Sodomy*, 127. Luther himself often described Italians using not only "die welschehochzeiten" ("welsche" being a derogative colloquialism for "Italy"), but also the more general "welschepracticken," or Italian actions/practices.

65. The description of Roman Catholic clergy as sexually illicit provided the laity with an opportunity to remove clerical authority. See Puff, "Localizing Sodomy," 180.

66. Frankfurt is an interesting locale for case studies due to the relatively free hand it enjoyed in legal cases. As a free city within the empire and one which, at least early in the sixteenth century, was sympathetic to Protestant causes, its records present fertile ground for evidence of the terms this study seeks. Moreover, Boes has done an incomparable job at investigating how accusations of sodomy were prosecuted within the city during the sixteenth and seventeenth centuries.

Boudin sprang from the accusations of Thomas de Fuhr. Both Boudin and de Fuhr were pastry bakers in the city who were in direct competition with each other. Boudin asserted that these commercial concerns were the underlying reason for de Fuhr's complaint.

In a pre-trial summation he [Boudin] rebutted de Fuhr's charges of sodomy by proposing professional envy rather than sexual misconduct as the underlying reasons for the accuser's claim. In a lengthy and detailed statement, the suspected recounted that several years previously de Fuhr's maid, after having been beaten by her employer, sought employment in his, Boudin's, household. To this he had agreed. Consequently, the maid had diverted many customers from de Fuhr to her new employer. De Fuhr, greatly upset about this, had brought unfair practice charges against the suspect, which were heard and consequently dismissed by the mayor. Boudin claimed that de Fuhr was terribly angry about the loss of his maid and customers and about the dismissed charges and had only two things in mind: to prevent him, Boudin, from continuing his trade and to have him removed from Frankfurt. The suspect did, however, concede that he was aware that several years previously a, *bos Geschrey*, a bad rumour, had circulated about him.[67]

During Boudin's trial, the testimony of a host of witnesses presented consistent accounts of Boudin attempting to seduce younger men when he was drunk. The witnesses were always keen, in their stories, to indicate that they repulsed Boudin's advances and, instead, re-directed him to more natural courses, namely his wife. Moreover, the testimonies reveal not only a lengthy—almost two-decade long—pattern of such behaviour, but an accompanying societal indifference to his actions, probably because they had failed to produce a "public scandal." What is most interesting in this situation is that neither *weicheling* nor *knabenschender* appear in the wording of the record. Boudin, by his lack of sexual control, inebriation, and desire to entice, should have easily fulfilled the lexical requirements to be called a *weicheling*. That Boudin's sexual enticements were directed solely at younger men should have also marked him as a *knabenschender* were the word simply to indicate a pederast. That neither term appears in the record, however, should give pause as to whether the terms were meant to be, or could be, applied to Germans. Certainly, the dating of Boudin's case at the end of the sixteenth century might be too early for him to be marked, as a *knabenschender* were Luther's neologism still not widely understood. The same could not be said for a later Frankfurt case.

Heinrich Krafft was a shopkeeper in mid-seventeenth-century Frankfurt. Like Boudin, Krafft seems to have had a penchant for soliciting

---

67. Boes, "On Trial for Sodomy in Early Modern Germany," 29–37.

younger men when drunk. Unlike his predecessor, however, Krafft did not enjoy a long career of carousing. Legal records are sparing with the details of Krafft's life, but it was recorded that he was a shopkeeper, a citizen, and a married man. Although he was a shopkeeper and thus part of civic business, it appears that Krafft's social position was not nearly as secure as Boudin's had been. Whereas individuals were keen to point out that Boudin had never acted upon his solicitations and was easily rebuffed, Krafft's accusers were more than happy to describe his rough advances in detail, even though such advances never progressed beyond sexual harassment/assault to rape.[68] More interesting still is that Krafft was noted to have engaged in *knabenschade* or *knabenschändung*.[69] On one hand, this accusation against Krafft would seem to point towards a growing understanding of the *knabenschender* within later early modern Germany. Certainly, one might reasonably expect Luther's neologism to gain traction in common and legal dialects the longer it was extant. Mid-seventeenth-century lexicons, as previously examined, did provide accounts for the term being associated with pederasty. On the other hand, it is worth noting that Krafft was born French and only later migrated to Frankfurt, and whether he enjoyed full citizenship is unknown. Thus, it is plausible that the term was applied to a foreigner whereas it might not be applied to a "true" German or, in the case of Boudin, a well-liked neighbour. This "outsiderness" would only seem to be further evidenced by examining other instances of *contra naturam* sexuality within early modern Germany.

The "non-German-ness" of Luther's translation seems distinctly illustrated, particularly regarding *weicheling*, in the case of Philip of Hess. Philip, Landgrave of Hesse, was one of the most prominent Protestant princes of the sixteenth century and, in many ways, was largely responsible for the spread of Lutheran ideals. Martin Bucer, Philip Melanchthon and Martin Luther himself lived and were sheltered within Philip's realm. Married in 1523 to a fellow noble, Christine of Saxony, Philip, per most outside observers, led a normal married life, which included the siring of children, for the following sixteen years. This all changed in 1539 when Philip fell in love with Margarethe von der Salle.[70] Margarethe's shrewd mother would not allow her daughter to become the Landgrave's concubine. Instead, Philip could only be allowed the pleasures of Margarethe should he marry her and make her his legal wife.[71]

68. See Boes, "On Trial for Sodomy in Early Modern Germany," 39–41.

69. See Boes, *Crime and punishment in early modern Germany*, 159.

70. See WABR 9:13f.

71. Rockwell, *DieDoppelehe des Landgrafen Philipp von Hessen*, 316–17.

Philip, along with his doctors, would initially claim that he suffered from a condition known as *triorchidism*, or the possession of a third testicle. Although this exceedingly rare congenital abnormality might be seen as either a sign of a curse or as a blessing in the early modern world, Philip and his doctors chose to play their cards in a manner that presented the landgrave as a man of insatiable sexual appetite.[72] Such an appetite was beyond his control, not because of his personal nature, but because of his biological nature, which avoided the appearance of effeminacy. Thus, in part, Philip seems an ideal candidate to be labelled a *weicheling*. Philip's doctors argued he needed unduly frequent coitus, which Catharine alone was unable to provide. In addition, Philip claimed his disdain for Catharine and—both due to his need and his want—his betrayal of his wedding oath only three weeks into his marriage.[73] Armed with this expert medical advice, Philip initially conferred with "his" reformers, but without success.[74] The reformers initially counselled Philip to take Margarethe as a concubine and to be outwardly faithful to his original wife. This was not a workable solution for Philip, Margarethe, or her mother.[75] Ultimately, the reformers would be, by their own admission, forced by necessity to give approval to Philip's bigamous marriage.[76] To assuage their consciences and "to avoid scandal," the reformers encouraged Philip to keep the marriage a secret. Luther suggested Philip publicly treat Margarethe as a concubine, knowing "in his heart," as Luther said, that she was his true wife.[77] Philip, for his part, picked and chose the parts of Luther's advice as he saw fit. He gladly accepted the reformer's sanction of his new marriage; however, Philip presented his two

---

72. WABR 8:640.36. How Philip characterized his insatiability is quite interesting. Were he simply sexually insatiable, it is likely that he would have been called μαλακοί or *weiche*. Sexual incontinence, such as a lack of control over desire and lust—as Philip was claiming—were hallmarks of this category. It was also not out of the realm of possibility for a ruler to be castigated as such (as we shall see in the case of Henri II of France.) Claiming physical disability, however, granted him the ability to say it was "not my fault, God made me this way." In its own way, this was both an adequate and yet dangerous excuse. Certainly, many could understand the woes of nature's dispositions; however, for a ruler to claim physical disability could be dangerous. Early modern monarchs were to be both physically virile and emotionally composed. They were to be the epitome of society because they were God's chosen rulers. Claiming disability might have adequately explained Philip's need, but it also was a quite risky move.

73. WABR 8:631.

74. Luther to Philipp of Hesse, Nov 1526, WABR 4:138.

75. WABR 8:638–43.

76. WABR 8:638–43.

77. Luther, *Luther: Letters of Spiritual Counsel*, 288–91.

wives openly. This duly occasioned the expected scandal and damaged the reputations of both Philip and of the German reformers.

The story of Philip of Hess, his bigamy and the subsequent support received from his reformers is more than simply a juicy anecdote. Philip's indiscretion, lack of control and adultery should have marked him as the *uber-weicheling* of his time. That Philip and his doctors conspired to present his insatiability as an unfortunate result of a biological defect would seem to illustrate that they were aware of the risk behind his actions. To be so sexually insatiable that one could not and did not accept the confines of the conjugal household should have been anathema to the Protestant reformers. Philip was, at least lexically, the avatar of the oversexed *cinaedus* and should have been labelled and condemned as a *weicheling*. That Philip was not condemned as such presents several alternatives: firstly, Philip really did suffer from triorchidism and could not be blamed for his lust, although this seems extremely unlikely. Secondly, the Protestant reformers recognized Philip's status as a *weicheling* and were simply afraid of crossing the man who held their physical destinies in his hands. Thirdly and finally, Philip displayed traits of the un-masculine character, but was not meeting the requirements, in the minds of the reformers, to be labelled a *weicheling*. Somewhat obviously, the second consideration seems most likely to have been the over-arching consideration for much of the situation.[78] Nonetheless, Luther and company, by not at the very least warning Philip of his potential status as a *weicheling*, left open the possibility that the term simply did not apply to the situation.

While political necessity might have swayed Protestant hands in the case of Philip and his bigamy, the *weicheling* was not an indictment levelled at even lesser figures within the Reformation. Michael Kramer was a priest in the town of Dommitsch in the early 1520s. A keen supporter of Martin Luther, Kramer eventually married a local servant girl. This disregard of his vows landed Kramer in dispute with the bishop of Naumburg, culminating in Kramer's arrest. In 1523, Kramer, escaped custody and spent a considerable amount of time on the run from officials.[79] In 1524, whilst her husband was away, Frau Kramer grew tired of waiting and took a new husband in a new locale. When her original husband was able to return to Dommitsch, the re-married Frau Kramer refused to return to him. As Frau Kramer had the backing of her local council, her husband chose not to engage in what might have been a protracted and very public

78. Luther is relatively blunt about political necessity forcing his hand in the situation with Philip. See Luther's letter to Elector John Frederick, June 10 1540, WABR 9:131–35.

79. See Plummer, "Much-Married Michael Kramer," 89–90.

dispute to win her back. Instead, he chose to re-marry and begin a new life. By the summer of 1525, however, the new Frau Kramer had also left her husband.[80] The spectacle of Kramer and his wives caused scandal amongst the local populace, both Protestant and Catholic. The scandal became so widely known that Luther was forced to intervene. What is interesting for our study is the somewhat ambivalent tone Luther took towards the affair. Kramer should have, by his actions, been a rather blatant *weicheling*. His lack of effort to win back his first wife, the expediency with which he took a second wife, and the rather bizarre loss of that second wife should have branded the man as a hallmark of anti-masculinity. Luther, however, never levelled such an indictment at Kramer. Blaming the entire misadventure on Kramer's wives and their lack of character, Luther opted to say little about the situation, aside from quoting 1 Corinthians 7:"But if the unbelieving partner desires to separate, let it be so; in such a case the brother or sister is not bound. For God has called us to peace."[81] In essence, Luther provided Kramer with a solution that, in the process, simply implied that his wives were "unbelievers" and thus Kramer was not to be blamed entirely for the sordid affair.[82] This failure to employ the indictment of *weicheling*, even in seemingly opportune moments, did not simply apply only to those to whom Luther was indebted, and sometimes not even to those who were not German. As Luther was rarely averse to using the colloquial, his failure to employ words he himself supplied for the verse under study, or even to allude to the verse in circumstances in which either or both could seem possible and even appropriate, is interesting.

All these cases, from Boudin and Krafft to Philip, emphasize both the silence and the "otherness" of the *weicheling* and *knabenschender* in early modern German writings and in Luther's work. Although Boudin evidenced, by lexical standards, traits of the *weicheling* and *knabenschender*, neither was ever applied to him. Certainly, Krafft's misdeeds were associated with the *knabenschender*, but whether this association was true to the

80. Plummer refers to this situation as Kramer's "trigamy." Regardless of how one counts the spouses, Kramer had two legally married spouses at the same time, as did his first wife.

81. See WA 12:123–25; LW 28:36.

82. Kramer's was, admittedly, something of an awkward and odd case. Frau Kramer I was almost certainly in an awkward and untenable situation without her husband. For her to remarry certainly made quite a lot of practical sense. At the same time, for Frau II to leave might simply say something about the masculine and marital qualities of Rev. Kramer himself. One almost might wonder whether we should see Rev. Kramer as an example of the *weiche* within his society. Certainly, if only for not challenging his first wife's defiance (in effect, allowing himself to be cuckolded before the entire community), he might be lacking in masculine fortitude.

way in which Luther meant the term to be understood is impossible to say. The same is true for Kramer and Philip; both evidenced traits of the *weicheling*, yet neither was ever identified as such, especially not by Luther. Thus, Luther had employed German words, which, in some way, seemed to have specific connotations for him and perhaps for his audience. These words related Paul's proscriptions not to a general practice or group of individuals, but to a more limited group, at least as far as Luther was concerned. This audience seems to have been evidenced both in Luther's acceptance and support of Rubeanus' assertion of the Roman Curia as *cinaedi* and in his own labelling of them as *buben*. Nonetheless, one cannot, even with the evidence, be quite sure just what Luther truly intended his terms to imply. While Luther seems to have been quite content to employ *weicheling* and *knabenschender* in his vernacular Bible, he was reserved about elucidating the terms, let alone contextualising them in situations in which they might be levelled against an offender.

How Luther and his followers viewed οὔτε μαλακοὶ οὔτε ἀρσενοκοῖται certainly speaks volumes about early modern Germany, but it does not speak for the whole of the German-speaking Reformation world. To expand the discussion, one must turn to non-Lutheran, German-speaking areas and the reformers there, to Zurich, Zwingli, and Bullinger.

Zwingli, at the height of his power, produced a vernacular Bible for the city of Zurich that largely followed Luther's own vernacular. Thus, it should not be surprising that Zwingli's text used *weiche* and *knabenschender* for the two key words in 1 Corinthians 6:9.[83] Unfortunately for this study, Zwingli himself said very little about οὔτε μαλακοὶ οὔτε ἀρσενοκοῖται in his exposition of 1 Corinthians 6:9, beyond declaring that these sinners were not children of God.[84] Zwingli's writings suggest an affinity between himself and Luther, even if such an affinity could only be in suggested by their lack of desire to discuss οὔτε μαλακοὶ οὔτε ἀρσενοκοῖται. Although Zwingli was equally obscurantist about the wider meaning of the words, he employed in 1 Corinthians 6:9, his successor, Heinrich Bullinger, provided a much clearer definition and stern indictment of οὔτε μαλακοὶ οὔτε ἀρσενοκοῖται:

> That is, "molles," who are as if unmanned (evirati), who are devoted to monstrous desires, of whom Greece has always had large numbers. Theophylact [of Ohrid] said, "one calls 'molles' those who suffer disgusting and vile things," and he links with them those who perform heinous acts, that is, those who use males in the place of women. CaeliusRhodiginus, *Antiquarum*

---

83. *Neus Testament Deutsch*, Kv3R.
84. Zwingli, *Annotatiunculae per Leonem Judae*, 46–47.

Lectio book 3, chapter 15 says it is in Pliny that there is a weakness [mollices] and defect of the pregnant, that a good few, when they are suffering, from time to time crave something, so that they even try and devour earth. From which men are metaphorically called "molles" who are given up to vile and unaccustomed enjoyments of desire. It follows therefore that "arsenoikoites" * signifies least disgustingly he who does the most filthy thing by himself that he could. *Pederasty.[85]

To begin, one may note the narrowness of Bullinger's interpretation. While many other definitions, seen above, implied both same and opposite-sex sins for the μαλακοὶ, Bullinger's understanding of the μαλακοὶ was much more focused. Although within the parameters of his contemporaries, Bullinger directly equated the μαλακοὶ specifically with same-sex interactions. The *molles*, for Bullinger, were those who sexually exchanged women for men.[86] Bullinger agreed with his contemporaries understanding of *molles* as being unmanned or unmanly characters—even going so far as to equate their actions with the strange and helpless cravings of a pregnant woman. Nonetheless, Bullinger provided a specific understanding of what he believed the *molles* to be doing, all while not providing the boundaries within which a person would actually "be" one of the *molles*. Same-sex activity, as above, could indicate several lexical identities. Thus, one is left to wonder whether the author understood the *mollis* to be a pederast or the more general *contra naturam* "sodomite." Bullinger was clear that being μαλακοὶ involved males having sex with males, but he was frustratingly opaque about the actual type of sex involved, such as whether he understood sodomy as being part of broad *contra naturam* sex or uniquely involving pederastic actions. This ambiguity continues with Bullinger's definition of the ἀρσενοκοῖται. The Ἀρσενοκοῖται, for Bullinger, were extraordinarily hideous. As the author seems to have included sodomy, to some extent, with the *molles*, one might

---

85. Bullinger, *In Priorem D. Pavli ad corinthios epistolam, Heinrychi Bullingeri Commentarius*, 67. The original states *id est molles uelut euirati sunt, qui prodigiosae libidini inseruiunt, quales Graecia semper plurimos habuit. Theophylactus, molles (ait) uocat qui foeda et nefaria patiuntur, subiungit enim et qui turpia factitant, qui scilicet masculis mulierum uice abutuntur. Coelius antiq. lectio lib 3 cap 15 (ait) praegnantium Plinio est mollices quaedam et defectio, cum languentes modo hoc modo illud appetunt, adeo ut terram quoque vorare appetent nonullae. Proinde metaphoricos homines dicuntur foedis et insolitis libidinum concupiscentiis dediti. Sequitur ergo arsenoikoites* quo rem per se foedissimam quam potuit minime foede significauit. *Paedicare/Paedico* We might note Bullinger's use of classical sources. There seems to have been a significant attempt to cast ideologies as being historically continuous, while also understanding that Greco-Roman worlds, while not wrong in their understandings of ἀρσενοκοῖται and μαλακοὶ, were wrong in their employment of such things.

86. The *molles* will be discussed in much greater detail in chapter 2.

speculate that his understanding of ἀρσενοκοῖται was perhaps directed at the specific action of pederasty. Bullinger describes the ἀρσενοκοῖται as he who "does the most filthy thing by himself he could." At the same time, Bullinger footnotes ἀρσενοκοῖται and specifies it as *paedicare/paedico*.[87] This double definition is somewhat problematic. Bullinger seemingly equates the actions of the ἀρσενοκοῖται with a primary description that evokes masturbation. At the same time, he footnotes this specific term and clarifies it as meaning pederasty. Ultimately, the author could have intended the term to include "both and," as both actions were *contra naturam*.

These definitions by Bullinger seem to add considerable nuance to the somewhat vague descriptions and definitions that were prominent in both Luther's writings and in those of wider Germany. Where Luther's German society seemed loathe defining *weicheling* and *knabenschender*, Zurich's later reformers seemed quite ready. Similar to Luther's Germany were the usages of *weicheling* and *knabenschender* in Zurich society or, more specifically, the lack thereof. The case of Zurich reformer, Werner Steiner, his sexual misdeeds, and the absence of *weicheling* and *knabenschender* as qualifiers was similar to those previously discussed with reference to Luther.

Werner Steiner was a Zurich reformer and friend of Bullinger; he was also an accused sodomite. In 1541, evidence was produced that, Steiner, while working for a parish priest in 1518, had shared a bed with a young traveling farmer. Steiner and the farmer later admitted that Steiner had offered to teach the traveller the pleasures of mutual masturbation.[88] Steiner, as the records indicate, tried to win his bedmate's trust by bribing him with trinkets. The farmer declined Steiner's offer and is said to have found a local prostitute for the two to share instead. This lurid scene, and Steiner's attempt to teach someone a *contra naturam* practice, was costly for the reformer. The farmer's family, upon learning of his awkward encounter, demanded large sums of money from Steiner. Eventually, such payments were brought to light along with Steiner's original actions. Ultimately, Steiner confessed to attempting to teach the farmer how to masturbate and was punished with house arrest.[89]

What is interesting in this story is Steiner's action and the level of similarity it bore to the *cinaedus* and the *weicheling*. Steiner clearly wanted to entice his bedmate into lurid sexual experiences, even preying upon his vanity by giving him trinkets and suchlike. This seems to echo the

87. Bullinger, *Priorem*, 68. In this way, Bullinger seems to, again, combine an understanding of the χιναδεύς and μαλακοὶ.

88. Puff, *Sodomy*, 97n142.

89. Puff provides far more detail about the story. See Puff, *Sodomy*, 97–100.

definition of *cinaedi* in lexicons of the time. Moreover, Steiner was either too ashamed or too nervous to refuse to pay the farmer's family the bribe money they demanded for over twenty years. Were the *weicheling* to have illustrated a character found in all societies, including German-speaking ones, Werner Steiner would seem to have fit that description. Nonetheless, the term is nowhere to be found in either Steiner's confession, the accusations of the farmer and his family, or the legal writings of the time. Thus, one might assume that, similarly to Luther, the labels of *weicheling* and *knabenschender*, although found in the Zurich Bible, had no reference to the actual population of Zurich. This leaves the possibility, as suggested above, that Zurich reformers, as did Luther, envisaged Paul's comments to be directed at the types of individuals associated with the Roman Curia. Thus, an obscure verse that is opaque in the original may well have led the German reformers to associate μαλακοὶ and ἀρσενοκοῖται with Roman clerics, specifically, and to debauched Italians in general.

In the early modern German world, lexical examples suggest that definitions of *weicheling* and *knabenschender*, while malleable, operated within certain lexical parameters. In Luther's Germany, the μαλακοὶ and ἀρσενοκοῖται were spelled out in the *weicheling* and the *knabenschender*, terms that had accessible everyday meanings, but that seemed to contain considerable innuendo and euphemistic qualities within them. On one hand, *weiche* simply meant soft or weak.[90] As the study has shown, however, the term was often a euphemism for unmasculine or emasculated. This weakness could clearly include those who were sexually and/or emotionally incontinent. The *knabenschender*, unlike the *weiche*, was more problematic within the lexicon of early modern German. The *knabenschender* was a term created by Luther that was a straightforward neologism with all the problems that entails for definition.[91] In his wording, Luther was most likely attempting to stay as lexically authentic to the Apostle Paul as possible, matching Paul's neologism with his own. The term, although absent from sixteenth-century lexicons, was found to be strongly associated with *contra naturam* sexuality, particularly pederasty, by the mid-seventeenth century.[92] The terms seem to have been rife with euphemistic intent and, given Luther's emphasis on the topic in other writings, most likely hinted at the sexual practices of Roman Catholic priests. The rationale for this inference required a close reading of the sexuality and politics of the German Reformation in this study.

90. Grimm, *Worterbuch*, 1311–23; Dasypodius, E2 1ᵛ; Maaler, *Spraach*, 488.
91. Lexer, *Handworterbuch*, 655–56.
92. Frisius, *Novum*, 455; Grimm, *Worterbuch*, Bd.11, Sp. 1325; Passor, *Lexicon*, 403.

Sex and sexuality in early modern Germany show continuity and change. The religious and socio-cultural ideal of the (Lutheran) conjugal household, together with clerical marriage, altered the idea of the "goodness" and "naturalness" of the sex act fundamentally. Nonetheless, concepts of sexual propriety, sexual roles and sexual function remained widely unchanged within the early modern German world, despite the Protestant Reformation. Thus, a new, positive view of the sex act inherent in the establishment of the conjugal household, for both the laity and the clergy, did not usher in libertinism. Instead, German society, overall, was widely conservative regarding sexual propriety. For Luther, Bullinger and others, acts of illicit sex were often understood as being found in the "other," or that which was decidedly non-German and not part of the Protestant Reformation.[93] The most glaring aspect of this "otherness" could be embodied within the person of the Roman Catholic priest, one who shunned marriage, the conjugal household and the licit sex lauded by Protestant reformers.

Germans and their reformers were able to accept a range of sexual licence when it involved a person of power or usefulness—or just a well-liked neighbour. Individuals not protected by their necessity, status or power faced the full weight of social disapproval and the severe exactions of the law.[94] This was most evident in the writings of Luther and other reformers when sexual deviancy was conflated with Italians and the Roman Curia. Luther, locked in a struggle he considered of eternal importance, was more than willing to make use of and encourage the prejudices and stereotypes his fellow Germans accepted for all things Italian. This polemic, however, required a kernel of truth to be effective. Italian cities such as Venice and Florence were notorious for sodomy and pederasty long before the Protestant Reformation; they barely discouraged these views, as seen later in this study, by establishing courts and police units specifically designed to control sodomy. Moreover, this polemic was particularly effective against the Papacy since reports regularly circulated in Germany about the sodomitical sinfulness of Rome.[95] Contained within this vernacular warning was a fairly astute reading of German prejudices. Luther was explicitly warning his listeners of a vice that Germans associated with

93. This is like Bale, who considered all Roman Catholics to be synonymous with sodomites. See Betteridge, "Place of Sodomy in the Writings of John Bale and John Foxe," 12.

94. This understanding is seemingly supported in Luther's own writings in which he gives preference to pastoral care and consideration instead of legal code. See "On Marriage Matters," (1530), LW 46: 319; WA 30III: 247.

95. Rubeanus' letter was just one such instance. See "Crotus Rubeanus and Luther," in WABR 1:542.

Italians while simultaneously castigating the Catholics for their supposed moral laxity and sexual deviance. Luther and others all issued writings that connected the actions of the *weicheling* and the *knabenschender*, the *cineadus* and the catamite, as *contra naturam* and intricately associated with the Roman Catholic Curia. Luther conflated the Roman church's leadership with catamites and male whores, while others, such as Zwingli, refused to discuss the specifics of the text, but deemed any offenders to not be children of God. Given the climate of the German Reformation, one must consider whether this was a not particularly subtle insinuation about Roman clergy, the mortal enemy of the Protestant Reformers. Locked in a tremendous struggle with the Roman Catholic faith for the very soul of Germany, the reformers were not afraid to level charges against their spiritual adversaries. Thus, in Germany, one finds 1 Corinthians 6:9 to evidence both a strong commitment to the *ad fontes* initiative, but also to provide an opening for criticism such as that later given by More. Luther was certainly concerned with the literal word of interpretation, but that word might easily be extrapolated into an attack on those who opposed him.

CHAPTER TWO

France: Malignment and Alignment across
a Broad Reformation

T ransitioning from the world of sixteenth- and seventeenth-century
Germany, the study arrives in the world of early modern France
and the wider French-speaking and influenced world. The Protestant
Reformation, in these worlds, was largely united under the banner of
the "Reformed" community but, as the study will show, it was not entirely dominated by Calvin and the Genevan reformers. Contrary to the
Lutheran world, which quickly moved to discouraging individual reading
of the Bible by the laity, the Reformed world actively encouraged such a
practice.[1] Believing the engagement with and the integration of the biblical
text to be critical to the life of the individual, these reformers constructed
a textual apparatus to facilitate such a reality. This apparatus enabled amplification and clarification for the average reader by cross-referencing and
commenting on numerous passages within the biblical text. One text for
which little or no cross-referencing seems to have been provided was 1
Corinthians 6:9.[2] At the outset, such a dearth might seem to be a great
hindrance to this study. Nonetheless, as the chapter will show, inclusion
in the Reformed textual apparatus or not, the wealth of sources in the
French-speaking world contributes to a much more robust and potentially
less inflected definition of οὔτε μαλακοὶ οὔτε ἀρσενοκοῖται.

The study begins its examination of French vernaculars with perhaps
the most important translator in early modern France, Jacques LeFevre
d'Étaples. LeFevre was a humanist contemporary of Erasmus, and while,
like Erasmus, he was a life-long Roman Catholic, he produced works that
were precursors of and foundations for later Protestant texts. Of particular
note for this study are LeFevre's pre-Reformation translation of and commentary on the Pauline epistles (1512), written in Latin and based largely

1. O'Sullivan, "Introduction," 3.
2. See Higman, "Without Great Effort, and With Pleasure," 116–20.

38

on the Vulgate, and his full vernacular translation of the New Testament, published in 1523. Examined together, these two writings, separated by approximately a decade, present an interesting juxtaposition of both the translation and the understanding of οὔτε μαλακοὶ οὔτε ἀρσενοκοῖται both within early modern France and at the dawn of the Protestant Reformation.

In his pre-Reformation work, LeFevre translated μαλακοὶ and ἀρσενοκοῖται as *molles* and *cinaedi*, thus both following and deviating from the standard Vulgate translation of . . . *neque molles, neque masculorum concubitores.* . . .[3] In this opening example, LeFevre provided broad parameters for οὔτε μαλακοὶ οὔτε ἀρσενοκοῖται as they were understood via the Vulgate and in the Latin language. This employment of *molles* for μαλακοὶ was traditional but problematic, as the term had varied connotations. A *molles* was a character who could have different definitions depending upon time and location. Nicholas of Lyra said, "Mollices is a species of the sin against nature in which some pollute themselves by making themselves ejaculate."[4] Thus, in this instance, it seems that the *molles* was a masturbator. By the time of the early Protestant Reformation, however, the term had changed, as illustrated in French dictionaries such as Estienne's, in which the term included:

1. *Qui a perdu sa force naturelle*

2. *Delicat*

3. *Enmaniere de femme*

1. He who has lost his natural force (impotent).

2. Delicate

3. In the manner or way of a woman.[5]

3. *Biblia Sacra Veteris et Novi Testamenti,* 121; d'Etaples, *Epistolae divi Pauli Apostolicum commentarii.* LeFevre's commentary was originally published in 1512, but neither the 1515 reprinting nor the 1517 edition, which I use here, contain any deviations. See Margolin, *Bible in the Sixteenth Century,* 158.

4. Nicholas of Lyra, *Biblia Sacra,* 239, 687. As I am using a late printing of Nicholas, there is the possibility of this definition having been added to or reduced by a later editor. Lyra's Latin verse was *Neque est autem mollices quedam species peccati contra naturam qua aliquisse ipsum polluit per emisionem seminis in seipso procurando.*

5. Estienne, *Dictionnaire francois latin contenant les motz et manières de parler francois, tournez en latin,* 315. Just as there seems to have been a significant amount of change between Nicholas and Estienne, it would seem that Estienne's definition, while certainly being echoed, was added to and more sexually refined by the seventeenth century; as Jean Benedict stated, "Weakness and laxity, as opposed to the virtue of perseverance. People so indulgent and so effeminate that (they) neglect what is necessary for salvation. Voluntary pollution—through touch, imagination, and delectation with men or women. *Bardashes* or passive sexualpartners." See Benedicti, *Les Sommes des*

The differentiation between these definitions is problematic for this study. Lyra provided an understanding that was sexual and sodomitical, if focused on the singular sodomy of masturbation, while Estienne at most implies the lack of the sexual in his first definition. Indeed, the later definition is both vaguer and more problematic. Moreover, it is impossible to say which definition LeFevre would have favoured, as he deigned to not indicate this in his commentary. That he was writing just prior to the dawn of the Reformation makes it seem plausible that the author could have held to an understanding, which was closer to later Reformation understandings. At the same time, by not ever actually detailing his understanding of the *molles*, LeFevre's early translation is problematic. At the very least, one might consider LeFevre's *molles* to be masturbators with possible undertones of effeminacy and "weakness," but unfortunately the exact "type of person" being condemned by Paul remains elusive. Certainly, the *molles* could have been masturbators, but they could just as well also be weak, abnormal males or, as suggested by dictionaries such as Estienne's, emasculated creatures as much by their sexual deeds as perhaps by their choice of clothing or social manner.[6] In general, they seemed potentially to be everything that smacked of emotional incontinence. Nonetheless, just what LeFevre had in mind in his Latin text is difficult to decide without, as mentioned below, some recourse to his later vernacular translation.

In a similar fashion, LeFevre's *cinaedi*, for ἀρσενοκοῖται, was a broad translation. The term in early modern France, as in early modern Germany, referred to those who incited lust or lustfulness in others, those who pursued or hired boys for sex, and/or those who generally engaged in bawdy or lustful behaviour.[7] Thus, it would seem that LeFevre, prior to the

---

Peches et le Remeded"iceux, 154–55.

6. *Enmannier de femme* is something of a fine colloquialism. One is left, perhaps intentionally, to wonder whether the offender has strayed in the realm of sexual comportment, social comportment, or perhaps a combination of both, as later definitions, such as Benedict's, seem to imply. Estienne, being highly trained in the classics, was almost certainly referencing the more classical understandings of *molles*, as opposed to Luther, who seemed to draw direct understanding of the terminology from his contemporary world (Roman priests). See Martin, "Le temps de Robert Estienne," 1:230–35. This concept of emasculation might also be drawn from more classical sources, such as the second century *Acts of John,* which described the effeminate man as follows: "You who delight in gold and ivory and jewels, do you see your loved (possessions) when night comes on? And you who give way to soft clothing, and then depart from life, will these things be useful in the place where you are going?" See Schneemelcher, *New Testament Apocrypha,* Section 36.

7. Ambrosii, *Dictionarium,* M5^V; Dasypodius, *Dictionarium,* E3^R and Pareus, *Lexicon,* 75. All of these lexicons received printings in both French and German spheres of influence and would thus have influenced both nations.

Reformation and in the common understanding of the time, implied that the ἀρσενοκοῖται could be defined by lustfulness and sexual incontinence, along with pederasty.[8] Whereas the *molles* suggested a general emotional incontinence, in the pre-Reformation world, the *cinaedi* embodied an incontinence of a specifically sexual nature. This would seem to suggest, based on LeFevre, a general understanding among early French humanists of οὔτε μαλακοὶ οὔτε ἀρσενοκοῖται. What is clear, however, is that it is difficult to determine what LeFevre meant via his use of Latin without a vernacular cross-reference.

LeFevre's vernacular Bible of 1523, *La Nouveau Testament*, was the first and, as was the case with Luther's German Bible, the foundational text for French vernaculars.[9] In this instance, LeFevre's rendering into French of 1 Corinthians 6:9 translated οὔτε μαλακοὶ οὔτε ἀρσενοκοῖται as *ni les volupteurs et ni les bougeros*.[10] LeFevre's work, which set the pattern for later translations both inside and outside France, was quite direct, not unlike Luther's translation. *Volupteurs* and *bougeros* were both specific. There was a consistency of definition throughout the sixteenth and seventeenth centuries of translating *volupteurs* as "those who are voluptuous, weak in resilience, those devoted to luxury."[11] Just as Estienne's definition of *mollis* seemed to be an evolution of the previous definition by Nicholas of Lyra, so too, by his choice of *volupteur*, did LeFevre present an evolution with regard to *molles*. The *volupteur* was the epitome of the sensuous within society. They were certainly emotionally incontinent, as were the *molles*, but theirs was a

8. Legal texts of the period, such as Jean Papon's *Arrestz Notables Des Covrts Sovveraines De France*, have little to say about sodomitical, pederastic, or same-sex sexual cases. Very few were discussed and contained surprisingly little detail. While one might expect some level of veiled secrecy from biblical commentators or even lexicographers, that legal cases do not exist seemingly points to a culture that generally is either not greatly concerned about policing this kind of sexual misconduct or that the sources simply have not survived. Crompton has pointed out that, in a seventy-five-year period, France executed only seventy-seven persons for any sort of sodomy. This is an average of just over one per year, a singularly small amount for a nation of fifteen million. See Crompton, *Homosexuality and Civilization*, 326–27.

9. Darlowe and Moule make it clear that, until the eighteenth century, all French vernacular texts were either copies or re-issues of LeFevre's text or the texts of Olivetan and Castellion. See Darlowe and Moule, *Historical Catalogue of the Printed Editions of Holy Scripture*, 876–88.

10. d'Etaples, *La Nouveau Testament*, lx4 [R].

11. Estienne, *Dictionnaire Francois-Latin*, 522; Nicot, *Le Grand Dictionnaire Francois-Latin*, 969. Perhaps more famous for introducing tobacco to France, hence "nicotine," Nicot was a successful French diplomat who also compiled several leading French dictionaries. See *Nouvelle Biographie Universelle Depuis les Temps les plus Reculés Jusqu'a nos Jours*, 38:19.

specific type of incontinence. The definition offered for a *volupteur* indicated one who was controlled by passion and a desire for pleasure. That is, one
whose disposition or physical attributes predisposed him to that which was
decadent and indulgent. This definition was distinctly feminine in its connotation at every point without the dictionaries making the specific gender-
related point that Estienne made for *mollis*. Women were the embodiment
of lust and sensuality within the early modern period. As explored below,
men, particularly in the Protestant world, were supposed to be in control
of their passions; to be indulgent of one's sinful impulses, in any direction,
was to be "effeminate," since masculinity was equated with self-control, particularly in sixteenth- and seventeenth-century France. Men were also to be
aware that they were capable of being dragged down into carnality through
the lustful wantonness of women.[12]

LeFevre's *bougeros* is also much more interesting and appears to have
been, if not slang, certainly a very common/low status word, as the term
does not appear in early lexicons such as that by Estienne. Nonetheless,
later lexicons translated *bougeros* as "paederasts or buggers."[13] This, again,
did not contradict LeFevre's use of *cinaedi*, but did provide a much more
specific focus for the sexual incontinence: pederasty and anal sex. As
with *molles* and *volupteurs*, LeFevre's choice of *bougeros* provided a more
pointed, though not entirely dissimilar, definition. Thus, the commentary
and translation by LeFevre represent not a "new enterprise" of sorts, nor
a translation of the text for personal needs, but instead a refinement and
continuation of the previous Latin Vulgate. LeFevre, although perhaps
the most important, historically, was not the only vernacular translator of
1 Corinthians 6:9 in early modern France.

It is critical, for this particular chapter of the study, to note that the
situation in France differed from that of the other vernacular regions in the
study. In other locations, such as Germany and eventually England, Protestantism became the dominant religion through the Reformation. France,
however, was never a Protestant nation, but simply a nation with Protestants
within it. Moreover, even amongst Protestants, as discussed in the introduction, there was not always unanimous agreement regarding methods and
methodologies. Thus, although LeFevre engaged the humanist concept of
ad fontes translation, some of his contemporaries did not. This is evident in

12. Roper, *Oedipus*, 61–63.

13. Thierry, *La Dictionnaire Francois-Latin*, 81, 675; Hus, *Dictionnaire Francois-
Latin* 92; Desainliens, *Dictionarie French and English*, E6[R]; Stoer, *Le grand diction-
nairefrançois-latin*, C[R]; Miege, *New Dictionary French and English*, 45, 82.The term, of
course, links sexual heresy with actual heresy, thus emphasising the sense of an outcast,
apostate and perverse group of individuals.

Francois Bonade's neo-Latin commentary of 1537, which largely followed the Vulgate and extrapolated upon 1 Corinthians 6:9:

> Slaves to idols, nor (the) soft, the adulterer, the greedy, the drunken man, imposter, shall reach the heavenly kingdom and sleeper, swearer, liar, bloody murderer,(they) shall know severe justice at the end . . . [14]

This explanation of οὔτε μαλακοὶ οὔτε ἀρσενοκοῖται is interesting. The author, although certainly aware of the option of *ad fontes* translation, provided a translation of 1 Corinthians 6:9 that was somewhat literal to the Vulgate understanding of οὔτε μαλακοὶ οὔτε ἀρσενοκοῖται. With regard to μαλακοὶ, the author simply employed *mollis* as his understanding of μαλακοὶ. While this is familiar ground for this study, one might question whether the author, by virtue of his employment of the Vulgate, was referring to the medieval (and thus Vulgate-oriented) *mollis*, or to the *mollis* in Estienne's later dictionary. Similarly, *concubitor*, defined as "bedfellow" in Ambrosius, almost certainly acted as a colloquialism for male same-sex activities and seems to relate at least in part to the sources for Paul's neologism. It is unclear, however, in comparison to LeFevre, whether the author intended the term to connote general sodomy, or the pederasty that LeFevre specifically posited by using the term *bougeros*. It is possible that the author simply assumed that the reader would have an understanding and knowledge of οὔτε μαλακοὶ οὔτε ἀρσενοκοῖται to the point of not needing to expound upon his understandings in any deeper format. In a way, this is a plausible explanation. While it is not possible to ascertain what modernity might call the "target audience" for many written pieces in the past, it is entirely likely that the author in question was writing for an audience that was fully aware of, or at least passably familiar with, the traditional, Vulgate-based understandings of οὔτε μαλακοὶ οὔτε ἀρσενοκοῖται. It is also equally plausible, perhaps even more so, that the author was writing for an audience that was not familiar with the ideas about οὔτε μαλακοὶ οὔτε ἀρσενοκοῖται that were developing in the early

---

14. The original being: . . . *Idolis famulas, non mollis, adulter, auarus, ebrius, impostor, caelicola regna tentum* . . . *concubitor, iurans, mendax, homicida cruentus, tandem iustitia tela severitas sciunt* . . . See Bonadus, *Divi Pauli Apostoli gentium*, 24. Bonade's translation falls into an interesting category known as "neo-Latin" translation. This was largely a product of Protestant reformers, although, in Bonade's case, one might wonder about the efficacy of the action and whether or not the action was separate from or was part of the *ad fontes* concept. See Grant, "Neo-Latin Verse-Translations of the Bible," 205–11. Little else can be learned about the author other than that he was a theologian in the early part of the sixteenth century and hailed from the Saintes region. See De'hoefer, *Nouvelle Biographie Universelle Depuis*, 6:536.

modern period under the twin impact of humanism and Protestantism. Thus, the author simply provided traditional translations of οὔτε μαλακοὶ οὔτε ἀρσενοκοῖται, touching briefly upon both in an attempt to be lexically authentic, yet not expounding upon the terms in order to prevent the contemplation of, or worse, the occurrence of such things. Nonetheless, the neo-Latin of Bonade and the *ad fontes* approach of LeFevre seem to show a French vernacular enterprise that was far less "inventive" than that of Luther's in Germany and instead, whether in the refined version of LeFevre's vernacular or in the direct re-statement of Bonade, was in some respect comfortable with the interpretation conveyed in the Vulgate.

LeFevre's writings and the neo-Latin of Bonade, however, were not the only vernaculars to come from the early modern Francophone world. As the study seeks to further define οὔτε μαλακοὶ οὔτε ἀρσενοκοῖται, it must seek interpretations from the wider French-speaking region, particularly the exiled Protestant community in Geneva.

The vernacular translation, which would become the standard for the Reformed tradition, particularly in the early days of the Genevan Reformation, was that by Pierre Robert Olivetan. The translation, produced with the financial support of the Waldensians, received the blessing of Calvin himself for being a proper and trustworthy translation.[15] Olivetan rendered οὔτε μαλακοὶ οὔτε ἀρσενοκοῖται in 1 Corinthians 6:9 as *ne les effeminez, ne les bougres.* This translation seems, at first, to be somewhat standard and to reflect, in part, the older translations by LeFevre. *Bougres,* as above in LeFevre's work, was normally equated with pederasty.[16] At the same time, *effeminez* was a broad-reaching terminology, but essentially meant a general level of being "unmasculine" and was reminiscent of LeFevre's Latin *molles* than his somewhat narrower *volupteur.* Olivetan, however, provided a footnote that produced a more interesting understanding of his translation: *ou berdaches/bougerons* in reference to *effeminez.*[17] *Berdache,* borrowed from the Italian *bardache,* was the colloquial term for a catamite, or a young boy kept for the sexual pleasure of an older male.[18] *Bougeron* was the diminutive form

---

15. Wenneker, "Olivetan, Pierre Robert," 1207–9.

16. See n11 in this chapter.

17. Olivetan, *La Bible Qui est toute la Saincteescripture,* L2R.

18. Desainliens, *Dictionarie,* D8R; Florio, *Queen Anna's New World of Words,* 55 (this definition also appears in Florio's 1598 edition on page 38); Richelet, *French Dictionary,* 75. With regard to catamites, Calvin himself called them the debauched, saying, "Hic estillesensusperversus, haecilla cupiditas ignominosus, hoc illud desiderium impurum, de quo Romanis loquitur!" [This is the perverse sense, the disgraceful craving, this filthy desire, about which the Romans speak.] See Calvin, *Lexicon iuridicum iuris Caesarei simul, et canonici,* 154.

of *bougre*, previously defined above, and as such was the youthful member in a pederastic relationship. This clarification of *effeminez* via *berdaches* or *bougerons* illustrated that, in essence, Olivetan was referring to a particular type of same-sex sexual interaction with his prohibition, namelypederastic sex. Thus, it would seem that Olivetan created a construction whereby he linked *berdaches*, *bougerons*, *effeminez* and *bougres* as the passive and active partners in pederastic unions and did in fact, suggest that the two terms were actually referring to the same group(s) of individuals—those involved in pederastic sex. This produces the clearest and narrowest understanding of the "types of person" Paul was excluding from heaven seen thus far in the study. For Olivetan, Paul was targeting (and limiting) his condemnation of those engaged in pederasty.

Although not a member of the Protestant mainstream, Sebastien Castellio produced a vernacular translation that rivalled that by Olivetan. Castellio had numerous theological differences to Calvin and Calvin rejected his vernacular in favour of that of Calvin's cousin, Olivetan. Castellio translated *οὔτε μαλακοὶ οὔτε ἀρσενοκοῖται* as *nec douillets, nec paedicones*, a translation that largely mirrored those of his contemporaries, as *douillets* was a colloquial version of *molles* or *mollitudes,* suggesting an attempt, like Luther, to mingle textual authenticity withcolloquial words.[19] Similar to that by Olivetan, Castellio's vernacular combined a somewhat nebulous definition of *μαλακοὶ* with the specificity of *paedicones* for *ἀρσενοκοῖται*. This, again, created a link between the hermeneutic worlds of Geneva and Paris and underscored that, while the *μαλακοὶ* could refer to a number of things, for these translators, the *ἀρσενοκοῖται* were most definitely pederasts. Whether or not the inclusion of *μαλακοὶ* was an indicator of a co-joined understanding of the two terms, as seen in Olivetan, or as a potentially separate actor as seen in LeFevre, Bonadus, and Castellio, is debatable. What seems clear, however, is the early modern French-speaking association of the "anti-masculine" or "weak/soft person" with *μαλακοὶ* and of pederasty with *ἀρσενοκοῖται*. In all these translations, there seems a harkening back to LeFevre's work, which in turn, as discussed above, is based extensively on the Vulgate, creating a continuity of sorts. Ultimately, while those working in French and Latin may have also included nebulous ideas of effeminacy in

---

19. Castellio, *Biblia, interprete Sebastiano Castalione,* O5[V]. Here, I am using Castellio's second, and substantially expanded, edition. It is interesting to note that, even though he was often theologically divorced from the mainstream of Geneva, in this instance both Castellio and Olivetan seem to offer strikingly similar translations. This, perhaps, points to an overwhelming consensus, at least within Geneva, of the understanding of 1 Cor 6:9.

their interpretation of Paul, it is clear that they were all united in specifically noting "the pederast" as being excluded from heaven.

Calvin himself, although never producing a biblical vernacular, was nonetheless prolific in terms of expository commentaries.[20] The titan of Genevaproduced a Latin translation that rendered the μαλακοὶ as *molles* and *paederastae* for ἀρσενοκοῖται.[21] As previously seen, Calvin's translations were a combination of old and new, providing both vague and specific definitions. To begin, one must first note that Calvin's definition of *molles* was little different from LeFevre's pre-Reformation commentary or Bonade's neo-Latin translation of *mollis*. This may have been, to some extent, an attempt by the reformer to balance necessary information with tantalising detail. Thankfully, Calvin's writings provide an opportunity to expand upon his understanding of the μαλακοὶ further. Commenting on the Pauline epistles, Calvin defined μαλακοὶ as follows:

> For "molles," I understand those who, although they do not prostitute themselves to lust in the common way, nonetheless, betray their lack of chastity through their meretricious speeches, effeminate gestures and clothing and other indulgences.[22]

According to his translation, Calvin understood *molles* in much the same way as did LeFevre's later vernacular, in that the *mollis* was self-indulgent. In contrast to his contemporary, however, Calvin seems to explore the concept a little further, implying that inappropriate behaviour for a male did not begin and end with sexual continence: general incontinence with regard to speech, gestures, self-display and, in short, self-indulgence in any respect signified such a character. In fact, Calvin specifically implied that the *mollis* was not sexually "degenerate" (*non prostituant se vulgo a libidinem*). While Calvin wrote this somewhat specific understanding of the *molles*, he still left several significant questions unanswered. "Meretricious speeches" may have been clear to Calvin and his readers but is quite alien to modern ears. Moreover, it adds an example of "soft" behaviour not encountered elsewhere. Whether these verbal flourishes were contained within mere verbosity, or if more was required to fit the definition is

---

20. The *Bible de Geneve de Jean Calvin* is attributed to Calvin, but this work is little more than a copy of Olivetan's vernacular—discussed previously in this study- and was more of an opportunity to employ Calvin's name and status than it was an attempt at an original and specific translation. See *La Bible, qui est toute la saincte Escripture.*

21. Calvin, *Opera Omnia Theologica Tomus V,* 311.

22. The original states *Per molles, intelligo qui tametsi non prostituant se vulgo ad libidinem, verbum tamen lenociniis, effoeminato gestu et vestito, aliisque deliciis impudicitiam suam produnt.* See Calvin, *In omnes Pauli apostoli Epistolas,* 209.

unclear. Despite Calvin's fascinating inclusion of "speech habits," in other ways his understanding of *molles* as a general form of emotional incontinence and effeminacy is completely traditional.

Certainly, one who did not prostitute himself to lust in the common manner seems the easiest place to begin digesting Calvin's comments. These characters could, quite easily, have been the masturbators that De Lyra previously mentioned. At the same time, one might also easily group pederasts and those who engaged in homo-social action as having been those evidencing a "lack of chastity" (*impudicitia*). This, however, could not be the end of the discussion, as *impudicitia* often simply implied sexual impurity and thus could also be attributed to those who were of what modernity might call a heterosexual nature who were being ruled by their passions.

"Unmanly behaviour" proves to be a much more nebulous concept to define. As previously discussed, the Protestant Reformation contained within it a certain degree of social utopianism that was based upon the proper comportment of men and women. In addition, there was a distinct concept that restraint and reservation were expected of men. Therefore, "unmanly behaviour" might be construed as anything that did not match the ideals of the conjugal household, established male patriarchy, or male dominance in social, political, and personal areas. Finally, Calvin's "other indulgences" are particularly difficult to define. Given that Calvin was one of the key architects of the Protestant Reformation and his work in Geneva was critical to establishing a Protestant society, one might conclude that "other indulgences" included virtually any of the sexual and social mores that Calvin preached.[23] This category might have included those who engaged excessively in sexual activity for pleasure and not simply for procreation, those who failed to establish ideal conjugal households and instead lived in relationships of cohabitation, those who remained single, and, in general, anyone who engaged in actions that were contra to the nature and purpose of the Protestant Reformation. Thus, one might ultimately define *molles*, per Calvin, as those whose passions, actions and/or ideals precluded their normal and orderly involvement in organized and civil society—a socio-sexual libertinism. This all seems in keeping with Calvin's ideas of what threatened the Reformation in Geneva in the sixteenth century.

Although his definition of *molles* required significant elucidation, the same could not be said of Calvin's usage of *paederastae*. As was the case with LeFevre, Calvin provided a clear translation of ἀρσενοκοῖται. For Calvin, pederasty was not simply a broad category containing all activities that embodied

---

23. Calvin's attitudes to drink, dance, and clothing seem to be definite places to begin with regard to these condemnations.

same-sex sexual relations but was instead a specific and defined category within the realm of sexual misconduct involving partially culpable youth and fully culpable adults.[24] This employment, by Calvin, seems to create a strict paradigm for interpretation amongst the earliest and predominant reformers. Luther, if one reads his neologism literally, LeFevre and Calvin were all in strict agreement that the ἀρσενοκοῖται were pederasts.[25]

Theodore Beza, the spiritual successor to Calvin, was silent about οὔτε μαλακοὶ οὔτε ἀρσενοκοῖται.[26] While Beza might have been reluctant to discuss the implications and understandings of οὔτε μαλακοὶ οὔτε ἀρσενοκοῖται in his day, this does not mean that other Genevan reformers were as reserved. Augustin Marlorat, writing in the mid-sixteenth century, discussed interpretations of the *molles, paederastae* and their places within Genevan life and society. Marlorat's *Thesaurus S. Scripturae* provided the following definitions:

> Molles: Those excluded from the kingdom of God [a clear reference to Corinthians]
>
> Paederastia: See sexual impurity and illicit sexual intercourse.
>
> Sodomia: you should not sleep with a man as with a woman, it is an abomination. (if) someone who sleeps with a man as with a woman, both of them [active and passive] do an abominable thing. They should be executed, excluded from the Kingdom of Heaven. It (the name) is handed down in a shameful sense. The Sodomites sinned in this way, and were destroyed with sulphur and fire.[27]

---

24. See Naphy, *Sex Crimes*, 108–9.

25. However, for Luther, these were specifically pederasts in the Roman Catholic curia and clergy.

26. It is perhaps somewhat salacious, but it is plausible that Beza's quiet treatment of 1 Cor 6:9 was due to the subject being too personal upon which to comment. Beza, in his younger days, produced poetry that spoke of his youthful self being torn between the love for another male and for a female. Such verse was later described as "lascivious, absolutely shameless, and detestable" by one of Beza's chief critics. As Claude de Sainctes would later allege, "Instead of your Audebert, you now have embraced Calvin, and so have substituted a spiritual male-whore for a carnal one, thus being still what you were—a sodomist." See Crompton, *Homosexuality and Civilization*, 323 and Garde, *Jonathan to Gide*, 289.

27. *Molles: a regno Dei excludendi. Paederastia–vide impudicitia et concubitus illiciti. Sodomia: Crimen contra naturam et damnabile. Cum mare ne concubito concubitu Muliebri: abominatio est. Qui concubuerit cum mare concubito muliebri: rem abominandam fecerunt ambo: omnino morte aficiuntor, caedis, ipsocum causa est in ipsis. Regno dei excluduntur A. In sensum reprobum traditi. Sodomitae hoc genere sceleris peccarunt qui sulphure et igne deleti sunt.* See Marlorat, *Thesaurus S. Scripturae*, 451, 497, 644. I am,

While Marlorat was relatively succinct in defining *molles* and *paederastia*, the same cannot be said of his understanding of *sodomia*. Marlorat's understanding of *sodomia* indicated a separation of action between *sodomia* and *paederastia*. Sodomy was a broad yet definable category for Marlorat; *paederastia* was a similar action butwas entirely separate. Although the two might be related, they were not so similar as to be grouped under one definition. Marlorat further commented on his understanding of οὔτε μαλακοὶ οὔτε ἀρσενοκοῖται in an exposition on the New Testament. Although Marlorat chose to employ a neo-Latin translation of 1 Corinthians 6:9 . . . *nequemolles, neque qui concumbunt cum masculis* . . . in this work, he also provided a fuller understanding by commenting:

> The soft are well known and understood, who, although they are not prostitutes, are commonly known as having the wantonness and allurement of a prostitute, effeminate gestures and clothing, and other ornaments of sexual impurity, which betray them. The fourth species is the most grievous, certainly the monstrous foulness, which in Greece was very much common. And all these are the precepts that forbid this one, Do not commit adultery.[28]

Of interest in this commentary is Marlorat's exposition linking the *molles* almost verbatim (including ruling out the concept of prostitution in the literal, "rent-boy" sense) with Calvin's previous definition but changing

rather obviously, using a posthumous edition of Marlorat's work. Although executed in 1562, Marlorat's work was published posthumously on a number of occasions.

28. . . . *est molles intelligit, qui tametsi non prostituant se vulgo libidinem, verborum tamen lenociniis, effoeminato gestu et vestitu, aliisque deliciis impudicitiam suam produnt. Quarum genus omnium est gravissimum, prodigiosa scilicetilla foeditas, quae in Graecia nimis usitate fuit. Et haec omnia uno hoc praecepto prohibentor, non moechaberis.* . . . This echoes Calvin and his "those who do not prostitute themselves in the common way" or, more frankly, receiving money for sex. Marlorat, *Novi Testamenti Catholica ExpositioEcclesiastica*, 689. This is, again, a posthumous edition of Marlorat's work. It is entirely plausible that the neo-Latin of the piece was placed there at a later date by an editor. However, Marlorat may have employed a neo-Latin translation intentionally instead of a more *ad fontes* understanding, as the practice was not unheard of within sixteenth-century France. See footnote 12 of this chapter. It is also possible that Marlorat, via his attribution of pederasty to the Greeks was aware of Plato's summary of pederasty, which stated "When an older lover (ἐράστεσ) and a young man (παιδίκα) come together and each obeys the principle appropriate to him—when the lover realises that he is justified in doing anything for a loved one who grants him favours, and when the young man understands that he is justified in performing any service for a lover who can make him wise and virtuous—and when the lover is able to help the young man become wise and better, and the young man is eager to be taught and improved by his lover—then, and only then, when these to principles coincide absolutely is it ever honourable for a young man to accept the lover." See Nissinen, *Homoeroticism*, 59.

Calvin's attack on speech patterns to one on gestures and clothing. Marlorat was descriptive in his exposition that μαλακοὶ signified a subservience to lust, unmanly actions, a preoccupation with dress and manners and had its roots in Greece. The closing statement, however, indicates that μαλακοὶ was directly connected to the sin of adultery. This might seem to imply a strictly sexual understanding of Marlorat's definition. Such an association, however, would be false. Adultery was more than just sex outside of marital boundaries; it was the breaking of mutual fidelity for personal or individual gain.[29] These μαλακοὶ may, in the mind of Marlorat, have encompassed sodomy within the boundaries of the term, but they were also much more than that. These creatures were not only sexually incontinent but were also incontinent in terms of the basic morals of life. The μαλακοὶ were characterswho were incapable of emotional reservation, who lived for passion and pleasure, and who were not afraid to break boundaries of fidelity—in any aspect—to gain such things.[30] They were, perhaps, the whores who whored only for pleasure, the needy who were not truly needy, and the wanton who had no reason to want.

While Marlorat did not provide a direct interpretation of ἀρσενοκοῖται in his commentary on 1 Corinthians 6:9, he did provide a detailed commentary on the term in its other biblical location, 1 Timothy 1:10:

> Heinous crime, according to its many kinds, abominable to God, nature and mankind, and worthy of divine vengeance, also punishable by harsh and severe laws. P. Scantius made a law by which those who lay with boys were punished with severe torment. NeverthelessValerius writes that they were punished in various ways . . . Which however, the Italians, approving this among themselves now call them "Florentinians" [i.e. people acting like Florentines]. But they give in this time suitable enough punishments. This, and the vice of whoredom God has ordained to be reproved in the laws governing marriage,

29. It is possible that Marlorat, in his connection of pederasty with adultery, might have been echoing the classical poet Martial, who said "Wife, you catch me in the act with a boy, And pointedly state that you too have an ass. Juno said as much to her horny Thunderer, Yet still he sleeps with big Ganymede. Instead of his bow, the man who came from Tiryns Used to bend Hylas over; do you suppose That Megara, Hercules' wife, was bereft of buttocks? Runaway Daphne put Phoebus on the rack, But his tortures were banished by the Spartan lad. Briseïs often lay with her back to Achilles, Yet his beardless friend was closer still. So wife, don't flatter your bits with masculine names, And don't convince yourself you have two cunts." See Martial, *Epigrams*, 11.43.

30. Given the epithets leveled at Henri III, as will be shown later in this chapter, one cannot help but wonder whether Marlorat, or perhaps his editor, had the king in mind when describing his understanding of μαλακοὶ.

especially that which was recommended by custom against worshippers of idols.[31]

Of particular interest in Marlorat's translation is his summary of Roman law and his fixation with the direct and concrete consequences for the ἀρσενοκοῖται. Previously, authors had stated their severe distaste and disdain for ἀρσενοκοῖται, even excluding them from eternal life. Marlorat, while echoing such criticisms, raised the bar by suggesting direct penal consequences.[32] Those who engaged in the actions of the ἀρσενοκοῖται were in direct and concerted opposition towards God and were at the same level as the idolater and the whore. As such, these ἀρσενοκοῖται should receive the same punishment, as might idolaters and whores. However, it is interesting that Marlorat's writing neglected to provide a complete or succinct understanding of how or what he envisioned ἀρσενοκοῖται to be and/or encompass. Although he did cite various historical authors and legal codes such as the Lex Scantinia, which itself might strongly imply pederasty, he did not actually define ἀρσενοκοῖται.[33]

While his definition was somewhat vague, one might infer that Marlorat, by his reference to Florence, understood ἀρσενοκοῖται similarly to the way it was used by Calvin. Florence was, at the time in which Marlorat was writing, infamous for its association with pederastic unions. Pederasty was so rife within the city that the local authorities, realising the situation in which they found themselves, took to fining convicted pederasts instead of punishing them capitally, lest they decimate their male population.[34]

31. Originally Crimen infandum secundum species suas non paucas Deo et nature et hominibus abominabile, ac caelesti ultione dignum, acerbis quoque et duris legibus vindecandum. P. Scantius legem tulit qua puerum concubitores gravi supplicio afficerentur. Varie tamen eos fuisse punito Valerius scribit ... Quod tamen Itali ad hoc sibi applaudentes Florentinari nunc vocitant. Dabunt aut et isti quo tempore poenas satis dignas. Hoc et scortationis vitium legibus matrimonii Dominus reprimere statuit, quibus contra colibus ex idolatorum consuetudine maxime suffragavit. See Marlorat, Novi, 895. Marlorat's inclusion of Valerius only makes the previous two footnotes seem more plausible.

32. Not unlike the Carolina seen in the study's first chapter.

33. The Lex Scantinia is much debated now but was certainly understood as a law prohibiting sexual abuse/violence against the person of a child/youthful citizen and, by extension, seems to have been able to encompass the "crime" of allowing oneself (as a citizen) to be sexually "abused" (penetrated).

34. This will be described in much greater depth in a later chapter; however, for further detail, please see Rocke, Friendships, 205–35. Florence also appeared in other early modern French accusations. In 1534, it was reported that "In this year and in the month of January, a merchant from Florence named Antoine Mellin was brought from Lyon before the parliament, appealing the death sentence of the lay justice of Lyon for having been found a bugger and having committed this sin unnaturally on a girl and on a young boy." The emphasis is on the assailant's Florentine background despite his

While the city was supposedly replete with pederastic unions, one should note that the instances of adult males engaging in acts of sodomy was rather small, and the activity seems to have been, in many ways, taboo.[35] Thus, it is probable that Marlorat had the concept of pederasty—and not, perhaps, the broader concept of *sodomia*—in mind when he levelled his invective against the Florentines.

Marlorat's writings and this study's understanding of them hinge on the concept of Marloratmaking a clear distinction between pederasty and sodomy. While Marlorat's writings are only one person's understanding, a wider survey of other early seventeenth-century writers seems to reinforce the concept. To begin, Martin Becan defined sodomy, in a legal context, as:

> Concerning sodomy the law is this: you should not engage in coitus like a women with a man, it is an abomination. Likewise: If any one lies with a man in coitus like a woman, they should be put to death. Their blood shall be upon them. This is usually called the sin against nature . . . Leviticus 20: 13: If any one lies with a man as a woman, both have committed an abomination and should be put to death: their blood shall be upon them.[36]

This definition provides an understanding of sodomy linked, almost inextricably, with an impression of adult same-sex sexual intercourse. Moses Pflachero wrote that sodomy was *qui coierit cum masculo et mortemoriantur*, or "those who lie with men shall be put to death." This seems to suggest, as one might expect, that the prohibitions of Leviticus guided the understanding of instances of adult sodomy within early modern France.[37]

---

residency in Lyon and is thus indicative of the French mindset. See Lalanne, *Journal d'un bourgeois de Paris sous le regne de Francois premier (1515–1536)*, 435–36.

35. Rocke, *Friendships*, 95.

36. The original saying: . . . *de sodomia sic statutum est: cum masculo non commisceris coitu foemineo, quia abominatio est. et iterum: Qui dormierit cum masculo coitu foemineo, morte moriantur. Sit sanguis eorum super eos. Solet hoc vocari peccatum contra naturam. . . Leviticus 20: 13: qui dormierit cum masculo coitu femineo uterque operati sunt nefas morte moriantur sit sanguis eorum super eos.* See Martinus Becanus, *Analogia Veteris Ac Novi Testamenti*. See Becanus, *Analogia Veteris Ac Novi Testamenti*, 504–5. Becan, although he was a Jesuit priest, is important for this study as his non-Protestant definitions help to develop a picture of sodomy within the overall French-speaking world, not just the world of French Protestants.

37. This summarization of sodomy with Leviticus is quite telling when taken in aggregate with the lack of cross-reference 1 Cor 6:9 receives in early modern Reformed sources. Neither Olivetan, Calvin nor any other offers a cross reference to Leviticus. This would seem to point towards the thought, as explored later in the chapter, that the authors of the time understood the passage to be something perhaps related but distinct from Leviticus. Bullinger, writing in the more German Zurich, did cross-reference the passage, but only to Rom 2:3, with neither New Testament source linked further to

This reinforces a vision that sodomy was mainly equated with same-sex adult interactions, although it did not exclude the actions performed by *cinaedi* and *paederasti*. French legal tracts of both the sixteenth and seventeenth centuries further indicate a more comprehensive view of sodomy that covered all varieties of non-procreative sex. Within such writings, sodomy was equated with masturbation, same-sex relations of all types, bestiality, and any type of non-procreative sexual act, even those between a man and a woman.[38] Therefore, one may understand the ἀρσενοκοῖται as being a sub-category of a larger taxonomy of sodomy. What seems prominent, however, is that while they were associated, the terms ἀρσενοκοῖται and sodomite were not fully interchangeable.

Genevan translations, as well as the translation by LeFevre, raises question of why the translators of the time were so focused on pederasty when translating ἀρσενοκοῖται. One potential explanation of this fixation is based on the politics of the Reformation. The Protestant Reformation, as seen previously in Germany, was not only a religious reformation, but was also a political and social reformation. During the Reformation, the concept of the conjugal household was, again, central to the construction of societal ethics. Whereas those who were engaged in either child abuse or adult-oriented sodomy might constitute a relatively small number, the cities of Venice and Florence, to the south of Geneva, proved that pederasty could be an irksome vice, given the right social characteristics.[39] Men in their twenties dallying with youths were distracted from their duty to focus their aspirations on a future in which they would establish and maintain a strong household. At the same time, late marriages prevented men from exercising sexual functions, which would have been an obvious temptation, especially when young men were frequently huddled together in crowded quarters. Apprentices, servants, or farm labourers, as well as those who were not yet financially able to marry and set up a household, were doubtless often the victims of sexual frustration, or even of romantic yearning. While child abuse and other instances of sexual action *contra naturam* were a scandalous, yet relatively small part of

Leviticus. See Pflachero, *Analysis typica omnium cum veteris,* 104. Little seems to be known about Pflachero, other than he was a Protestant and had a noticeable publication record. His works were published in both Germany and France.

38. See Benedicti, *Somme,* 160–62. See Rochette, *Les Proces Civil et Criminel Divise en Cinq Livres,* 2:21-24.

39. Chojnacki, *Women and Men in Renaissance Venice,* 32–40. We might wonder again if the writings of Martial were not impetus for such concern. Clearly, boys had long been seen as a supplement to women and, if we take Martial's writings at face value, could even become somewhat superior to them in desire. Thus, there might very well have been a well-placed fear of what could happen were pederasty be allowed to gain a legitimate hold within the city. See Martial, *Epigrams,* 11.43.

early modern life, pederasty presented itself as more of a genuine challenge to the social building-blocks of the French/Genevan—and wider—Reformation. Thus, it seems completely plausible that Calvin, LeFevre and others recognized the potential damage that pederasty might cause to the social dynamic of the conjugal household and chose to focus their efforts on this particular subset of sodomitical actions.

Pederasty seems to have often been on the mind of Francophone writers, from Paris to Geneva, when discussing οὔτε μαλακοὶ οὔτε ἀρσενοκοῖται. Nonetheless, this does not account for all instances, as there are two variants that muddle the picture of pederasty being the intended translation of ἀρσενοκοῖται for Francophone writers. Firstly, there are the biblical vernaculars of the early modern Dutch world. Although initially influenced theologically by Lutheranism, the Dutch quickly fell under the influence of the Genevan Reformed movement. In this regard, they serve to link the spreading Lutheran movement that, as will be shown, also had an initial impact in England, to the wider Francophone-dominated Reformed movement. Just as these ties of the Dutch Reformation were multi-faceted, so too were the biblical vernaculars of the movement.

Erasmus of Rotterdam's 1520 *Novum Testamentum*, while providing the impetus for much of the vernacular Bible translation, was decidedly faithful to the Vulgate in its interpretation of 1 Corinthians 6:9. Erasmus' *neq molles, neq qui concubit masculis* was just as enigmatic as was Jerome's previous iteration in the Vulgate.[40] This, however, began to change with the work of Willem Vorsterman.

Vorsterman's 1528 *Vorstermanbijbel* translated οὔτε μαλακοὶ οὔτε ἀρσενοκοῖται as *noch oncuyscheyt, noch wikenzwaken*, providing far more interesting detail than did other translations.[41] *Oncuyscheyt*, derived from *oncuusch*, held a meaning of "unchaste, unclean in mind, obscene, luxurious, and unclean (physically)."[42] Such an understanding is nothing new for this study. Insome ways, it seems quite like the *volupteur* described by LeFevre. The use of *noch wikenzwaken*, however, is another story entirely. While it is most likelyto be a type of colloquialism, the literal translation of the phrase is "neither the effeminately weak." At the outset, this seems to be a re-iteration of terms more often used for the μαλακοὶ than for the

40. Erasmus, *Novum Testamentum Totum*, 486.

41. Little is known about Willem Vorsterman's life, aside from his prodigious-second only to Hillenius's—printing of books in the early modern Netherlands. See "Vorsterman, Willem." See also *De Bibel*.

42. See *Thesavrvs Thevtonicæ Lingvæ*; Kiel, *Etymologicvm Tevtonicae Lingvae*, 930; and van Boendale and de Vries, *Der lekenspieghel, leerdicht van den jare 1330*, 202, 445, 699.

ἀρσενοκοῖται; there is, however, a plausible explanation for this. The *wiken*, an offshoot of both *wekelijk* and *verwijd*, could connote the "emasculated or unmanned."[43] Thus, one might view the text as castigating the "effeminate unmanned" character, or those who eschewed their masculine obligations in society. This, as will be shown below, particularly in the chapter about Italy, was not an uncommon understanding for the time. The ἀρσενοκοῖται was, by its *contra naturam* actions, very much "unmanned" and thus an "effeminate" part of early modern life.

The *Liesveltbijbel*, which was originally published in 1526 but culminated in its final, and arguably most complete edition in 1542, both echoes and clarifies the earlier work by Vorsterman. For οὔτε μαλακοὶ οὔτε ἀρσενοκοῖται, Liesvelt offered *noch die tegan nature oncuyscheyt, noch die wieken*.[44] This was, again, quite similar toVorsterman's version. However, Liesvelt's work did clarify that the *oncuyscheyt* were unclean against nature, thus defining the text as applying strictly to those whose immorality was *contra naturam*, and not simply just the generally impure.

Although Roman Catholic in origin, the 1548 *Leuvense Bijbel*, largely produced by Nicholas van Winghe, provided a surprisingly vernacular translation of 1 Corinthians 6:9. For οὔτε μαλακοὶ οὔτε ἀρσενοκοῖται, van Winghe's text stated *noch sodomiedoende, noch onnatuerlijckeoncuyscheytbedzijuende*.[45] Perhaps what is most interesting about this is the blunt association of the μαλακοὶ with the broad category of sodomy, and the ἀρσενοκοῖται with "unnatural impurity in bed/sexual relations." This translation would thus seem to suggest that the previously broad category of sodomy was indicative of the μαλακοὶ in sixteenth-century Dutch life. At the same time, ἀρσενοκοῖται was indicative of unsavoury sexual practices, most likely non-copulative actions; the 1560 *Biestkensbijbel* only increases this intrigue.[46]

---

43. See *Thesavrvs Thevtonicæ Lingvæ*, NP; Schueren, *Teuthonista of Duytschlender*, 323.

44. *Den Bijbel,* NN1ᵛ. Van Liesvelt was a popular printer of religious works in mid-sixteenth-century Antwerp. He is most noted perhaps both for bringing Luther's Bible into a Dutch print and by doing so losing his head after running afoul of Roman Catholic authorities. See Greenslade, *Cambridge History of the Bible,* 3:123.

45. Winghe, *Den Bibelinhovdende het OvdtendeNiev Testament,* liv. Van Winghe was the Augustinian cannon in Louvain and largely the Roman Catholic church's answer to Liesvelt and his increasingly reform-minded printings. See Greenslade, *Cambridge History of the Bible,* 3:123 and Corbellini, *Discovering the Riches of the Word,* 237.

46. Moreover, *bedzijuende* was also used by the *Leuvense Bijbel* in Rom 1:27 to indicate the type of relations that men and women exchanged with one another, thus implying a decided sexual connotation of the term.

Produced by Nicholas Biestken and strongly influenced and favoured by Luther and Lutherans, the *Biestkensbijbel* translated οὔτε μαλακοὶ οὔτε ἀρσενοκοῖται as *noch de weecklingen, noch de jongenscheynders.*[47] This was, as seen in chapter 1 of this study, an almost literal transposing of Luther's German text with its Dutch analogues. With its blatant similarity in wording, including the requisite compoundneologism for ἀρσενοκοῖται, one should not be surprised by the similarities in the definitionsin Biestken's and in Luther's Bibles. Both the pliable, wanton weakling and the "young boy abuser" are hardly new concepts for this study to encounter. What remains unknown, however, is whether Biestken's translations carried the same potential invective as Luther's, most likely damning the Roman Catholic clergy.

The 1562 *Deux-Aesbijbel*, largely produced for the exiled Reformed Protestant Dutch community in England, provided yet another translation for 1 Corinthians 6:9. In this, οὔτε μαλακοὶ οὔτε ἀρσενοκοῖται was translated as *noch oncuyscheyt/oncuyssche, noch die by mannenliggen.*[48] As with the above, this adds considerable intrigue to the definition of μαλακοὶ and ἀρσενοκοῖται. The *oncuyscheyt/oncuyssche* is well understood from the above definitions. The text's understanding of ἀρσενοκοῖται as *mannenliggen*, however, is worth noting. This somewhat non-descript translation is out of line with its contemporaries but, possibly due to the location, does seem to echo the English understanding of Wycliffe, as shown below in chapter 3.

Perhaps a basis for Dutch translation can be found in the mid-seventeenth century *Statenvertaling*. Produced in 1637, after the Synod of Dordt, and meant to be the first truly "Dutch" translation in terms of both language and influence, the text is reminiscent of its 1562 forerunner mentioned above. Translating οὔτε μαλακοὶ οὔτε ἀρσενοκοῖται as *noch ontuchtighe, noch die by mannenligghen*, the text provides a welcome continuity within the otherwise previously disjointed world of Dutch vernaculars.[49] While the Statenvertaling was -and arguably still is- the predominant translation for Dutch Protestantism since the mid-seventeenth century, it might not be seen as the final word in Dutch vernacular translation.

The 1640 commentary by Willem Hessels van Est indicates that, despite the organic vernacular, the Dutch understanding of οὔτε μαλακοὶ

---

47. Diest, *Den Bybel*, Fol. 70r. Little is known about Biestkens who, for a time, was not even thought to be an actual person. What is certain is that he was a mid-sixteenth century printer, possibly in Emden, and was a strong Lutheran proponent. See Hollander, *Religious Minorities and Cultural Diversity in the Dutch Republic*, 83–85.

48. Wingen and Dyrkinus, *Biblia*, Fol. 63ᵛ. This was the Bible that would be *the* Bible for the Dutch Reformed church until the advent of the Statenvertaling of 1637. See Metzger, *Oxford Guide to Ideas and Issues in the Bible*, 516.

49. *Biblia, dat is, De gantische H. Schrifture*, Fol. 90ᵛ.

οὔτε ἀρσενοκοῖται was still, in several ways, largely tied to the Francophone world. A scholar of biblical interpretation, the Roman Catholic van Est lived and worked in the Catholic Southern Netherlands, particularly in Louvain, as well as in the Northern French Douai. As a result of his studies of biblical interpretation and his regional location, van Est was thus almost certainly familiar with both Protestant and Roman Catholic publications. Therefore, one might consider van Est and his writings as something of a "cross-section" of French, Dutch, Protestant and Roman Catholic understandings; his commentary on the Pauline epistles reveals as much. In his commentary on 1 Corinthians 6:9, van Est discussed both the familiar term of *sodomia* and -separately-ἀρσενοκοῖται, providing each with unique, yet similar definitions. Most telling, however, was that the author used different biblical passages for each. For van Est, *sodomia* was summed up succinctly in the writings of Leviticus. Ἀρσενοκοῖται, on the other hand, was cross-referenced to Romans 1, 1 Corinthians 6:9, and 1 Timothy 1:10.[50] Thus, one might strongly suspect that, for van Est and perhaps for many in his time, sodomy itself was a larger categorisation that dealt primarily with the potential, or lack of potential, for human procreation within a sexual act. Ἀρσενοκοῖται was used to refer to a non-procreative sexual act of a specific type, perhaps pederasty.[51] Therefore, it may be assumed that the Dutch interpretation of 1 Corinthians 6:9 was both comfortingly similar and yet frustratingly different from the rest of the Francophone-inspired movements. One need not only look at Dutch writings, however, to muddy the waters in French/Genevan interpretation, as such material can be found much closer to the proverbial home.

LeFevre, Calvin and their contemporaries put forward vernaculars that were dependent on the ideals and constructs of sexuality being referenced or inferred in their interpretations. Words such as *bougres*, *volupteurs*, *bardaches* and *paederastes* all conveyed some type of sexualized understanding. These renderings, and others like them, provide significant clues regarding how this study might understand οὔτε μαλακοὶ οὔτε ἀρσενοκοῖται in 1 Corinthians 6:9. One must ask, however, what to do with translations that do not display such overtly sexualized renderings? There were, in fact, French

---

50. Est, *In Omni Beati Pauli*, 19, 248. This has already been seen in the much earlier mid-sixteenth century writings of Castellio.

51. The caveat we might insert here deals with *cinaedi*. Due to its wider lexical range, it is entirely plausible that the term could be interchangeable with sodomy. However, it would seem unlikely, when used to reference ἀρσενοκοῖται, that *cinaedi* would mean the whole of sodomy. Overwhelmingly, the translations of early modern France dealt with pederasts when speaking of ἀρσενοκοῖται, which, as we have examined, is also a part of the lexical range of *cinaedi*.

vernacular Bibles that did not render οὔτε μαλακοὶ οὔτε ἀρσενοκοῖται using directly sexualized understandings of 1 Corinthians 6:9. For example, some vernaculars rendered οὔτε μαλακοὶ οὔτε ἀρσενοκοῖται as *ni les effeminez, niceux qui habitent avec masles* instead.[52] This translation of οὔτε μαλακοὶ οὔτε ἀρσενοκοῖται is of interest in this study.

Effeminez, as a definition, is nothing new for this study. Whereas LeFevre's *volupteurs* held within it an intrinsic understanding of pleasure, particularly of carnal pleasure, *effeminez* simply meant non-masculine.[53] Thus, it seems that this rendering was potentially meant to discuss less of a sexual act and more of an over-arching condition within society andhad parallels with Calvin and others who discussed gestures and mannerisms. It is as though the translator was implying that those who failed to meet their masculine obligations were barred from the Kingdom of Heaven. This, in itself, seems to provide much to ponder. That the authors of these translations were so keen to utilize *effeminez* when there were other translational options, such as *volupteurs*, should solidify the notion that concepts of gender identity and comportment were of critical importance to those within early modern French-speaking realms. At the same time, neither the *volupteur* nor *effeminez* schools of translation were differed significantly; one spoke in a generalized sense about a "sensual" (feminine) character, while the other focused specifically on the gendered role/comportment. Both were addressing issues of countercultural masculinity. Both translations dealt with men who failed to achieve or uphold the societal understanding of what it was to be a "man" or "masculine." The difference between the two, however, was that the former, represented by LeFevre and Calvin, refined the term to speak only to a specific type of male, most often one who had failed in the arena of sex and passion. The latter, while not severing an association with the former, applied the distinction in a broad and general sense to all of those who failed to uphold the social and cultural ideals of what it meant to be masculine. Just as the pederast was always a sodomite, so too was a *volupteur* always effeminate. Thus, extrapolated to its exegetical fullness, it seems that the translators of the latter renderings held social comportment and adherence as such critical ideals that they were willing to label all those who failed to keep them as unable to inherit the Kingdom

52. See Laurents, *La Bible, qui esttoute la saincte Escriture du vieil et Novveau Testament;** Marot, *La Nouveau Testament* (Amsterdam: Chez la Veuve de Schippers 1692); Unknown, *La Nouveau Testament* (Paris: Par Antoine Cellier, 1655); Unknown, *La Bible* (Geneva: Imprinted Matthieu Berjan, 1605);* Unknown, *La Nouveau Testament* (Paris: S.I., 1655); Unknown, *La Bible* (Geneva, S.I., 1637). * = Those which substitute *bougres* for ἀρσενοκοῖται in 1 Tim 1:10.

53. Estienne, *Dictionnaire*, 162.

of God. This understanding, in and of itself, provides much to think about, not only concerning early modern theological understanding, but also how theology and society might have interacted at such a time or place. Based on this study's investigation, one can infer that social order and theology were not mutually exclusive items.[54] Instead, the two concepts were intertwined items that influenced, supported, and subsisted through and via one another. Theology was defined by social policy and social policy was often defined by theology in early modern French-speaking territories. This is not to say that the two did not have separations and differentiations, but it would seem, particularly in the case of this study, that the two were more often connected than not. Again, it was one thing entirely to utilize *volupteurs* as LeFevre did. This levelled a prohibition at one specific part of society that engaged in specific actions. On the other hand, to utilize *effeminez* as a translation was to place a prohibition on an entire segment of society, the offending actions of which ranged across a relatively broad spectrum. Such a translation provides an interesting window into the early modern worldview: Social comportment, by virtue of this hermeneutic, seemed to be not simply a casual or fond concept for the early moderns. Instead, social comportment was such a critical ideal and building block of societal makeup that the early moderns were willing (literally) to "damn to hell" any who did not function according to these ascribed set of actions. This study is thus not far off in imagining that he early modern translators, when employing *effeminez* in their translations of 1 Corinthians 6:9, were saying,"If you do not uphold the masculine structures and expectations that we have, you are worthless to our vision of society."

While the intricacies of employing *effeminez* as a rendering of μαλακοί are highly interesting, even more complex is the translation of ἀρσενοκοῖται as *niceux qui habitent avec masles*. Rendered literally, this translates as "neither the males who live with males." This translation gives cause for considerable pause. While tempting, it would be simplistic to overlook the usual role of circumlocutive euphemisms and to see this as simply implying a prohibition against those engaged in cohabitation with others of the same sex. Men of that day and age were almost completely moulded around the expectation of taking a wife and creating a family when reaching a certain thresh-hold of masculinity. Instances of male cohabitation certainly did exist, but were mainly linked to situations that involved guild membership and labour, and which represented a transient, pre-adult stage in the life of the individual.[55] Those who were involved in guild apprentice programmes

---

54. Roper, *Oedipus*, 57.
55. We might also include soldiers in this category.

of the time were generally expected to live and work under their master-craftsman's roof, sometimes with other males with whom they would learn, live and share quarters.[56] These men were not generally considered "men" in the eyes of society until they had attained both a mastery of their craft and membership of the guild that controlled their craft.[57] Thus, they could spend a significant amount of time in the service of the master-craftsman and in living arrangements that placed them with other males. With the economic and social power that craftsmen's guilds had at the time, it is unlikely that there would have been a significant prohibition in the translations in question levelled against the guilds or apprentices.

Another potential explanation for this rendering of ἀρσενοκοῖται is to ascribe the meaning of the translation to a dedicated homo-social sub-culture. Ostensibly, this sub-culture included men who lived with other men, whether secretively or not, and engaged with them on a sexual and emotional level. Such engagement, whether suspected or proven, through sodomy convictions or other similar instances, could have spurred the translators of these biblical texts to include such infractions in their exegesis. This would appear to be plausible. The verb used in the renderings, *habitent*, was specifically designated to mean "living with," while the phrase itself employed the masculine gender, indicating that the text referred explicitly to male actions.[58] Unfortunately, this creates significant problems, particularly with the verb. Were the word to be *habitant* or another similar variant, one could assume a more sexualized understanding. As this was not the case in any of the translations, one is left to sit with *habitent*. Again, this seems to imply that some form of co-habitation was occurring, or was at least suspected, within or around the locales of the translators. The other problem one finds with this type of understanding is that there is little or no historical evidence to support this concept of adult male cohabitation at the time of the publications of these vernaculars. In the historical records, one does not find evidence in the locations in which these texts were produced, of the existence, or rather acknowledgement of the existence, of homo-social sub-cultures until the early to mid-eighteenth century.[59] This is not to say

56. Roper, *Household*, 20–37.

57. Black, *Guilds and Civil Society in European Political Thought from the Twelfth Century to the Present*, 123–28.

58. Estienne, *Dictionnaire*, 304; Mace, *Dictionnaire*, 314; Miege, *Dictionary of Barbarous French*, 68.

59. As Robert Oresko has pointed out, we can only decipher such situations from legal cases. Such cases do not appear in legal record, in notable numbers, until the eighteenth century. See Oresko, "Homosexuality and the Court Elites of Early Modern France," 105–28. See also Rocke, *Forbidden*, 88.

that one may not find evidence of sodomy via civic trials in the seventeenth century. Much to the contrary, there are a few recorded sodomy trials within the seventeenth-century French-speaking world. It is also not the case that one cannot find evidence of an understanding of the homo-social action of sodomy being viewed as a specific sub-culture in the seventeenth century.[60] In fact, sodomy trials in sixteenth- and seventeenth-century Geneva indicated an understanding of the true sodomite as having qualities, desires and experiences that were different from those of the average "normal" citizen.[61] Nonetheless, these lines of thought were not sufficiently developed to indicate the specific existence of a dedicated homo-social sub-culture at the time. If all these vernaculars were of the latter half of the seventeenth century, perhaps one might understand them to be precursors to the revelation of the homosocial sub-cultures that were made known within the early to mid-eighteenth century. Again, this fails to hold true, as the vernaculars stretch across the breadth of the seventeenth century.

Thus, while it may seem plausible that the vernacular renderings of ἀρσενοκοῖται in question were referencing a defined and designated homo-social sub-culture in their regions, the historical record would seem to make this understanding highly unlikely. Therefore, the study must seek another understanding of these interpreters' renderings of ἀρσενοκοῖται.

As the study endeavours to understand this pericope, it might do well to review the pertinent facts that may provide clues regarding to how the translators might have viewed the text. To begin, the grammar in the phrase that was used to render ἀρσενοκοῖται seemingly indicates that the translators were dealing with a situation that, again, applied strictly to men. Certainly, one must allow that masculine plurals, as encountered in this instance, have long been used to address both men and mixed gender groups. Thus, it might be suspected that these reforming authors were admonishing against cohabitation just as much as they were same-sex interactions. Moreover, the cohabitation of unmarried males and females was certainly documented as having been a significant source of concern for certain

60. Monastic life, in particular, was an enterprise, which was often associated with sodomy, and very well could have been the author's intent. The Third Lateran Council included a stipulation that clerics who were caught in *peccatum contra naturam* be forced into penance within a monastery. (*Quicumque incontinentia illa, quad contra naturam est, propter quam venit ira Dei in filios diffident et quince civitates igne consumpsit, deprehensi furring laborare, si cleric furring eiciantur a clerk vel ad poenitentiam agendum in monasteriis detrudantur*). In a great many ways, this stood to encourage Protestant notions that monasteries were full of sodomites. See *Decrees of the Ecumenical Councils,* 1:217.

61. Naphy, *Sex*, 93–94.

members of the reforming communities.[62] A mixed-gender connotation for the translation, coupled with the usage of *habitent*, might certainly account for the ire of the translators being focused on those who engaged in non-married cohabitation within the translators' times and locales.[63] Unfortunately, the lexical framework of ἀρσενοκοῖται does not, in any instance, seem to support a usage that includes women as being its active agents with reference to those who cohabited with men.

A further option for the definition, given the conditions examined previously, is that the authors of these texts were focusing their ire on Roman Catholic clerics, especially on monastics. As seen previously, for Luther, the Roman Catholic priest was, in a great many ways, thought to be the antithesis of Protestant sexual morality. Moreover, these characters did *habitent* with other men inside a monastery. Although largely driven by religious differences, this characterisation was, again, more than a simple polemic.[64] There were a great number of examples, both historical and contemporary, to support this claim. A substantial number of priests—and even more than a few popes, such as Julius II and III—were thought (or were known) to have not-so-secret lovers and offspring.[65] This flouting of both clerical vows and maritally oriented sexuality might have occasioned these biblical translations by Protestant malcontents.[66] This theory seems to find some outside support within the early seventeenth-century translation by the Bernese Protestant Benedict Aretius. Aretius translated μαλακοὶ traditionally as *mollices*. Aretius' translation of ἀρσενοκοῖται as *pelicatus*, however, is fascinating.[67] Translated literally, Aretius rendered ἀρσενοκοῖται

62. Karant-Nunn, *Reformation*, 40.

63. Including, perhaps the ostensibly celibate men and women clinging to their monastic vows as these were often thought of as—rather inevitably—being involved in cohabitation. Luther's entire proposition of the conjugal household revolved around the thought that sexuality was an inherent part of human existence. To deny such desire, was to lie to oneself. Eventually, the person would forsake chastity for adultery of some type. See "*The Estate of Marriage (1520)*" in LW: 45.

64. Though, it should be made entirely clear: there was considerable polemic involved in all accusations. As Crompton has illustrated there was more than a bit of xeno-homophobia directed at both Spain and Italy within early modern France. So great was this association that sodomy was commonly known as "le vice Italien" and "le vice ultramontain." As early modern scholar Joseph Scaliger noted *In Spagna gli preti, in Francia i Grandi, in Italia tutti quanti*: "In Spain, the priests, in France, the nobility, in Italy, everyone." See Crompton, *Homosexuality and Civilization*, 321–23.

65. Though, there is, perhaps more than a bit of room to doubt the characterization of Julius II as being pederastic. Again, polemic cause was an incredibly handy tool for accusations of sodomy. See Crompton, *Homosexuality and Civilization*, 322.

66. I am, of course, assuming a Protestant orientation and origin to these texts.

67. Aretius, *Commentarii in Domini Nostri Iesu Christi*, 125. Aretius, though

as "concubinage."[68] If the author were referencing male concubinage with women, the rendering would seem to be redundant as it could be included in 1 Corinthians 6:9's later mention of adultery.[69] Concubinage, however, was most often associated with cohabitation. Given the status and nature of priestly relations at the time, one might wonder if the author, as Luther did previously, was directing his censure at priests who were less than celibate. In addition, the lack of definition or detail provided by the author might also incline us to assume some type of sodomitical or homo-social overtone. As such, it is probable that the author was expounding upon the specific act of men, priests or otherwise, keeping boys for sex, thus implying a prohibition of *pederasty*. This understanding is reinforced by examining the usage of ἀρσενοκοῖται in 1 Timothy 1:10 in these questionable vernaculars. In 1 Timothy 1:10, ἀρσενοκοῖται, in two of the vernaculars in question, was rendered in the same manner as it was found in 1 Corinthians 6:9. Several other translations, however, rendered the term as *bougres*. Aside from placing us in familiar territory, this provides a significant clue regarding how one was to understand the translators' more problematic rendering in 1 Corinthians 6:9. *Bougres* or "buggers," as has been seen, was synonymous with *paederastes*.[70] Pederasty amongst clergy members was something of a well-trumpeted, although not entirely common, occurrence in the late medieval and early modern eras. It was more common for priests to be cited for adultery, but cases of *propter puerum* were certainly not unheard of.[71] Luther's colleague even alleged that the Pope's entourage consisted of *impudicae mulieres ac prostituti pueri*.[72] This understanding of priestly pederasty, however, cannot fully account for an understanding of these translations, as such actions were not sufficiently frequent to occasion translations across the entire seventeenth century; in any event, the late-medieval stereotype of the licentious priest was receding before the Tridentine reform programme

---

educated in Strassbourg and Marburg, was far more associated with the Genevan Reformation than he was with the Lutheran. See Graf, *Geschichte der Mathermatic und der Naturwissenschaften in Bernischen Landen*, 25–29.

68. Estienne, *Dictionnaire*, 101.

69. It would not be outside the bounds of definition to speculate that the *cinaedi* were seen as engaging in *pelicati pelicatio*.

70. Thierry, *Dictionnaire*, 81.

71. Puff documents this well and, as he noted, *propter puerum*—on account of boy—became a common way of labelling pederastic crimes in legal records of the early sixteenth century. See Puff, *Sodomy*, 35–42.

72. "*Crotus Rubeanus and Luther*," in WABR 1:542. Crompton notes that there was quite a practice of priestly pederasty in parts of early modern France, with the offenders, when discovered, sent to monasteries for penance. See Crompton, *Homosexuality and Civilization*, 322.

at that time. This places the study in a position of cognitive dissonance with regard to how one should understand the usage of *habitent* in view of its male connotation. At present, the study seems to be caught between the realities that *habitent*, in its time, conveyed the meaning of "living together with," the fact that such relationships amongst men, outside of guild life, were virtually unheard of at the time, and a lexical limitation in ascribing the term to heterosexual engagements.[73] However, linking these translations to the wider field of pederasty—including, but not limited to, priestly incidents—produces a more plausible understanding.[74] An examination of legal proceedings from the time only bolsters this understanding.

One may argue that Geneva, because of its Calvinist principles, had the most restrictive views on sex and sexuality within the French-speaking world of the early moderns.[75] Nonetheless, even Geneva, as discussed previously, became familiar with situations involving pederasty. Such a case is described in Naphy's *Sex Crimes from Renaissance to Enlightenment:*

> In 1551, Jean Fontanna and Francois Puthod were arrested for "inappropriate acts"[76] initiated by Fontanna. The best evidence suggests that Fontanna was in his mid-forties while Puthod gave his age as about nineteen. He lived in the Fontanna house though he does not appear to have been a servant. Presumably, he was either a lodger or a ward of some sort. The two had come to the attention of the court when they were seen "wrestling" nude in a garden. . . . Under intense questioning, the court discovered that the two had been engaged in sexual relations for about a year, even though Fontanna had a wife and child. Fontanna admitted that they had mutually masturbated and engaged in intercrural sex and frottage. However, they both specifically denied that anal penetration had taken place, ever. . . Puthod told the court that he did not know if what they had done was good or bad, but if bad he begged for

73. Estienne, *Dictionnaire*, 247.

74. Puff noted that the trials of pederastic priests often became something of a "tug of war" between ecclesiastic and secular jurisdictions, often with the priestly offenders receiving light penalties due to being under ecclesiastic law. This, in and of itself, might explain something about the notoriety and knowledge within the Reformation of such a relatively small instance. See Puff, *Sodomy*, 42.

75. It has been noted that Geneva, in particular, was exceptionally stringent with its enforcement of rules concerning sodomy—including pederasty. Not all cases instances returned a death sentence, but at the very least they occasioned banishment (which, was perhaps almost as bad as a death sentence.) See Monter, "Sodomy and Heresy In Early Modern Switzerland," 1–2, 41–55.

76. One might note that the Genevan courts choose to not use the words sodomy or pederasty and instead applied a circumlocution.

mercy and forgiveness. The resulting sentence was. . . Fontanna
was ordered to be chained to a large stone for a year and a day
and Puthod was banished. There is some evidence, though, to
suggest that Fontanna was, in fact, executed.[77]

The legal case of Puthod and Fontanna poses a number of critical questions, particularly, the lack of comment regarding the fact that the youth
was staying with a married man and his family. Geneva, at that time, contained less than 20,000 souls.[78] One does not find any record of there being
any protest at Puthod and Fontanna's living situation, which suggests that
it did not appear unappealing or odd within the social settings of the day.
Geneva was also well known for its systemic methods of ensuring proper
social discipline and comportment. Genevans were not only constantly
under watch but were also watching for proper comportment within the
city-state. Given the highly regulated and inflammatory properties of sex
and sexuality within the day and age, one might assume that sexual con-
duct was the most regulated of all. With regard to the current examination, it should be remembered that, for sexual sin to have taken place, be
it willing or unwilling, a certain level of accessibility was required. Given
the preoccupation with social and spiritual order, it seems unlikely that
such considerations would not have occurred to Genevans. Were the living arrangements of a citizen suspicious, it seems unlikely that they would
not have received attention, criticism, or redress long before there was a
fateful tussle in the garden, as was the case with the men in our example.
That the sins of Puthod and Fontana occurred in the open, again, seems to
illustrate that it was nothing odd for a youth in Geneva to be housed with
a male who was not his father. Limited records prevent knowing the exact
way that Puthod and Fontana were found out by their neighbours, only
that they were engaged with one another in a public setting. This would
seemingly point towards either a distinct lack of discretion on the part of
the two defendants, or a social tolerance of young men being around, living
with, and/or engaging with older men. Again, this should not be mistaken
for an admission or claim that there was a sub-scene that approved of or
promoted homo-social sexual engagements. Instead, it should merely be
noted that the specifics of the act were of an offensive nature and not the
act of being in the garden together in itself.

Although this case allows a greater understanding of the nature
of and background to the translations, it does not bring one closer to a

---

77. Naphy, *Sex Crimes*, 90–91.
78. Naphy, *Sex Crimes*, 90.

distinct and concrete understanding of the translation in question.[79] Unfortunately, finding a succinct and explicit explanation of *niceux qui habitent avec masles* is something that will remain outside of the scope of this study. It may certainly be said that it seems likely that the translation was a euphemistic reference to male same-sex activities and, in the context of the other translation, probably implied pederasty. It would even be tempting to say that these understandings of ἀρσενοκοῖται, involving *habitent* and pederasty, were simply different ways of saying the same thing. However, this might be something of a stretch. A reality that must be accepted, albeit grudgingly, is that the definitions of cohabitation in these texts, whether they later alluded to *pederasty* or not, are vague to the extreme. Thus, it would seem that two options present themselves: Firstly, one might understand the texts simply to be colloquialisms, the meaning of which is now lost. The text would make complete sense to early modern ears but is now inaccessible. Secondly, the text is an example of a coded or restrictive dialogue. The text would have made little specific sense to the average reader—in any period—but could provide sufficient definition to be relevant. At the same time, for those with knowledge of the nature and actions of pederasty, the text could have spoken volumes.

While it is perhaps tempting to say that this study has now produced pertinent definitions for its key words, this is only partially true. Although the writings of LeFevre, Calvin, Bonade and others have established some crucial boundaries for οὔτε μαλακοὶ οὔτε ἀρσενοκοῖται, these boundaries do not establish the full context of the phrase. It is one thing to know what words meant within a society, but it is another to understand the wider tenets of that society and how such words might fit within such frameworks. For this study, this requires a discussion of sex, sexuality, and proper comportment within the early modern French-speaking world.

As in Germany, the era prior to the Protestant Reformation saw a distinct separation of gender guidelines and distinctions within early modern France. Men were to act like men and women like women. Failure to do so was not necessarily unheard of, but it was greatly condemned. Sex, as an act, was ideally to be avoided, except for procreation. Even when the purpose was procreation, sex, for some, was not to be enjoyed but was an act necessary to fulfil God's injunction to populate the earth.[80] Abstaining from

---

79. Roper, *Holy Household*, 20.

80. Salisbury, *Sex and the Middle Ages*, 1–3. We might assume that these that a large amount of sexual thought and reasoning of the pre-Reformation world traced at least in some respect, the root to Thomas Aquinas and his proclamations upon sex and sexuality, an epitome of the church's traditional teaching on the matter. These items may be found in: Aquinas's *Summa Theologia II-II* questions 153 and 154.

and denying one's urges and desires achieved holiness, or propriety, in the realm of sexuality. The rationale behind this view assumed that, by denying those things that came naturally from having a base nature, one might grow closer to God. To deny that which was natural on this earth was a way, by experiencing denial, to grow closer to the divine. Thus, partly because of the denial of their own physicality, monks, priests, nuns, and other celibates were seen as being closer to the divine and holier than those who engaged in sexual actions, even if they were only for procreation.[81]

It is appropriate to say that sex and sexuality in early modern Francophone lands were concepts that were simultaneously traditional and evolutionary in their understandings. French-speaking regions represented both a traditional understanding that was inherited from the Middle Ages and a new and re-defined ethic influenced by Protestant ideas.[82] This Protestant ethic was still easily defined as patriarchy, yet it also contained ideals concerning both sex and sexuality that were new and which differed from the ideals of earlier centuries.[83] The concept of the conjugal household, previously seen via the example of Germany, was one of the most distinct aspects of civic change within the Protestant Reformation, enabling a vibrant and frequent sexual outlet within the confines of the marriage bed.[84] Even the world of the Roman Catholics, which was largely predominant in early modern France, saw a significant movement towards pleasurable sexuality in marriage.[85] In a relatively short time, sex in France—much as in Germany—transitioned from a somewhat uncomfortable aspect of the human condition to a critical component of both social and ecclesiastic life.

French males, in the new Protestant construct of sexuality, continued to be dominant actors in any discussion concerning sex and sexuality at the time. They were expected to display certain characteristics in both their intentional and unintentional actions. Men were to be dominant, assertive leaders in both the home and within communities. They were thought to be the ideal of creation and potentially reflective of the spiritual or divine

81. Salisbury, *Sex and the Middle Ages*, 28–29. Again, the logic for this can be drawn from Aquinas, specifically parts 2 of question 153 in *Summa Theologia II-II*. We should note, however, that this was line of thought was far from universal in the early modern world.

82. For a fuller exploration of this topic see Mentzer, "Masculinity and the Reformed Tradition in France," 120–39.

83. For a fuller understanding of this, see Hendrix, "Masculinity and Patriarchy in Reformation Germany," 71–94.

84. Oliver, *Conjugal Spirituality*, 17.

85. Wiesner-Hanks, *Christianity and Sexuality in the Early Modern World*, 133.

truths of the world.[86] They were to be restrained, logical and contemplative beings. God worked through men and was most likely to be understood and experienced through the actions of men. Accordingly, men were the primary actors in civil and in ecclesiastic life. At the same time, men, even in the nobility, were not born masculine *per se*, but merely as males, upon whom masculinity and manhood would eventually be bestowed should they navigate particular social criteria and obstacles successfully. As Farr noted, masculinity within this early modern era required a learned and engaged relationship with a "cosmic, divinely sanctioned hierarchical structure securing the peaceful social relationships which defined Christian community."[87] Whereas femininity was seen as a definite status, achieved by virtue of being born with female anatomical parts, manliness required deliberate action and maintenance by the men of the time.[88] A significant portion of what one might call the economy of masculinity focused on masculinity in public life. Was a man a leader? Did he show ambition and, when necessary, aggression? Perhaps most importantly, what was a man's career outlook; was he apprenticed to a tradesman and guild, was he a soldier, was he a common farmer, or was he indentured to a house?[89] The last criterion was critical to allowing a male to achieve the ultimate in masculine economy: marriage.[90] While the procession from journeyman to master and fortunes of war did much to display the masculinity of a male, marriage was his ascent to the pinnacle of masculinity. Marriage presented the male with the ability to display all the attributes of masculinity within his own private world. His taking of a wife allowed him the opportunity to build a household, his own small kingdom, in which his wife would obey his will, provide him with children and care for the internal working of his home. The man's role was to be the economic provider for the home, in control of his wife's base sexual urges, and to ensure the correct comportment of all within his household.[91] Failure to do so caused the male and, in many cases, his entire household to lose standing in social, civic, and even economic matters.[92]

---

86. Kritzman, *Rhetoric of Sexuality and the Literature of the French Renaissance*, 13.

87. Farr, *Authority and Sexuality in Early Modern Burgundy*, 18.

88. Roper, *Oedipus*, 107, 125. See also Low, *Manhood and the Duel*, 71–72.

89. As Roper has noted, phallic culture of the time was very much a public expression. Whereas women were mysterious and unexplainable, men were to be defined and open; figuratively showing who and what they were for all to see. See Roper, *Oedipus*, 59.

90. To be unmarried could be cause for suspicion amongst reformers. See Wiesner-Hanks, *Christianity*, 63.

91. Wiesner-Hanks, *Christianity*, 62–63.

92. Karant-Nunn, *Reformation*, 7.

Women, conversely, were seen as the direct opposite of men. If men were the link to God's spiritual truth and enlightenment, then women were creatures with a base nature who were bound to the simplicity and corruptness of the earth. French females were often seen as lustful, weak and, perhaps most importantly, they were corrupt and corrupting.[93] Because of this view, men were to rule over women to lead them to the truth of God and to help to ensure right and proper civic order. In all of these things, passion, and the response of each sex to passion, was a prime differentiator between the two within early modern French society.

The concepts of *honnetéte* and *bienséance* were the guiding concepts of masculine comportment within early modern France. *Honnetéte* meant honesty, chastity, and civility, or, as Farr notes, the brake on passions in an individual. Similarly, *bienséance* meant comeliness, decency, a becoming attribute or, again as concluded by Farr, the love of virtue. Both concepts were key components not just of noble masculine society, but of all masculine society in early modern France.[94] Men were to be devoid of, or at the very least in tight control of, their passions. Women, on the other hand, were thought of as the embodiment of passion.[95] Unbridled passion was, in the eyes of society, the primary cause of social upheaval and instability. Thus, men and masculinity, through their ability to restrain their passions, were the saviours of society, while women and femininity were its potential undoing.

Given this background, one can begin to ascertain what it was to be οὔτε μαλακοὶ οὔτε ἀρσενοκοῖται at the time. In particular, the concept of μαλακοὶ, the *volupteurs*, becomes clearer. LeFevre, employing *volupteurs* as μαλακοὶ, thus implied men in the grip of the feminine vice of incontinence. This understanding of μαλακοὶ as an embodiment of the feminine displayed the gravity of LeFevre's and of Calvin's interpretations.[96] Women, again, were assumed to have the qualities of a *volupteur* as this was in their nature. Men, on the other hand, were expected to transcend this for the betterment of themselves and society. They were to be the saviours of society, its portals

93. Fradenburg and Freccero, *Premodern Sexualities*, 119. See also Roper, *Oedipus*, 41.

94. Miege, *Barbarous*, D4R; Miege, *New*, J4V, Sf2R; Farr, *Authority*, 14, 16, 22, 23, 43; La Cuisine, *Le Parlement de Bourgogne depuis son origine jusqà sa chute*, 1:243–53, 1:267–69; Baret, *An aluearie or triple dictionarie in Englishe, Latin, and French*, 860–66.

95. Farr, *Authority*, 13–32.

96. As Salisbury has noted in medieval thought the man who played the effeminate or passive role was not necessarily keen for other men, so much as he was keen to be a woman, or the embodiment of disorder for society. See Salisbury, *Sex and the Middle Ages*, 129.

to the divine and its rational actors.[97] The definition of ἀρσενοκοῖται as the *bougeros*, *bougre* or *paederastes* also becomes clearer. While not sacrificing their own masculinity *per se*, these were the creatures that necessitated or enticed the *volupteur* to sacrifice his masculinity.[98] This nefarious synergy is one that is not difficult to find within early modern French culture. When one examines early modern French society to find evidence of the *volupteur*, *mollis*, *cinaedus* or others, one finds evidence of both the characters and the problems they might create right at the proverbial top.

Henri III Valois has been the subject of much historical debate. In both contemporary and modern sources, Henri has often been portrayed as an effeminate, emasculated and dubious character, occasioning 900 polemics between 1584 and 1589 alone and being castigated by Catholics and Protestants alike.[99] Henri was described by one contemporary as having "prostituted himself to unnatural love, and had even turned his pleasures to passive rather than active, one noted the loss of that courage which had been seen before the birth of these enormities."[100] This description, while certainly polemic, harkens closely to the definitions given for *molles* by authors such as Estienne and Benedict. How and why a king could earn such an epithet details just who might have been οὔτε μαλακοὶ οὔτε ἀρσενοκοῖται in early modern France and the vitriol associated with them.

Firstly, it is historically difficult to label Henri as a sodomite or as a homosexual. If anything, Henri was a notable lover of women, particularly during his journey to Poland.[101] What associated Henri with definitions similar to those given for οὔτε μαλακοὶ οὔτε ἀρσενοκοῖται was not one particular thing, but a combination of many factors. In the first instance, Henri was a rather vain man, noted for the novelty of his wardrobe.[102] Ladurie noted that Henri's chamberlains were sent far and wide to collect all sorts of ornaments for the king.[103] In this regard, one might be reminded of Calvin's reference to the *molles* and their dress and indulgences. Certainly, Henri was far from alone

97. Borris and Rousseau, *Sciences of Homosexuality in Early Modern Europe*, 17. See also Roper, *Oedipus*, 41.

98. We should note that, just as with Luther, there was an association with sodomy and Italy in early modern France. Specifically, both the name and origin of sodomy were attributed to Italians. See *Les Proces civil et criminal divise in cinq livres*, 2:21–24.

99. Crompton, *Homosexuality and Civilization*, 330.

100. Römer, "Der Uranismus in den Niederlanden bis zum 19," 605.

101. Crawford, "Love, Sodomy, and Scanda," 518. Also, Ferguson, *Queer (Re)Readings in the French Renaissance*.

102. Crompton, *Homosexuality and Civilization*, 329.

103. Ladurie, *L'Etat Royal*, 235.

in the sense of being a vain ruler, but this was not Henri's only notable public flaw; instead, it was only the tip of the proverbial iceberg.

Henri was, in his rule as king, not only incredibly intelligent and charming, but also quite an indecisive ruler who was given to his passions.[104] Upon his accession to the throne, Henri inherited an extremely volatile political landscape. A significant portion of this volatility was the result of the infighting of rival Catholic and Protestant adherents within French politics. Henri, a moderate Catholic, was in constant struggle with both the Huguenots and with France's extreme Catholics. As part of this struggle, Henri vacillated between each faction, appeasing none and alienating most. Moreover, Henri's more successful ventures, such as the treaty of Beaulieu, were overshadowed by the leadership of his mother, the formidable Catherine de Medici.[105] So overshadowed were the king's abilities that Freer noted, after the Treaty of Beaulieu, a pamphlet circulated bearing the indictment: *Henri, par la grace de sa mere inerteroi de France et de Pologneimaginaire . . .*[106] Henri was, at least for some portion of his subjects, indecisive, inept and, perhaps most importantly, overshadowed by his mother, all aspects that would have served, in combination with his noted vanity, to mark him as an emasculated ruler. Thus, it should be no surprise that Henri was labelled "a King-Woman, or better, a Man-Queen" by one contemporary.[107]

While there was much occasion during his reign to doubt both Henri's competence and his emotional continence, the most substantial damnation must always involve Henri's famed *mignons*.[108] Henri's *mignons*, drawn from lesser nobility at the expense of higher houses, were colourful characters, said to ornament themselves in the excessive ways of women with large quantities of jewels, make-up, ruffles and other ornamentation.[109] They fawned and swooned over the king in the way that a lady was expected to fawn over a male courting her.[110] There is no doubt that *mignons* were not unheard of within the early modern French court, and the term could in

104. Crompton, *Homosexuality and Civilization*, 328–30.

105. Knecht, *Catherine de" Medici*, 184–86.

106. Crawford, "Love, Sodomy, and Scandal," 517–20. See also: Paulson, *Catherine de Medici*, 103–12.

107. Teasley, "Charge of Sodomy as a Political Weapon in Early Modern France," 21.

108. Per Ladurie, the *mignons* would lose all normality and display incredible attention and affection whilst attending Henri. See Ladurie, *L'Etat*, 235.

109. Freer, *Henry*, 120; We should note that the mignons display all the characteristics of μαλακοὶ in both their dress and actions as is defined by Johan Suicer. See Johan Suicer, *Lexicon Graeco-Latinum et Latino-Graecum*, A3^V.

110. Crawford, *Love*, 524–25.

fact mean nothing more serious than a "sweetheart or darling."[111] Henri's *mignons*, however, while certainly being the king's "darlings," were more commonly described as *mignon de couchette*, or bedroom favourites.[112] One might assume from such a definition that the *mignons* were most certainly the favourites of a king in a manner that might blur gendered boundaries.[113] One *mignon* was even derided as having served the king *son cul*, or with his ass, a less than couth reference to sodomy.[114] Whether or not Henri actually had sex with his mignons seems to have been beside the point for contemporaries, although the implication of sodomy undoubtedly added fuel to the fire and titillated the gossips. As will be seen later in the case of James VI and I, the elevation of a lower-class youth to a high-powered station smacked of only one thing: pederasty. Thus, it is again not surprising that Henri, much like one of LeFevre's original *cinaedi*, was derided as "an adulterer, a rake, incestuous, and a sodomite."[115]

Ultimately, there were a great number of things that doomed Henri's rule and reputation. His politics were roundly unstable and his personal tastes untenable to the morals of both Protestant and Catholic subjects. Certainly, one must note that Henri was never directly referred to as a *mollis*, *cinaedi*, *volupteur* or *bougre*, which is interesting as it recalls the failure to use similar words when discussing leading figures in Germany. At the same time, although the titles are absent, it is impossible not to see these

111. Miege, *Dictionary of Barbarous French*, 82. We should note that Miege also allows for the term to mean "wanton." Pierre De L'estoile noted in his memoirs: "The name of minions began, at this time, to make the rounds through the mouths of the people, to whom they were very odious, as much for their ways of acting, which were silly and haughty, as for their effeminate and immodest makeup and attire, but especially for the immense gifts and bounties that the king gave them, which the people thought were the cause of their ruination. . . . Their activities were gambling, blaspheming, playing bowls, dancing, tumbling, brawling, lechering, and following the king everywhere and in all societies, doing and saying nothing but to please him . . . " Given this description, one might certainly wonder, given some definitions, if the king was not an ἀρσενοκοῖται as his minions were certainly the height of the μαλακοί. See Brunet, *Memoires-journaux*, 1:142–43.

112. See L'Estoile, *Journal pour le règne de Henri III (1574–1589)*, 232.

113. It has been noted that Henri would have his mignons dress and act in the manner of women. Whether this was to elevate his masculinity or for reasons of sexual preference has never been sufficiently defined. This does, however, seem to fit with the way, as we shall see later in this chapter, that characters thought of as embodying οὔτε μαλακοὶ οὔτε ἀρσενοκοῖται could be defined as having symbiotic tendencies. A pivotal question in this instance is whether Henri was the μαλακοί, ἀρσενοκοῖται, or perhaps a bit of both? See Freer, *Henry III King of France*, 2:148.

114. L'Estoile, *Journal pour le règne de Henri III (1574–1589)*, 154; Gary Ferguson, *Queer (re)Readings in the French Renaissance*, 147–50.

115. Crompton, *Homosexuality and Civilization*, 330.

characters in the epithets created by Henri's contemporary critics. All of the above, namely incontinent emotions, indecisive politics and the elevation and actions of his *mignons* contributed to Henri's vilification. Overall, the terms could possibly have identified him as the *grande volupteur* or the *grande bougre* of his day—although, again, he was never labelled as such. Moreover, while Henri provided a face for the lexical terms given earlier in this chapter, his was a story that also explains why such characters were so vilified: regardless of whether they were peasant or noble, these were creatures who created chaos in society.[116]

At this point, one might begin to summarize holistically that which has been examined thus far. In all situations, regardless of the location, the term ἀρσενοκοῖται seems to have almost always been associated with pederasty. There is plenty of evidence in the writings of LeFevre, Calvin and those who followed their lead and employed their translations. For the somewhat blunt LeFevre, this was spelled out in the person of the *bougre*, a licentious, lustful, and debauched creature who enticed others to engage in sin and folly. Although pederasty was often associated with sodomy, the definitions by Marlorat, Bucanus, and van Est revealed that sodomy itself was a much larger category, of which pederasty was only a small subsection. While all pederasts might have been sodomites, not all sodomites were pederasts. Other writings, however, have shown that ἀρσενοκοῖται, although referring to pederasts or sodomy, could have a much broader connotation. In some instances, who the ἀρσενοκοῖται were has been found to be encoded and deliberately opaque; a particular frustration for this study, but one that is understandable given the logic of the early modern mind. This most likely was due to the associations of pederasty with sodomy and the destruction of the biblical Sodom and Gomorrah that was equated in the early modern mind. Ultimately, ἀρσενοκοῖται, while a problematic neologism, was indicative of an action that was quite unacceptable and seems almost always to be generally associated with sexual activity; specifically, with pederastic sin that often required colloquialisms, circumlocutions and/or euphemisms to translate.

While the ἀρσενοκοῖται were rather singularly defined and despised within the early modern Francophone world, who the μαλακοὶ were was far more dangerous and encompassing. From the writings of LeFevre, Calvin, Marlorat, Miege, and others, the term was understood to have signified the unmasculine or atypical malesin common society. These males would not have been inkeeping with the attributes of *honnetéte* and *bienséance*, the key

116. Henri's rule, along with his indecisive handling of critical affairs, particularly between Roman Catholics and Protestants, would have certainly illustrated this point to the early modern onlooker.

governors or masculine emotion in the early modern Francophone world. Such men would have been seen to be frivolous, overly passionate, overly decorative or concerned with appearance and, in general, ruled by passions and desires, thus makingthem more feminine than masculine. Moreover, this attribute could affect any male at any level or stratum of society and could or could not be connected to the sexual misconduct of the ἀρσενοκοῖται. Henri III displayed and enacted the attributes of the μαλακοὶnot only by his indecisive and un-engaged style of rule, but also by his emotional incontinence, displayed in his vanity and through his *mignons*.

Ultimately, both the μαλακοὶ and the ἀρσενοκοῖται were a type of malaise, both mental and physical. This malaise could affect any man at any given time and place and was possibly just as likely to occur in the common man as in the noble. The *bougres* fulfilled their sinful nature and pederastic desire by the emasculation of the *volupteurs,* while the *volupteurs* indulged their emotional incontinence through their submission to warped emasculation by the *bougres.* Thus, while French translators were still quite mindful of the gravity of that upon which they commented, there was little of the tepidness for definition that Luther offered. Instead, perhaps due to their commitment to the laity reading the biblical text, French reformersseemed to have understood the subjects to require definition lest ignorance breed destruction. Of note particular note is the authors' seeming restraint in employing the given terms, or their analogues, when demeaning one particular class of person. This is contrary to early modern Germany, which seemed to approach οὔτε μαλακοὶ οὔτε ἀρσενοκοῖται with only a slightly veiled inflection towards the Roman Catholic clerics. Instead, the French Reformation seem to be more preoccupied with providing a translation of οὔτε μαλακοὶ οὔτε ἀρσενοκοῖται that was not confessionally but, instead, societally driven. Given the cultural context of early modern France, the *volupteur* and *bougre,* μαλακοὶ and ἀρσενοκοῖται, were not only those who could not inherit the kingdom of God, as described in 1 Corinthians 6:9, but those who threatened the very fabric of society. Engaging fully with the concept of *ad fontes* translation, even with the implicit risk of propagating such sins, was far more preferable to the risk of silent, ignorant and undiscovered practice.

CHAPTER THREE

England: Twists, Turns, Plots, and Problems

That early modern England is the next stop in this study should come as no surprise. Although lagging somewhat behind its continental peers in the adoption of the Protestant Revolution, the nation is nonetheless significant. As was explained in the introduction, English thoughts about biblical translation engendered heated responses from various sources. The most famous of these responses came from Sir Thomas More with his castigation of William Tyndale and the process of vernacular Bible translation in early modern England.[1] As this chapter will show, however, the art of biblical translation in early modern England was neither new nor old, Catholic or Protestant. Instead, the process was quite reflective of the rest of sixteenth and seventeenth-century England: changing, occasionally messy, and often difficult to pin down.

While England did not adopt Protestantism until mid-way through the reign of Henry VIII, Protestant ideas were gaining ground long before then. Beginning with the work of John Wycliffe in the fourteenth century, England saw a significant amount of reform-based unrest and rebellion, which presaged aspects of the Reformation, as did Hus in Bohemia.[2] Wycliffe's fifteenth-century work, which was actually a series of translations, was a significant step in both outlook and process towards the vernacular Bibles that would result from the English Reformation. For οὔτε μαλακοὶ οὔτε ἀρσενοκοῖται in 1 Corinthians 6:9, Wycliffe's translation reads "neither lechers with kind, neither they that do lechery with men." Wycliffe's translation was, to say the least, cumbersome and seems

---

1. More was quite skilled in his use of what modernity would call a "hermenutic of suspicion," reading through the text itself to determine authorial intent. To More, Tyndal was a political producer, not translating from one book to another, but instead producing a new book altogether for his own interests. See Duerden, "Equivalence or Power?" 11–13.

2. For a succinct summary of the beliefs and calls of Wycliffe and his followers, See "The Lollard Conclusions" in *Fasciculi Zizaniorum Magistri Johannis Wyclif Cum Tritico Ascribed To Thomas Netter Of Walden,* 360–69.

to suggest Pauline repetition,"with kind" seeming to mirror "with men." The concept of what constituted "lechery" in the late medieval period was something that could be interpreted broadly.[3] Lechery, according to the *Oxford English Dictionary*, was often used to describe a type of powerful, and by its association with other similar sins, unnatural lust. This unnatural lust, however, could often, as the *OED* shows, be indicative of sins with the self, with women and, as Wycliffe noted, could also include men. Moreover, Wycliffe translated in such a way as to echo the Latin Vulgate in common English. Although this, again, might be seen as a forerunner to the Reformation, the actual textual approach had a different emphasis from the *ad fontes* effort that influenced later reformers. As such, Wycliffe's translation, while providing an English translation for the text, was decidedly ambiguous. As in the case of Germany and France, all this changed with the coming of the Protestant Reformation and its emphasis on a text that was both lexically authentic and socially accessible.

Equipped with these caveats and thus beginning to investigate the translations in early modern England, one notices that, from the Great Bible to Parker, Tyndale and Coverdale, there were identical translations for οὔτε μαλακοὶ οὔτε ἀρσενοκοῖται.[4] All these texts provided the translation of "weaklings" for μαλακοὶ and "offenders of the flesh with mankind" for ἀρσενοκοῖται. These translations were somewhat vague and did not

3. "lechery, n." OED Online. June 2015. Oxford University Press. http://www.oed.com/view/Entry/106833?redirectedFrom=Lechery (accessed September 08, 2015).

a. Habitual indulgence of lust; lewdness of living. †Also, an instance of this.

c1230 *Hali Meid.* 11 Þat is te lust of leccherie þat riuleð þer wiðinne.

a1325 (‣c1250) *Gen. & Exod.* (1968) l. 3510 Oc horedom ðat ðu ne do ne do, Ne wend no lecherie to.

c1380 *Eng. Wycliffite Serm.* in *Sel. Wks.* II. 79 Of þe herte comen yvel þouȝti, in yvelwordis; mansleyingis, avoutrieris, leccheries.

c1386 Chaucer *Parson's Tale* ₽762 After Glotonye thanne comth leccherie.

a1400 (‣a1325) *Cursor Mundi* (Vesp.) l. 10046 Þechastite o þisleuidi Ouercumms al lust o lecheri [*Gött.* lichery].

a1400 (‣a1325) *Cursor Mundi* (Trin. Cambr.) l. 6476 Do no lecchery bi no wommon.

a1420 T. Hoccleve *De ReginimePrincipum* 3656 Leccherye. . . is hogges lif.

4. See *The new testamen [sic] both in Latin and English after the vulgare texte*; *Biblia. The Bible, that is, the holy Scripture of the Olde and New Testament, faithfully and truly translated out of Douche and Latyn in to Englishe*; *The newe Testamēt as it was written, and caused to be writte, by them which herdeyt*; *The. holie. Bible. conteynyng the olde Testament and the newe*. Please note that I cite Parker as the Bishop's Bible as he has, historically, been seen as the main interpreter of the texts. It is entirely possible, however, that Parker had no hand in this area of translation.

illuminate how the translators might have truly understood μαλακοὶ and ἀρσενοκοῖται.[5] This is, again, not an entirely unexpected thing to note in a number of translations from early modern Europe. "Weaklings" and "offenders of the flesh with mankind" were phrases that were highly reflective of both the Latin Vulgate and how Wycliffe had once rendered ἀρσενοκοῖται when he translated the Vulgate into English.[6] Nonetheless, these translations seem to be reflective of an England that was, as the sixteenth century unfolded, never quite sure if it was Protestant or Roman Catholic. Thus, one might never be sure whether it was wise to follow a Protestant understanding of biblical translation and produce a vernacular rendering, or to adhere with the more historical renderings of Jerome's Vulgate and scholastic doctors.

As with those areas that were previously examined in previous chapters, the vagueness of the earlier translations requires contextualisation using extra-biblical sources. Heretofore, ἀρσενοκοῖται had generally been a difficult term to place, but a brief perusal of the *OED* in this instance explains that it might very well be the μαλακοὶ that will be difficult to define succinctly.[7] With regard to "weakling," the common English translation for μαλακοὶ, the dictionary says:

- *An effeminate or unmanly person.*

- *A person or animal that lacks physical strength, or is weak in health or . . . constitution.*

- *One who is weak in character or intellect.*

- *One who is weak in the faith or in spiritual attainments.*

- *appositive or as adj. Weak, feeble.*[8]

Certainly, one should note that the *OED*'s definition of "an effeminate or unmanly person" was specifically derived from Tyndale's Bible and thus might be given preference. This acknowledgement, however, does not necessarily signify an ignorance of the other renderings. In fact, although

---

5. It is worth noting that these translations, mundane though they appear, do follow a pattern established by the Vulgate and also kept within other Continental treatments of the time.

6. It is plausible that one might consider these to be ventures similar to the neo-Latin of France's Bonade.

7. Note: I am only including examples from the OED that were used within sixteenth- and seventeenth-century England.

8. "weakling, n." OED Online. September 2013. Oxford University Press. http://www.oed.com/view/Entry/226554?redirectedFrom=Weaklings (accessed October 10, 2013).

μαλακοί was specifically defined as "weakling," the translators failed to mention the type of weaklings they intended the term to indicate.[9] Thus, this study begins with broad and opaque renderings of the μαλακοί in early modern England.[10]

Ἀρσενοκοῖται, however, differed from μαλακοί. "[O]ffenders of the Flesh with Mankind," the common rendering of ἀρσενοκοῖται was, like its original, a euphemistic turn of phrase. An examination of the component parts of the text, taken from the *OED* as they were used historically, shows that the phrase was actually quite clear.

Offender:

- *A person who or (occas.) thing which offends; a person who infringes a rule or regulation; a transgressor or sinner. Also: a person who gives offence, displeases, or causes resentment, upset, etc.*

- *Law. A person who breaks the law, one who commits an offence.*

- *A person who attacks, one who takes the offensive position, an assailant.*

Flesh:

- *In euphemistic phrases with reference to sexual intercourse.*

- *to go after or follow strange flesh: a Biblical expression referring to sexual behaviour regarded as unnatural.*

- *Put for: Quantity or excess of flesh; hence, plumpness, good condition, embonpoint, esp. in phrases, to get, (†get oneself in), lose flesh; also (to be) in flesh: in good condition, corpulent. Cf. French être en chair.*

- *The sensual appetites and inclinations as antagonistic to the nobler elements of human nature. In theological language (after St. Paul's use of σάρξ) applied more widely to the depraved nature of man in its conflict with the promptings of the Spirit. sins of the flesh: esp. those of unchastity.*

- *after the flesh and variants: after the nature of the flesh; according to the flesh.*[11]

Mankind:

9. This definition does; however, seem to reflect Thomas Aquinas' understanding of *molles* or the μαλακοί, which we shall engage much more in the section covering Italy.

10. What we can be sure about, however, is that the μαλακοί does not, to the early modern English author, include a category of physical strength. To be μαλακοί, instead, is very much indicative of a personal or moral characteristic.

11. "flesh, n.". OED Online. September 2013. Oxford University Press. http://www.oed.com/view/Entry/71460?rskey=lcWtPy&result=1&isAdvanced=false (accessed October 17, 2013).

- *The human species. As a collective noun: human beings in general. Formerly freq. with pl. concord.*

- *The nature of man; human nature. to take (also fang, nim) mankind: to assume human form, to become incarnate.*

- *Human feeling, humanity. Obs. rare—1. The male sex; men or male people ingeneral. Cf. menkind n.*[12]

Examining these words, a bit more, it seems apparent that "offenders" was to have generally meant sin, misuse or mal-intent; "flesh" generally meant the human body, although it could equally refer to human nature; "mankind" most often signified the male person, although it might indicate all of humanity. With this in mind, the study finds a number of options for understanding ἀρσενοκοῖται in the vernaculars examined thus far. The ἀρσενοκοῖται were indicative of those who sinned against the physical nature or body of men or humanity, and those who used their bodies, in any capacity, against their natural functions or intent. While this seems to be a fitting option, particularly given the previous examinations of ἀρσενοκοῖται in other settings, it should be noted that, at this point, one could possibly make a connection between gluttony, obesity and ἀρσενοκοῖται, given the lexical options in the *OED*. This is quite curious. The authors seem clear that, with regard to ἀρσενοκοῖται, they were not discussing the glutton or the obese, but still employed terminologies that might include such attributes.[13] This could indicate insecurity regarding the authors' concept of ἀρσενοκοῖται; they may well have had difficulty translating the concept of ἀρσενοκοῖται—in history and from the continent—into English words and life.

In addition to this opacity, the terms examined thus far present a problem concerning how to proceed with this study. "Effeminateness" is a relatively easy word to find in various early modern English texts; however, "Offenders of the flesh with mankind," regardless of the previous assumptions based upon the *OED* is, for obvious reasons, not a phrase that leaps off many pages. The phrase seems to indicate a type of conservatism in early Henrician translation not, unsurprisingly, unlike the Vulgate. To

12. "mankind, n. and adj.1". OED Online. September 2013. Oxford University Press. http://www.oed.com/view/Entry/113548?rskey=DNXZeY&result=1&isAdvanced=false (accessed October 17, 2013).

13. This, may, in and of itself, be a hinting towards an understanding of overindulgence and over-eating being indicators of one's inclination to being part of the ἀρσενοκοῖται. We shall see this much again—and much more fully explained—within the section on Italy. Certainly, this was not an entirely unknown issue. See Ruggiero, "Forbidden Fruit," 31–52.

be textually authentic was fine and well, but so too was keeping one's head firmly attached to one's body.

The Geneva Bible, imported after the Marian exile and highly influential within early modern England and Scotland, translated ἀρσενοκοῖται as "buggery."[14] This singular definition provides the opportunity to begin to define a more solid understanding of ἀρσενοκοῖται. With reference to buggery, the *OED* charts the historic development of the term as follows:

- *Abominable heresy. Obs.*

- *Anal intercourse. Cf. sodomy n. Also: as a technical term in criminal law =bestiality.*[15]

This understanding of ἀρσενοκοῖται as buggery, much like effeminateness for μαλακοὶ, lends itself to investigation and examination more than does "offenders of the flesh with mankind," even though they might have meant the same thing.

Richard Huloet's *Abcedarium Anglico Latinum*, published in 1552 and on which many subsequent authors drew, defined buggery as *pederastia*.[16] This definition of buggery as *pederastia* raises a crucial point to bear in mind: There seems to have been an evolution of the understanding of ἀρσενοκοῖται that occurred after the reign of Henry VIII. The older understandings, brought forth by the *OED*, seem to point towards ἀρσενοκοῖται as potentially indicating generalized sodomy. This succinct definition of buggery—*pederastia*—again brings to mind questions of the relationship between ἀρσενοκοῖται and the buggery mentioned in the Geneva Bible. Huloet's definitions seem to question the relationship between sodomy and pederasty, and hint at the influence of a Francophone context in the Geneva

14. See *Bible and Holy Scriptures contained in the Old and New Testament*. Much as earlier Bibles reflected the religious uncertainties of the time, this imported text reflects the opposite. *The Geneva Bible* was reflective of a time where Protestantism had all but won the battle for primacy in the English world.

15. "buggery, n. and adj.". OED Online. September 2013. Oxford University Press. http://www.oed.com/view/Entry/24372?redirectedFrom=Buggery (accessed October 29, 2013).

16. Huloet, *Abcedarium Anglico Latinum*, DV. Very little is known about Huloet and his intentions with his lexicon. It is thought that Huloet hailed from Cambridgeshire and was interested in producing a lexicon to help in the instruction of youth. Regardless of intention, Huloet's lexicon is largely fashioned in a way that mirrors at least one contemporary French-English dictionary. It is thought that his text might also be based upon older Latin lexicons, which might tie his understandings, evidenced above, into a far older line of reason. See McConchie, "Howlet, Richard (*fl.* 1552)." This is much the same as later German lexicons, such as Grimm's, addressed the *knabenschender*, with several options being available, but one particular option the most common and likely.

Bible. As will be explained later in this chapter, buggery was not always ped-erasty, as it could also occur between adults of opposite sexes. One must question whether Huloet truly believed that all buggery was *pederastia*, or whether he was simply noting its most common expression.[17]

This potential dichotomy of buggery and *pederastia* seems to be supported by John Mayer's *Commentary upon the New Testament* (1631). Mayer's commentary, which addressed indications of both μαλακοὶ and ἀρσενοκοῖται, illustrated both the association and the flexibility of sodomy, buggery and pederasty. With regard to 1 Corinthians 6:9, Mayer stated:

> For some kind of sinners here named the effeminate, in the Greek malaki, soft, were such as were libidinous, affecting the curiosities of women in their ornaments, and associating themselves unto them, out into any act of fornication. Thus I finde it in the Expositors: but consider whether Ganimedes are not hereby meant, who like whorish women prostitute them-selves to the lusts of other men, because they are coupled with such an abuse themselves with them. Male-corrupters were such as defiled themselves with young boyes, after the manner of the Sodomites.[18]

To be effeminate, in the mind of Mayer, was both an inward and usually, al-though not necessarily, outward level of sin. The effeminate person eschewed socially acceptable levels of masculinity, particularly in aspects of dress and comportment, but this was not necessarily indicative of any active or out-ward lusts that might be known to the wider public. The effeminate male, for Mayer, was sexually out of control, although not necessarily engaging in sexual actions. While acknowledging this option for μαλακοὶ, Mayer also proposed that the term was best and perhaps most commonly understood as referring to the *Ganimede*. This coupling, as Mayer stated, was performed in the "manner of the sodomites," which ostensibly meant anal sex. Thus, these μαλακοὶ might very well simply burn with lust and be controlled by

17. This definition was echoed in other lexicons throughout the sixteenth century. See Levins, *Manipulus Vocabulorvm. A Dictionarie of English and Latinewordes*, E1[R]; and Hollyband, *Dictionary*, V2 [R].

18. Mayer, *Commentary upon the New Testament*, 184. Mayer was a noted bibli-cal commentator of the early-seventeenth century. His works were published "with an intelligent rather than educated audience" in mind. Thus, we might suppose his defini-tions were influenced not just by scholarship, but also by wider colloquial understand-ing; resonating with both lay and learned audiences. Thus, perhaps echoing Luther, he created an interpretive method, which valued not just lexical authenticity, but also common relevance. See Keene, "Mayer, John (*bap.* 1583, *d.* 1664)." Mayer's writing also seems to be heavily influenced by Calvin's definitions, seen previously in this study's chapter over early modern France.

ostentatious things. It was also just as likely that, due to their sexual perversions, the μαλακοὶ sought sexuality and sexual occasions in the forbidden manner of the Sodomites. Those who were μαλακοὶ would not always be ἀρσενοκοῖται, according to Mayer, but the ἀρσενοκοῖται would always, by definition, be μαλακοί. Mayer's definition also provides a plausible manner in which to understand the differences between sodomy and pederasty. Pederasty was the sexual copulation of older men with younger men. These older men, according to Mayer, were the ἀρσενοκοῖται, while the youngerwere the μαλακοί, and the action in which they engaged was the sin of Sodom. It is this stipulation of "in the manner of the Sodomites" that is critical. Mayer was explaining that the actions undertaken in pederasty were in the style of the Sodomites, but not necessarily exactly like those found in Sodom. Thus, possibly also emphasising Huloet's understanding, the μαλακοὶ and the ἀρσενοκοῖται could be a number of things, but they were best understood as the intrinsic parts of a pederastic relationship.[19]

In a similar fashion, Henry Cockeram (1647) defined pederasty as "a lusting after of boys" and sodomy as "belonging to sodomy or unnatural lust," seemingly separating the two terms by definition and giving significant emphasis to definitions such as those by Mayer and Huloet.[20] Pederasty, in this definition, was a specific subset of unnatural lust, whereas unnatural lust itself was more broadly encompassed by sodomy. With these writings and definitions in mind, we find ourselves entering a semantic "grey-area."[21] This dichotomy of function was reflected in early modern works that sought to translate 1 Corinthians 6:9. In these instances, one finds μαλακοὶ and ἀρσενοκοῖται commonly translated as "Nor wanton persons/weaklings, nor buggerers."[22] While this understanding seems to

19. This, again, helps to understand the differences and similarities between sodomy and pederasty. The pederast could be engaged in actions quite similar to the sodomite, but the sodomite was not necessarily a pederast.

20. Though, we very much might argue that Cockeram intended his audience to assume that a lusting after of boys was "unnatural" and thus would fit well within the bounds of sodomy. While he would define the terms in separate and not necessarily obviously linked manners, he does not make them mutually exclusive by any means.

21. Cockeram, *English Dictionary*, 250, 325. While there is considerable discussion as to just where Cockeram drew his understanding from, it is impossible to deny the success and influence of his lexical writings. Writing to provide an understanding of "hard words" rather than an exposition of the wider English language, one should look at his definitions for this study as perhaps attempting to refine wider understanding. See Beal, "Cockeram, Henry (fl. 1623–1658)."

22. See Hume, *Treatise of the Felicitie*, 31. Ferrarius, *Work of Ioannes Ferrarius*, Fol. 135; Bale, *Image of Both Churches*, 426; Jewel, *Exposition Upon the Two Epistles*, 109; Atersoll, *Badges of Christianity*, 57; Greenham, *Works of the Reverend Richard Greenham*, 301.

represent the majority of translated texts, there are a number of texts that list buggery and sodomy as individual and different sins.[23] Presumably this differentiation between sodomy and buggery was reflective of the definitions given by Huloet and others, according to which buggery could be indicative of all things contra-copulation, including anal and oral sex, as well as with frottage. Buggery in common usage, however, was often best thought of as *pederastia*, while sodomy was indicative of the wider field of sexual sins attributed to the towns of Sodom and Gomorrah.

Edward Leigh's *Critica Sacra or Philologicall and Theologicall Observations upon all the Greek Words of the New Testament in order alphabeticall* (1650) adds to the levels of distinction and differentiation already seen in this work. Leigh's definition of $\mu\alpha\lambda\alpha\kappa o\grave{\iota}$ was in the same vein as many of those mentioned previously; understanding the $\mu\alpha\lambda\alpha\kappa o\grave{\iota}$ as "those that wear soft apparel" and that "the apparel shows the effeminateness of the mind." At this point, this is not new ground to cover.[24] Leigh, like many of his contemporaries, associated those who were $\mu\alpha\lambda\alpha\kappa o\grave{\iota}$ with having an inward sickness that became apparent in outward behaviour and display. Leigh's definition of $\dot{\alpha}\rho\sigma\varepsilon\nu o\kappa o\widehat{\iota}\tau\alpha\iota$ covered little new ground by simply offering the Latin Vulgate translation and no formal definition. Within his margin notes, however, Leigh suggested that the Latin *cinaedi* were analogous to $\dot{\alpha}\rho\sigma\varepsilon\nu o\kappa o\widehat{\iota}\tau\alpha\iota$.[25] Although the *cinaedus* has been encountered in other locales, one now must consider what it was to be such a character within early modern England. The *cinaedus*, in the late seventeenth century, was described as "one abused against nature, a bardash, a wanton dancer, a gelded youth, or shower of tricks, a tumbler."[26] This

23. See Alleine, *Vindiciae Pietatis*, 49; Hildersam, *CLII Lectures upon Psalme LI*, 507; Keach, *Display of Glorious Grace*, 157.

24. In this, Leigh seems to be more in-line with classical translations, as seen in this study's introduction, than a number of other contemporaries.

25. Leigh, *Critica Sacra*, 41, 162–63. Leigh's conflation of the *cinaedus* with the $\dot{\alpha}\rho\sigma\varepsilon\nu o\kappa o\widehat{\iota}\tau\alpha\iota$ is notable. Certainly, we have seen this type of approach elsewhere— namely Germany—but the supposed similarity is curious. If authors, such as Dale Martin, are to be believed, there was a definitive distinction between the ancient $\chi\iota\nu\alpha\varepsilon\delta\upsilon\sigma$ and the $\dot{\alpha}\rho\sigma\varepsilon\nu o\kappa o\widehat{\iota}\tau\alpha\iota$. Understandings such as Leigh's seem to support that there was either a complete misconception, in the early modern period, of how the ancients viewed such things or that the distinction was not nearly as wide as Martin and others might suppose. At the same time, it is plausible, given his Puritan outlook that Leigh chose to conflate the terms to provide a close and "understandable" creature that would resonate in wider society. Moreover, that the term is Latin, might suggest that Leigh, like Luther, did not believe the term had an analogue in common English, thus making it a sin of "other persons." See Sutton, "Leigh, Edward (1603–1671)"; Martin, *Sex*, 45.

26. Littleton, *Linguae Latinae Liber Dictionarius*, U3R. Littleton was a noted seventeenth-century philologist and clergyman. Having been described as neither Calvinist

definition requires examination. The one abused "against nature" is a familiar turn of phrase, but the other descriptors are more opaque. Those "against nature" were the enticers of society. These were the persons who cared nothing for commonly held rules of social comportment and who focused instead on attracting and commanding the attentions of others in society, particularly the attention of other men. The "bardash," derived from the French *bardache*, was another term for catamites, or males who were kept, economically, for sex by other men.[27] Wanton dancers, somewhat obviously, worked to intrigue the mind and engage the fantasies of their audiences, all of which could lead to a gross loss of manners and comportment. In a similar manner, the showers of tricks and the tumblers were those who captivated and controlled the attention and desires of their viewers by holding them in their sway. In summary, the *cinaedus* focused the attentions and passions of upright and moral males on areas in which they might—either contemplatively or actually—circumvent the moral foundations of wider society. The *cinaedus* was thus the embodiment of awkward lust, combustible passions, unfocused excitement, and irreconcilable desire. Although early modern English standards of propriety varied considerably from 1540 to 1700, a lack of propriety could still occasion significant concern and question.

Largely echoing this definition of *cinaedus*, Thomas Cokayne's *Greek English Lexicon* (1658) described the ἀρσενοκοῖται as "a wonton dancer, one past all shame. Scripture sometimes calls such one a dog, from the lustful nature of a dog."[28] For the μαλακοὶ, the lexicon offered "effeminate—an impure and lecherous man."[29] Just as in the case of Leigh, describing the ἀρσενοκοῖται as having the free and indiscriminate lusts of a dog paints an interesting portrait. In previous chapters, the study has usually seen

nor Lutheran, but entirely Anglican, Littleton's writings might be seen as uniquely English in their outlook and interpretation. Key, "Littleton, Adam (1627–1694)."

27. This is, itself, drawn from the Italian word for prostitute. See Richelet, *Dictionnaire*, 75.

28. We have seen this previously in our examination of early modern Germany. The concept of ἀρσενοκοῖται as a dancer is neither new nor exclusive to early modern England. We might speculate, however, whether this was picked up during the Marian exile and subsequently exported back to England at the end of such times. See Frisius, *Novum*, 106.

29. See Cokayne, *Greek-English Lexicon*, 168, 195. Cokayne is thought to have published his lexicon with the intention of expounding upon the more difficult words of the Bible. That Cokayne held no place as either a theologian or a proper lexicographer, makes his definitions seem somewhat circumspect. At the same time, his words, accurate and educated or not, stand to provide a window into the understandings of this study's critical terms for those in society who were not a part of the academy. See Life, "Cokayne, Thomas (1587–1638)."

descriptors of lust and uncontrollable passion associated with those who were μαλακοί. While acknowledging the overlap, Cokayne's definition requires one to recognize that, although England drew largely on continental influence, it also had its own opinions and understandings. Whereas ἀρσενοκοῖται seems to be somewhat different, one can see in the definition of μαλακοί familiar territory with the term "effeminate." Moreover, the inclusion of the term "dancer" is worth noting. Much as is the case with "dog," the study has seen this term used as a descriptor in other locations in early modern Europe.[30] In previous instances, however, this has often been associated with those who were μαλακοί and not the ἀρσενοκοῖται, the rationale being that a dancer was one who enticed and who urged the wrong thoughts in a person's mind. The dancers, themselves, were already corrupt and sought to tempt others into their corruption. This is, again, a somewhat peculiar description of ἀρσενοκοῖται—one that echoes both Wycliffe's "lechery" and Mayer—as it portrays the ἀρσενοκοῖται as actors who were almost inherently also μαλακοί by nature. Thus, for Cokayne at least, the terms μαλακοί and ἀρσενοκοῖται were intertwined. To be μαλακοί was often to also be ἀρσενοκοῖται. What is not clear, however, is whether the μαλακοί were inherently the ἀρσενοκοῖται or whether there was the possibility of being μαλακοί without being ἀρσενοκοῖται.

Andrew Symson's *Lexicon Anglo-GraecoLatinum*(1658) translated the terms as:

μαλακοί: they that wear soft clothing—transfereth to the mind, the apparel shews the effeminatenesse of the mind

ἀρσενοκοῖται: an abuser of himself with mankinde—male copulation.[31]

Symson's definitions provide some level of contextualisation for the terms. The μαλακοί werepersons who, as seen in continental translations of the time, epitomized the effeminate status of a male or a perceived lack of masculinity. For Symson, this lack of masculinity was most easily identified in the type and style of apparel and was indicative of a larger mental condition of softness or un-masculinity. Though the author was long and convoluted in his definition of the μαλακοί, he was quite succinct in his definition of

30. See this study's chapter over early modern Germany, particularly the works of Johann Frisius.

31. See Symson, *Lexicon Anglo-Graeco Latinum Novi Testamenti*, 3, 167. Symson, while born English, spent the majority of his life in Scotland. As such, his writings, along with those of Poole, examined below, provide an opportunity to understand this study's words in both England and Scotland as both writers were published in both arenas. See Jackson, "Symson, Andrew (c.1638–1712)."

ἀρσενοκοῖται. Essentially reiterating the translations examined previously, Symson did add one defining characteristic: firmly defining the term in the masculine sense. Many early modern English vernacular translators often provided a translation that used "they" and was somewhat ambiguous in its gender, allowing for either male or female offenders. Symson clarified that ἀρσενοκοῖται was meant to distinguish men who were abusing themselves or attempting to copulate with other male members of society.[32] Perhaps even more notable was Symson's omission of "boys" or "youth." This omission is all the more interesting by the divergence between Cokayne's and Symson's definitions, particularly with regard to the ἀρσενοκοῖται. As examined previously, Cokayne found those who were μαλακοὶ often to be ἀρσενοκοῖται. These creatures were often involved in emotional incontinence in the same way as a dog in heat or an exotic dancer might be. Symson, however, ignored this emotional categorisation and simply professed a physical actinstead—that of male copulation. Therefore, one finds two similar yet divergent definitions for the ἀρσενοκοῖται.[33]

Examining Thomas Blount (1661), one finds a different perspective based not on the tradition of bible translation and commentary, but on English common law. Blount is somewhat of an oddity in this chapter as he is both the only Roman Catholic whose work is sampled and was also trained as a barrister, as his definitions attest. Nonetheless, his work provides a perspective regarding how this study's focus words were understood and employed in both legal and non-Protestant circles. Blount defined buggery as

> *carnalis copula contra naturam, & haec vel per confusionem Specierum*, sc. a man or a woman with a bruit beast, *vel sexuum*; a man with a man, or a woman with a woman. See Levit. 18.22, 23. This offence committed with mankinde or beast is fellony without Clergy; it being a sin against God, Nature, and the Law; And in ancient time such offenders were to be burnt by the Common-Law. 25. Hen. 86.5. Eliz. 17. Fitz. Nat. Br. 269. My Lord Coke (Rep.12. pag. 36.) saith, that this word comes from the Italian, *Buggerare*, to bugger.[34]

32. This would, again, seem to key upon issues of copulation; mainly the fact that men could not copulate with one another and thus their actions were a waste of sexual vitality.

33. Symson does leave something of a "door" open to Cokayne's definition. It is entirely plausible that those involved with male copulation would in fact be the type of person Cokayne described. We should allow that Symson might, in fact, simply assume that his readers would know such things as true.

34. Blount's Latin is lifted from legal definitions, which only seems further to prove his intention to echo the wider setting of regal and civic decrees. See Blount, *Glosographia*, G5ᵛ. See Mortimer, "Blount, Thomas (1618–1679)."

Blount's understanding of buggery, written in the middle of the seventeenth century, might have intentionally echoed the regal and legal writings seen later in this chapter. It is interesting that Blount also defined sodomy as buggery.[35] Moving forward, Blount, in his *Glosographia*, further defined pederasty as "the loving of young boys, commonly taken in the ill part, as signifying the abuse of them against kind."[36] This definition provides a specific context for the interpretations of ἀρσενοκοῖται examined previously. The author describes pederasty as being the anal copulation of older men with younger boys or youths. This anal sex, which by nature prevented procreation, was the signifier of abuse against humankind, which was against the natural order of sex.[37] Blount also noted that, within pederasty, was the role of the "Ingle." An Ingle, according to Blount, was "a boy kept for sodomy, a Ganymede."[38] Interestingly, Blount noted:

> Ganymede (Ganymedes) the name of a Trojan Boy, whom Jupiter so loved (say the Poets) as he took him up to Heaven and made him his Cupbearer. Hence any Boy, loved for carnal abuse, or hired to be used contrary to Nature, to commit the detestable sin of Sodomy, is called a Ganymede, or Ingle.[39]

This definition of a Ganymede is interesting. In a roundabout way, Blount linked all the terminologies of sodomy, pederasty, buggery and the ingle, in a circular manner. Buggery and sodomy, for Blount, were unnatural or non-procreative actions. Pederasts, who sought to hire ingles to fulfil their desires, enjoyed the action of sodomy and/or buggery. These terms, for Blount, thus existed within something of a self-contained and circuitous system of being.

Adam Littleton (1678), writing in the latter part of the seventeenth century, also commented on buggery. Most interestingly, whereas other authors linked sodomy and buggery, Littleton linked both sodomy and buggery to pederasty.[40] This inclusion by Littleton, however, does less to

35. Blount, *Glosographia* (1674), 594.

36. Blount, *Glosographia* (1661), Gg2ᴿ.

37. This would seemingly provide us with some clarity as to what it was to abuse one's self against mankind. Though, we cannot say that this defined "against mankind" or "against kind" in totality.

38. Blount, *Glossographia* (1661), Y1ᵛ. As this study will illustrate in the next chapter," Ingle" and "Ingler" were also words that were used by Blount's contemporaries to describe the rampant pederasty within early modern Italy. See Florio, *Queen*, 51.

39. Blount, *Glossographia* (1661), S4ᵛ.

40. Littleton, *Linguae Latinae Liber Dictionarius*, D3 R, Ee3 R. Littleton defined the same terms as: *Buggery: Pederastia, Venus postica (rear intercourse) To Commit Buggery: Paedico A buggerer: Pederastes, paedicator Sodomy: sodomia Pederastia Sodomite:*

provide certainty than it does to muddle the picture further. By his singular definition of buggery as pederasty, Littleton called into question a
number of definitions given previously. As with Huloet's definitions from
more than a century earlier, one is left wondering whether the author was
referring to the most common form of the offence, or was being coy for
some other, undisclosed reason.

The Complete Christian Dictionary (1678) by Thomas Wilson, largely
reminiscent of the explanation found in the Oxford English Dictionary,
suggests that an effeminate was described as "one that is lustful, addicted
unto strange and filthy lusts," or "they that wear soft apparel. The apostle
transfereth it to the minde, where it's taken in an evil part, for the apparel,
often shews the effeminateness of the mind."[41] This, again, is reminiscent
of a previously offered understanding that the μαλακοὶ were often associated with outward and physical signs of a supposed lack of masculinity—
largely echoing Symson, but not Cokayne. Wilson's definition, however,
similarly points to an inward and uncontrollable lust, one that seems to
have been quite similar to the definition of those who were ἀρσενοκοῖται
as offered by Cokayne.[42] Wilson also noted buggery as "bestial unclean-
ness against nature" and cited Leviticus as his rationale, ostensibly linking
the term with general sodomy.[43]

Although it was published in Edinburgh and not until the very
beginning of the eighteenth century, the annotations by Matthew Poole
(1700) begin to offer a more distinct manner in which to understand
the biblical translations seen previously, particularly as theological writings circulated between England and Scotland. Poole offered the same
translations of μαλακοὶ and ἀρσενοκοῖται in 1 Corinthians 6:9 that were
seen previously: "nor effeminate persons, nor abusers of themselves with

---

Sodomita, Pederastes, paedico.

41. See Wilson, Complete Christian Dictionary, 186. Wilson was a late sixteenth-
and early-seventeenth-century English clergyman. His dictionary was originally published in 1612, but underwent subsequent additions and refinements, hence the later
publication seen here. See Wright, "Wilson, Thomas (1562/3–1622)."

42. By now, we must allow that the placement or understanding of this inward and
uncontrollable lust was, at best, occasional and at worst, completely arbitrary. That this
lust must not be of a kind satisfied by heterosexual encounters must be allowed. If
such were the case, then many men of the day would themselves be either μαλακοὶ
or ἀρσενοκοῖται. Moreover, men were rather expected to be lustful to a certain extent
and were commonly seen as having their passions boil over and overwhelm them.
(i.e.: ejaculation in coitus or vomiting from too much ale.) Thus, we should allow that
μαλακοὶ and ἀρσενοκοῖται were something spectacularly applied. See Roper, Oedipus,
119–20, 153 and Breitenberg, Anxious Masculinity in Early Modern England, 39-50.

43. Wilson, Dictionary, 78.

mankind." Thankfully, Poole also provided a commentary to the passage, which stated "nor persons that give up themselves to lasciviousness, burning continually in lust. Nor such as are guilty of the sin of Sodom, a sin not to be named amongst Christians or men."[44] This direct link of the ἀρσενοκοῖται with the biblical sodomite was supported by Poole's later translation of ἀρσενοκοῖται in 1 Timothy 1:10, where he succinctly translated the term to mean "sodomite."[45]

All these lexical examples seem to indicate multiple schools or traditions of interpretation. On one hand, one might identify a theme relating to those who identified μαλακοὶ and ἀρσενοκοῖται as being entirely about pederasty. On the other hand, one can certainly identify a school of thought that indicates the terms to be indicative of womanliness and pederasty. Nonetheless, one can still point to potential instances in which the terms were thought to mean womanliness and general sodomy. In other words, there was significant "confusion" (in the sense of divergence) amongst early modern English writers, but not individual lack of clarity. This might, in part, indicate that the English situation was much more complex, perhaps showing the diversity of reformation influences in England, namely moderate Erasmianism, hard Calvinism, Lutheran/Reformed conformist and Anglican *via media*. Thus, the translations and commentaries mirror the diversity of the English religious situation, even if they are not necessarily mapped onto it. This diversity in translation for the μαλακοὶ and ἀρσενοκοῖται requires the study to look to other sources in the hope of extrapolating an overall meaning for the μαλακοὶ and ἀρσενοκοῖται in 1 Corinthians 6:9.

As shown previously, developing a context for the key words of this study requires an engagement with and an analysis of words that have associations with gender roles, sex, and sexuality. These concepts, in common with other areas examined in this study, were both fluent and fluid in early modern England. Moreover, a level of local desire to avoid discussing

44. In this, Poole seems to be suggesting that there are two types of people caught up in being μαλακοὶ and ἀρσενοκοῖται. Those who are given to lust—even lust in what we might term completely heterosexual ways—and also those who men who have sex with other men.

45. This is similar to the writings of Becanus et al. from France. Poole, *Annotations Upon the Holy Bible Volume Two*, 4D^V, 4X3^R. See also Becanus, *Analogia Veteris Ac Novi Testamenti*, 504–5. Poole's work is something of an oddity as the author only reached Isa 58 before dying. The remainder of the work was completed by various authors and attributed to Poole. Thus, one cannot be sure just who wrote Poole's work and from what perspective. At the same time, the work was incredibly popular, perhaps accounting for its printing in Edinburgh, and generally well received by scholars, thus marking it as, at least largely, having relevance to and comprehension of contemporary discussions and ideas. See Keene, "Poole, Matthew (1624?–1679)."

concepts which, simply by talking about them could occasion scandal, complicated the discussion. Despite this reticence, these issues played important political and public functions. This tension between scandal-avoiding quiet and useful (political) invective existed and evolved in the context of an England undergoing radical and oscillating changes in the century after the Reformation, culminating in a change of dynasty and, eventually, the execution of a monarch.

In such a fluid time, the terms $\mu\alpha\lambda\alpha\kappa o\acute{\imath}$ and $\acute{\alpha}\rho\sigma\varepsilon\nu o\kappa o\~\imath\tau\alpha\iota$ present an interesting proposition. English biblical interpretation (and translation) was heavily influenced by ideas arising from continental Lutheranism and Calvinism/Reformed Movement scholars.[46] It is hardly surprising, therefore, that there were many similarities between the vernacular translations and the societal situations in continental Europe and England. In general, and as discussed previously, sex and sexuality experienced a conceptual renaissance throughout the Protestant Reformation. The concept of the conjugal household, again, flourished within the Reformation; changing sex from something of a "tolerated taboo" to a regular, indeed integral, part of the Protestant "godly household." However, sex and sexuality remained within relatively specific boundaries. Sex remained patriarchal, initiated, and controlled by the husband. Sex, to be licit, was confined to the marriage bed, both to strengthen the relationship between husband and wife and to assist in legitimate procreation. Moreover, sex, being fundamentally tied to procreation, was still expected to involve acts that enabled procreation. Thus, all forms of frottage, as well as anal and oral sex, were against nature and, in that sense, constituted "sodomy."[47]

Therefore, any discussion of biblical sexual terms in the vernacular requires an understanding of how sex (as an activity) was understood in the wider context of ideas about sex (with divinely ordained purpose) and gender. Masculinity, in early modern England, not only differed in interesting ways from continental norms but, during the period in question, was in considerable flux.[48] Much like their continental counterparts, males were not seen as being inherently "masculine" simply by virtue of biological constitution. Instead, masculinity was a concept and attribute that was very much a limited resource to be attained and kept. This virtue might be

46. For example: Bishop Cranmer having been trained in the ways of Protestantism from the Strasbourg Lutherans and the Marian exile producing a large expatriate community in Reformed Switzerland. See MacCulloch, *Thomas Cranmer*, 60–66.

47. Hendrix, *Masculinity*, 71–89; Salisbury, *Sex*, 3, 29; Roper, *Oedipus*, 37–40; LW: 1:10; WA 42:79; and WATR 3:129.

48. See Breitenberg, *Anxious*, 1–4, 19–24.

attained, maintained, or lost within the acts of the joust, the duel, political action and/or social responsibility.[49]

In and of itself, this was little different from masculinity in early modern France or Germany. What distinguished England from its continental counterparts, however, was its flexibility regarding homo-social male engagement. Whereas France adopted a "masculinity" that prized the restraint and control of passions and emotions, early modern Englishmen were expected to be passionate, playful, and expressive, particularly with one another.[50] Male friendships in early modern England were finely gradated, allowing them to vary from warm relations, through homo-social interaction, to fairly open homoeroticism.[51] These actions even found considerable expression in the worlds of Henry VIII and of James VI and I. Within the writings of both kings were letters to male friends that were suggestive of passionate and perhaps even intimate relationships.[52] All of this is indicative of the challenge that faces this study with regard to early modern England: While England was part of a wider European cultural milieu, it was also decidedly "English" in some of the understandings of gender, sex and sexuality that were so inherently tied to the words of 1 Corinthians 6:9.

To extend the examination, the study now examines legal discourse of the period, specifically to see whether sodomy, buggery, effeminateness or any of the other terms associated with improper sexuality, both here and in previous chapters, had any place within the legal texts of the time and whether such texts have any relationship with English vernacular renderings.

The foundation for what would become the basic understanding of sodomy—ostensibly including buggery and pederasty, the two most common translations of μαλακοὶ and ἀρσενοκοῖται—had its first mention in an early modern British legal text during the reign of Henry VIII, who decreed in 1533:

49. See Low, *Manhood*, 71–80.

50. See DiGangi, *Homoerotics of Early Modern Drama*, 134–36.

51. See Bray, "Homosexuality and the Signs of Male Friendship in Elizabethan England," 2–4.

52. Great Britain Public Record Office, *Letters and Papers, Foreign and Domestic, of the reign of Henry VIII, preserved in the Public Record office, the British Museum, and elsewhere in England arranged and catalogued by J.S. Brewer under the direction of the Master of the Rolls, and with the sanction of Her Majesties Secretaries of State* Vol. 6 Part 1 (London: Longman, Green, Longman, Roberts & Green, 1862–1932), 759, 911. James, who married only one woman and fathered many children, as opposed to his predecessor Henry, was thought of as a significant sodomite by many contemporaries. Michael B. Young has explored the ambiguity that James' sexual favourites and favours has occasioned in recent times. See Young, "James VI and I," 540–67.

> Forasmuch as there is not yet sufficient and condign punish-
> ment appointed and limited by the due course of the laws of
> this realm, for the detestable and abominable vice of buggery
> committed with mankind or beast.[53]

It should also be noted that Henry's issuance of this statute most likely resulted from his increasing frustration with the Pope. Moreover, Henry was well aware of the wealth to be found in the abbeys and religious houses of England. Thus, it is not surprising that Cromwell's visits of 1535 found numerous instances of *contra naturam* sexuality in such places and confiscated their lands and wealth. In 1543, Henry would even write to the Scottish regent and encourage him to do the same, speaking of the wealth that might be gained from such actions. This created, in a way, the pretext to associate *contra naturam* sin with that which was one's enemy—in this case Roman Catholic—at least for a time.[54]

Edward VI repeated his father's decree, but added clauses that protected the spouses and heirs of offenders from suit, limited the timeframe for offences and, most interestingly, excluded those who stood to benefit financially from bearing witness in such cases.[55] Edward's sister, Mary I, upon her accession to the throne, repealed all felonies and treasons instituted by Henry and Edward that had not been illegal before their reigns effectively (and certainly unintentionally) legalized "sodomy."[56] Elizabeth I reversed Mary's blanket repeal of statutes by issuing a decree relating to sodomy:

---

53. *Whole Volume of Statutes at Large, 2 Parts in 1 Volume,* 637. (Part 1) Forasmuch as there is not yet sufficient and condign punishment appointed and limited by the due course of the laws of this realm, for the detestable and abominable vice of buggery committed with mankind or beast. It may therefor please the king's highness, with the assent of his lords spiritual and temporal, and the commons of this present parliament assembled, that it may be enacted by authority of the same, that the same offence be from henceforth adjudged felony, and such order and form of process therein to be used against the offenders, as in cases of felony at the common law. And that the offenders being hereof convict by verdict, confession, or outlawry, shall suffer such pains of death and losses, and penalties of their goods, chattels, debts, lands, tenements, and hereditaments, as felons been accustomed to do according, to the order of the common laws of this realm. And that no person offending in any such offence shall be admitted to his clergy. And that justices of peace shall have power and authority within the limits of their commissions and jurisdictions to hear and determine the said offence as they use to do in cases of other felonies. This act to endure till the last day of the next parliament.

54. See Crompton, *Homosexuality and Civilization,* 363.

55. *Whole Volume of Statutes at Large, 2 Parts in 1 Volume,* 72–72 (Part 2).

56. *Whole Volume of Statutes at Large, 2 Parts in 1 Volume,* 199–200 (Part 2).

the punishment of the said detestable vice of buggery, and every
branch, clause, article, and sentence therein contained, shall
from and after the first day of June next coming, be revived,
and from thenceforth shall stand, remain, and be in full force,
strength, and effect forever, in such manner, form, and condition as the same statute was at the day of the death of the said
late king Henry the eight . . . [57]

Thus, within a thirty-year period, sodomy became a felony, was legally refined, "decriminalised," and subsequently reinstated as a felony, although
only in its original broad definition.[58] Considering this variability in the law,
one might expect some permanent fluidity of definition and understanding
of sodomy in English society. By the time of James VI and I, however, the
concept of sodomy (and by proxy buggery) as a felony was firmly established, as is evident in Edward Coke's *Institutes of the Laws of England*:

[Sodomy is] a detestable and abominable sin, amongst Christians not to be named. . . Bugeria is an Italian word. . . Pederastes or Paiderestes is a Greek word, "lover of boys," which

57. It is interesting to note that Mary's repeal must have been unintentional. In her
rush to repeal anti-Catholic legislation, it would seem that the ill of sodomy was "swept
under the proverbial rug." "Wherein the parliament begun at London, the third day
of November in the one and twentieth year of the late king of most famous memory,
king Henry the eight, and after by prorogation holden at Westminster, in the five and
twentieth year of the said late king, there was one act and statute made, entitled "An act
for the punishment of the vice of buggery," whereby the said detestable vice was made
felony as in the said statute more at large it doth and may appear. Forasmuch as the said
statute, concerning the punishment of the said crime and offence of buggery, standeth
at this present repealed and void, by virtue of the statute of repeal made in the first year
of the reign of the late queen Mary: sithens which repeal so had and made, divers evil
disposed persons have been the more bold to commit the said most horrible and detestable vice of buggery aforesaid, to the high displeasure of almighty God. Be it enacted,
ordained, and established by the queen our sovereign lady, and by the assent of the
lords spiritual and temporal, and the commons of this present parliament assembled ,
and by the authority of the same, that the said statute before mentioned, made in the
five and twentieth year of the said late king Henry the eight, for the punishment of the
said detestable vice of buggery, and every branch, clause, article, and sentence therein
contained, shall from and after the first day of June next coming, be revived, and from
thenceforth shall stand, remain, and be in full force, strength, and effect forever, in such
manner, form, and condition as the same statute was at the day of the death of the said
late king Henry the eight, the said statute of repeal made in the said first year of the
said late queen Mary, or any word general or special therein contained, or any other act
or acts, thing or things to the contrary notwithstanding." *Whole Volume of Statutes at
Large, 2 Parts in 1 Volume*, 449 (Part 2).

58. It is rather interesting to note that Elizabeth skipped the definition of Edward
VI, and its subsequent protections, and instead gave preference to the definition from
her father's court.

is but a species of buggery. The emission of semen maketh it not Buggery, but is evidence in case of buggery of penetration; and so in rape the words be also "he knew him/her carnally," and therefore there must be penetration, and emession of semen without penetration maketh no rape. If the party buggered be within the age of discretion, it is no felony in him, but in the agent only. When any offense is felony either by the Common law or by statute, all accessories both before and after are incidentally included. So if any be present, abetting and aiding any to do the act though the offence be personal, and to be done by the one only, as to commit rape, not only he that doth the act is a principal; but also they that be present, abetting, and aiding the misdoer, are principals also. . . [59]

This description provides sufficient information to say that sodomy, or buggery, was something that could apparently be committed with either a person of like age and sex, or with a youth.[60] This concept of buggery involved penetration and ejaculation and assumed the unwillingness of the passive partner; again, all things that would defy the social norm of sex and its procreative role at the time. Coke seems to make particular note of pederastic unions, perhaps hinting at knowledge of their supposed frequency within certain parts of the continent. His clarification that pederasty was but a subcategory of sodomy certainly implies the notion of adult couplings. Although this helps to establish a legal definition of sodomy, the study has yet to understand how this was actually employed in legal cases of the time.

The case of Humphrey Stafford in 1607 shows sodomy, following Coke, as it applied to clear instances of pederasty and rape. Stafford was accused by two youths (aged 17 and c. 14) of committing sodomy upon them:

The two boys upon their oaths did directly charge him with the fact, and the particulars thereof: as the time when, the place where, the manner how, the circumstances both precedent and consequent. . . showing that the boys had received hurt thereby, and that they were forced to use the help of a Surgeon for their care. Master Stafford denied the fact, affirming and protesting that he was guiltless therein, excusing himself that if he had offended it was in wine.[61]

59. Coke, *third part of the Institutes of the laws of England*, 58–59.

60. Interestingly, Coke leaves aside any mention of bestiality. Whether this is to be understood as concomitant or was simply not of concern to the author is unclear.

61. We must assume that Master Stafford penetrated these boys without their consent, at least, according to their record at trial.

The accusations, medical proof and a lack of an effective defence damned the defendant. Master Stafford, unable to defend himself, was summarily executed within the month.[62] In this, one can see an extremely clear example of Coke's understanding, together with the wider regal decrees concerning sodomy, being executed. Although it is impossible to say whether there was ejaculation in this case, there was significant physical evidence of penetration that, with the boys' testimonies, was sufficient to condemn Master Stafford under Jacobean legal code.[63] Tidy cases such as this, however, were not the norm in early modern England. There were, in fact, cases that were much murkier.

The trial of Mervin Touchet, Lord Audley and the Earl of Castlehaven is as complex a case as it is a scandalous picture of the world of sexuality, power and legal code in early-modern England. The case immediately falls into the realm of the bizarre. Brought to light by the complaints of James Touchet, the earl's eldest son, the case combined charges of sodomy, rape, and the *lèse majesté* of what might be called "noble-icide," or a willingness to co-mingle the blood of nobility with that of servants and commoners.[64] According to James Touchet, the earl had spent lavishly on his servant Henry Skipworth at the expense of his son's inheritance. This lavish spending on a common servant at the expense of a noble heir would have been a strong indication of pederasty to the early modern English observer. More troubling, the earl was said to have encouraged Skipworth to engage in adultery with James Touchet's new wife because, as the earl is alleged to have said, he would prefer a son sired by Skipworth to one by his own offspring. The subsequent Privy Council investigation produced even more damning accusations. Touchet's wife testified that the earl had encouraged Skipworth to commit adultery with her while he and other servants watched. Anne Touchet, the earl's wife, testified that her husband, "from the first week of their marriage had shunned her in favour of prostitutes and male servants," a somewhat thinly veiled reference to some form of sodomy, at least with his servants.[65] By male servants, Anne was referring to two servants with whom

62. *Arraignment, Judgment, Confession, and Execution of Humphrey Stafford, Gentleman.*

63. Ejaculation was useful to aid in proof of sodomy, but was, again, unnecessary at the time to convict in sodomy trials.

64. This would be, at the time, considered a *lèsemajesté*, or an offence to the king's grace. *Lèse majesté* was technically seen as an act of treason, but one which would have been difficult to punish as it was difficult to quantify legally. In some instances, current one included, the term could be used to describe a violation of accepted noble norms. See "Lèse majesté" in The Oxford English Dictionary, 2nd Edition (London: Clarendon, 1989), Vol. 3—840."

65. Herrup, *House in Gross Disorder*, 18.

the earl had supposedly committed sodomy, namely Giles Broadway—who was also accused of raping Anne—and Lawrence Fitzpatrick.

Scandalous incidents involving sex and power were not new to the nobility of early modern Europe.[66] Notably strange, in this case, was the number of family members testifying against their patriarch. Son, daughter-in-law, and wife all provided the inquiry with damning evidence. That the servants, Fitzpatrick and Broadway, also incriminated the earl was also somewhat of an oddity.[67] Both servants agreed that immoral acts had indeed taken place but argued the semantics of the charges against them. Broadway claimed that, although the rape of Anne might have been attempted with the earl's help, he had never penetrated her, nor ejaculated in her; thus, rape (by Jacobean standards) had not occurred. Similarly, both Fitzpatrick and Broadway admitted sexual activity with the earl but denied their culpability on technical grounds. Broadway stated that the earl "had used his body as the body of a woman, but never pierced it, only emitted between his thighs."[68] Again, Coke stipulated that

> The emission of semen maketh it not Buggery, but is an evidence in case of buggery of penetration; and so in rape the words be also "he knew him/her carnally," and therefore there must be penetration, and emession of semen without penetration maketh no rape.

This was, technically speaking; a good defence for both men, as far as the letter of the law was concerned, the point being that emission of semen was not enough to convict. Both might have appeared to engage in buggery,

---

66. Though we may, perhaps, enjoy romanticized thoughts of the early moderns as having been a more sexually simplistic society, there is little reason to suspect this was actually so. From the accusations against Henry III of France and his mignons, to the bigamy of Philip of Hesse, and even the marriages (and subsequent divorces) of Henry VIII, there existed many instances where sex and power were intermingled.

67. The confessions of the servants, Fitzpatrick and Broadway, should both be considered with a healthy dose of skepticism. One might wonder why the servants, readily admitting to such a crime as sodomy, never brought the offence to light previously. We might speculate that, to some degree, the two servants submitted to the earl's will as the patriarch and head of the house. Additionally, we might speculate that since, as Broadway states, there was never penetration, there might not have been cause for concern or anger. (Though, Fitzpatrick's confession at his execution would seem to muddle this thought.) It seems rather altogether likely that the servants, seeing the position of their employer versus the crown, sought to ally with the side having the most power and turned on their employer. We might assume they did this in order to escape execution; however this was not to be the case. Both would be judged guilty of sodomy and rape and put to death. See *Case of Sodomy in the Trial of Mervin, Lord Audley*, 33–38.

68. *Complete Collection of State Trials*, 1:264–71.

but for such to be legally true, there needed to be evidence of penetration. The presence of semen could be an aid to prove that rape or buggery had occurred, but it was penetration, not ejaculation, that proved the offence. The earl himself capitalized on this in his defence, arguing that his wife had been unfaithful with Broadway by her own admission and thus negated her own legal protections as his wife. Moreover, the witnesses were incompetent as they had been co-opted by his son in a plot against him, and the charge that he was an accessory to rape, and thus guilty of felony, was questionable because, as Broadway testified, there was no penetration, only emission upon her belly while the earl held her. Such actions, again by legal statute, were not, strictly speaking, indicative of rape. Oddly enough, the earl did not try to defend himself against the accusations of sodomy.[69] It seems that the earl, presented with the testimony against him, relied on playing on the finer points of English law. Unfortunately for Lord Audley, those deciding his case were not interested in his defences, technically valid though they were.[70] All three men mentioned in the case were summarily convicted and executed. Lord Audley's case, for the purposes of this study, describes an understanding of sodomy whereby the action was somewhat fluid, with legal standards not always holding exactly true. It seems obvious that Audley did in fact penetrate at least the thighs of his servants. Whether this peri-anal penetration was enough to satisfy legal requirement or whether Audley's judges were simply more concerned with his other offences, one cannot entirely say. For this study, it is interesting to note the ways in which Audley, his servants and his wife are and are not indicative of several of the descriptions that have been used to describe the μαλακοì and ἀρσενοκοῖται. Skipworth, by being

---

69. *Case of Sodomy in the Trial of Mervin, Lord Audley*, 6–7.

70. While one might debate just what exactly damned Mervin Touchet, it would seem most likely that it was his failure to adhere to socio-political norms. The earl'sdefence showed a keen awareness of English law and under examination appears quite robust with-regards-to the issues of rape and sodomy. What is glaringly absent, however, was a strong repudiation of his intent to supplant his son's seed with a servant's. Socio-norms of the time were entirely predicated around strict concepts of status, birth, privilege, and, importantly, blood-lineage. That the earl was, by his son's account, trying to supplant his legitimate issue and prejudice his children's rights would have been inexcusable and shocking. Combining this grotesque offence with the scandalous vices of rape and sodomy was undoubtedly convenient for prosecutors striving to convict a leading noble largely on the testimony of his wife, his servants and a son who would materially benefit in case of a conviction—all of which should, otherwise, have fatally undermined the prosecution. Ultimately, one might argue, it was this critical departure from the regulated norms of society which caused the earl to be convicted of both rape and sodomy. Interestingly enough, the earl's trial presents the first time that English precedent in trial included homo-social acts without penetration or ejaculation.

something of the earl's pet, could certainly have been a μαλακοί.[71] Moreover, Audley, by engaging in non-copulative and downright odd sexual liaisons, could easily have fit the definition of an ἀρσενοκοῖται.[72] On one hand, it is interesting to note that none of the English (or Latinate) versions of either μαλακοί or ἀρσενοκοῖται appear in the entire sordid affair and its extensive literature.[73] On the other hand, one must question whether the gravity of the case was motivated by politics and the contempt of Audley's son or if this, combined with the opprobrium reserved for the μαλακοί and ἀρσενοκοῖται, was what caused legal standards to be circumvented.

A further case to consider is that of Bishop John Atherton. The Protestant Bishop of the largely Roman Catholic Waterford and Lismore, Atherton was convicted of and executed for sodomy in 1640. Pamphlets from the mid-seventeenth century, published soon after Atherton's execution, indicate that Atherton, although vigorous in defence at his trial, confessed to buggery with a servant and to bestiality with a cow.[74] By the early eighteenth century, however, works were published that described how Atherton had run afoul of several influential—Roman Catholic—members of his diocese. It was suspected that they had concocted a plot to find Atherton guilty of sodomy and, by his execution, to be rid of him.[75] In an eighteenth-century recounting of the incident, it is noted:

> He had (to use the softest expressions) several failings and bad qualities, which could never fail to raise him enemies enough. He was of a proud, passionate, and litigious temper; and, as his affairs forced him, so his inclinations induced him to contend and go to law; in which he had so much knowledge, as made him able and active in the recovery of his dues, a fault of the first magnitude in a clergy-man in some men's opinions.

> But for all the noise and clamour raised against him for his going to law, there was a great deal (and too much) to be offered for his justification in so doing. When he came to the Bishoprick of Waterford, it was so scandalously impoverished by usurpation upon its lands that the revenue or income thereof (as I have received from good testimony) was reduced to the poor

71. At least as would have been later defined by someone such as Blount.

72. Again, as might have later been defined by Leigh.

73. It is entirely plausible that, in the mind of the judges, the μαλακοί and ἀρσενοκοῖται, were being referenced, though, not directly as that could lead to further sins.

74. Bernard, *Case of John Atherton, Bishop of Waterford in Ireland*. Note: Bernard died in 1661, so this would most definitely be a reprinting of his earlier written piece.

75. King, *case of John Atherton, Bishop of Waterford in Ireland*.

inconsiderable sum of sixty pounds per annum. Upon this account, he was forced to go to law for a competent livelihood and to sue divers persons for the recovery of lands justly belonging to his bishoprick and as unjustly detained from him. He had so good success therein that he recovered and settled by law several considerable estates upon his see, which are at this time enjoyed by his successor. But made without doubt all those from whom he regained the church-lands his own, if not the churches, inveterate enemies. Besides having given out that he designed to try for greater estates which were in the hands of some great men, but as he thought of right belonged to the bishoprick, raised that malice (if not conspiracy) against him, which as you have read ended in his ruin; which is common opinion, and belief of almost every body in and about Waterford. . . .But I am afraid he went further; for he confesses himself guilty of taking advantages and over-reaching men.[76]

It would seem that the Bishop was a man fixated on what he thought he should have, rather than on what he could have. Ignorance of the political milieu surrounding him seems to be the primary cause that brought about his ruin. Atherton's fixation on want and desire might certainly have made him open to questions of being part of the μαλακοὶ as defined by Cokayne and can perhaps explain the severity of the case. At the same time, it is entirely plausible that Atherton was simply a greedy and unpleasant man, being idealistic and self-centred. King notes that Atherton, due to his legal activities, had few friends and yet was quite surprised when he was suddenly imprisoned and charged with sodomy.[77] Atherton is said to have neither denied nor accepted to the charges, which might ultimately account for his undoing. It appears that the Bishop assumed his trial would be lengthy and that cooler heads and distant authorities would rescue him. Atherton, although initially denying the charge of sodomy, accepted his guilt and sentence as the will of God for sins he had otherwise committed.[78] It is interesting that one finds no mention of physical evidence being

76. It seems, from the later histories of Atherton, that he was something of a "firebrand" in his episcopacy. Moreover, he seems to have been pastorally ignorant of his standing within the social community at large and the impact or effect his various policies had made. King, *Atherton*, 14–15.

77. King, *Atherton*, 15.

78. Most curiously, or conveniently, as it might be, the records of Atherton's trial have been lost. We are left to draw out truth from Bernard's condemnation of Atherton and King's defence of him. One might speculate, however, that the bishop, seeing the finality of his situation, sought to find as graceful an exit as possible, where things ultimately backfired. See King, *Atherton*, 18.

submitted. Atherton's acceptance of his guilt, however, would seem to make such admissions unnecessary.

Finally, a case between a Mrs Williamson and a Mr Thomas Ivie provides another perspective of the early modern English legal setting. In the proceedings, Mrs Williamson reported that Mr Ivie had "buggered his wife" as being one of her grievances.[79] The use of "bugger" shows that buggery, while being strongly associated with same-sex interactions or *contra naturam* sexuality such as sodomy, bestiality, or pederasty, could be levelled at heterosexual acts that were outside of the accepted realm of "natural" (procreative) sexuality. Mr Ivie could hardly have entered into a pederastic or bestial relationship with his wife. He could, however, very easily have forced her into non-copulative sexual practices such as anal or oral sex which, by their nature, precluded procreation and were thus indicative of both buggery and the wider taxonomy of sodomy.

Each of these four cases involved different situations and stations and had a number of different themes moving through them; a combination of actual happenings, accusation and what seem to be politically motivated subtexts. Nonetheless, all four were deemed to have met the definition of sodomy in their own locales and times. Unfortunately, this is a problem for this study. In the cases examined thus far, there was one accusation of rape, two of homosexual sodomy and one of heterosexual buggery.[80] While the cases mentioned previously show that all these offences were condemnable and thus provide clues to the status and station of those who were μαλακοί and ἀρσενοκοῖται within English society, they do not describe the differentiation between the accusations. Coke made it clear that pederasty was a sub-category of sodomy, hinting that sodomy was a wide and perhaps nebulous concept, contrary to some definitions.[81] As such, the question is just how far

79. Ivie, *Alimony Arraignd*, 19.

80. Moreover, there seems to be one thing that united them: sexual power imbalances. In all four instances we see accounts of men buggering those who were below their own station in life, never the inverse. This was, in many, though not all, ways indicative of classical pederasty; whereby the powerful, in compensation for sexual services, shared the benefits of their station with those who were lesser. Certainly, in the instances laid out previously, we might question the benefit for those who were weaker, particularly in the Stafford case, but there nonetheless remains the trope of the powerful dominating the weak. It seems this tells us something critical about sodomy within early modern England. Sodomy, in its legal realm, was largely noted as pederasty, though it was much more broadly understood as well. In a great number of instances, however, there seemed to be this element of weak and powerful, penetrator and penetrated.

81. Crompton suggests that English concepts of "sodomy" should be understood as deriving from Aquinas, whose writings on the topic will be examined in the next chapter. As such, sodomy might be best understood, per Crompton, as inclusive of

any subcategories might stretch—specifically, whether non-procreative sex was analogous to the ἀρσενοκοῖται and the buggered pederasty previously presented by lexicons. The ἀρσενοκοῖται, simply defined as the pederasts within buggery, as proposed by Huloet et al., would be one situation. The ἀρσενοκοῖται, defined as the buggerers, indicative of the wider category of general sodomy, as Wilson and Littleton seem to indicate, with both hetero and homo shades of sexual action included, would be another thing entirely. At the very least, these instances, as in the previous examples from the lexicons, seem to describeunderstandings of the μαλακοὶ and ἀρσενοκοῖται as sodomy and buggery, which were not proved beyond doubt.

Although some plausible definitions of those who were μαλακοὶ and ἀρσενοκοῖται have been suggested, there is still considerable debate as to who or what such creatures might actually be. In an attempt to expand on this, the study now examines how and whether these vernacular biblical terms, or the words and concepts linked to them, were used in popular society at the time. When using popular or public writings of the early modern period, it is important to clarify, at the outset, what it is the study wishes to know. The focus terms μαλακοὶ and ἀρσενοκοῖται were not widely discussed in their direct forms in much of the literature in any locale of the early modern world. However, the terms were associated with sodomy, bestiality, effeminateness, and pederasty, which were all addressed in some form at some time in the contemporary popular literature of any given culture.

Much has been said about the homoeroticism of both early modern drama and literature in early modern England, and it is beyond the bounds of this study to try to cover or consider every instance of homoeroticism in early modern English drama and stage. Such examination would be, and most likely has been, a lengthy study in itself. Nonetheless, it is critical at this juncture to survey some aspects of the period briefly, particularly looking to see how μαλακοὶ and ἀρσενοκοῖται, via their translations, might have been understood or understood by wider society at the time. Unfortunately, even this brief examination presents significant problems.

As Alan Bray noted, one would be hard pressed to find literal examplesin non-legal discourse that concerned sodomy, buggery and so forth in early modern England.[82] Instead, one finds stock characters or tropes on display. Therefore, it is somewhat naive to search through early modern literature to find specific examples of sodomy and buggery, as was the case in legal

---

male-male sexual relations, including pederasty, bestiality, and, as he argues as the most commonly known, masturbation. Crompton does allow that sodomy may be inclusive of male-female anal or extra-genital sex but sees this as a minor consideration. See Crompton, *Homosexuality and Civilization*, 363–64.

82. Bray, *Homosexuality in Renaissance England*, 34–36.

record. Instead, the study must examine these stock characters and tropes to see whether there was, in common society, a correlation between the legal and lexical examples noted previously. Examples in common literature that correlate to the examples studied previously would support a wide meta-understanding of those who were considered μαλακοὶ and ἀρσενοκοῖται in early modern England. The opposite, however, would present a situation in which one might have to acknowledge that the common translations of μαλακοὶ and ἀρσενοκοῖται meant one thing in legal or formal discourse, another in lexical definition, but something else in common usage.

Turning first to the work of Christopher Marlowe, one must examine Marlowe's *Edward II*.[83] A full examination of the play, its sexual overtones and its full meanings are far beyond this study. In the characterisations of Edward and Gaveston, however, there is much that tells of early modern understanding of the μαλακοὶ, the ἀρσενοκοῖται, and how the understanding of these characters played out in reality. In the character of Gaveston, one finds a prime example of the μαλακοὶ. Gaveston is interested in pleasure, sensuousness, beauty, sexual temptation, and other fineries. Gaveston's speech, in preparation for returning to England and entertaining the new king, is an example of the μαλακοὶ:

> Music and poetry is his delight;
> Therefore I'll have Italian masques by night,
> Sweet speeches, comedies, and pleasing shows;
> And in the day, when he shall walk abroad,
> Like sylvan nymphs my pages shall be clad;
> My men, like satyrs grazing on the lawns,
> Shall with their goat-feet dance an antic hay.
> Sometime a lovely boy in Dian's shape,
> With hair that gilds the water as it glides,
> Crownets of pearl about his naked arms,
> And in his sportful hands an olive tree
> To hide those parts which men delight to see,
> Shall bathe him in a spring; and there, hard by,
> One like Actaeon, peeping through the grove,
> Shall by the angry goddess be transformed,

---

83. Certainly, there are other works of Marlowe's that might be examined for information over sodomy, buggery, and pederasty in the early modern world. *Edward II*, however, is fascinating in its examination of an English topic in English society. Nonetheless, we cannot deny that homoeroticism was a fascination for Marlowe in much of his writing. See Boas, *Christopher Marlowe*.

And running in the likeness of a hart
By yelping hounds pulled down and seem to die.
Such things as these best please his majesty.[84]

Gaveston's speech gives public shape and personification to the definitions found in Blount, Leigh, Huloet and others. Here was a man who was the favourite of the king and who was concerned only with providing his master with sensuous pleasures galore, focusing particularly on the pleasure of watching a beautiful naked boy.[85] Edward, for his part, was infatuated with Gaveston and gave him with significant power and prestige within his court. Ostensibly, as Gaveston was given to a continuous search for pleasure and as Edward was so infatuated with him, one might assume that the two were involved; both could be seen as being reflective of the μαλακοὶ and ἀρσενοκοῖται, with Gaveston the *cinaedus* and Edward his enabling lover.[86] Again, although there is much to say about the innuendos and tropes on display in Marlowe's writing that is not applicable to this study, in Marlowe's representations of Gaveston and Edward, one finds personification of many of the lexical definitions examined previously.

Apart from Marlowe, one cannot engage with the topic of sodomy in early modern English literature and not include a brief note about the writings of John Bale. Bale's extremely acerbic denouncements of the Roman Catholic church are well noted in a number of studies on early modern English literature. His works, *The Three Laws of Nature, Moses, and Christ, Corrupted by the Sodomites, the Pharisees, and Papists*(1536) and *The Actes of the EnglyshVotaryes* (1546), were texts that were both highly incendiary regarding the Roman Catholic Church and notable for their accusations of sodomy, particularly pederasty, amongst its leaders.[87] While Marlowe's dramatic portrayal of sodomy affected English life explicitly, Bale's was notably religiously xenophobic in its personification. Catholic priests were, according to Bale, "none other than sodomites and whoremongers all the pack."[88] This should indicate that, while not nearly as prominent as other locales

---

84. Marlowe, *Edward II*, I.I.53–70.

85. It has been speculated that Edward II was really an allusion to the relationship of James VI and I with his cousin Esme Stewart, Lord Lennox. While this is again, sadly, outside the purview of this study, it is nonetheless interesting. See Normand, "What Passions Call You These? Edward II and James VI."

86. Thus, as usual, the socially dominant man is the sexually active and the man of lower status the passive.

87. Crompton, *Homosexuality and Civilization*, 364–65.

88. Bale, *Actes of the EnglyshVotaryes*.

such as Luther's Germany, sodomy as demonisation of the Roman clergy
was certainly present within early modern England.

Perhaps most telling regarding the opaque nature of the μαλακοί and
ἀρσενοκοῖται in early modern society was their application in actual royal
life, not simply in literature. The definitions of those who were μαλακοί or
ἀρσενοκοῖται, as presented in this chapter, were applicable to specific kings
of early modern England: Henry VIII and James VI and I. Henry has often
been portrayed in history as a virile and masculine king. He was a king who
stood up to the Pope, the king who established an English faith, and the
king who largely did simply as he pleased. However, according to some definitions of the period, he could have been considered part of the μαλακοί.
He was ostentatious in terms of spending on clothes, frivolities, and what-
not, both on himself and on his friends and family.[89] Moreover, he had a
significant problem producing heirs, often thought to be a sign of divine
displeasure with a monarch and his or her rule. Although Henry produced
heirs in the form of his daughters Mary and Elizabeth, it took him quite
some time to produce his only male heir, Edward. In this regard, Henry was
a king who, quite simply, could not fulfil his royal duty. He was unable to
be "manly" in the greatest sense of national duty. All these things should,
given the potential definitions of the μαλακοί, have caused considerable
question, if not accusation, regarding Henry. The fact of the matter is that
these factors did not produce any accusations, contemporary or otherwise.
There are admittedly a number of reasons for such accusations not to have
occured. It is plausible that the king, although meeting the lexical criteria,
simply did not meet the mental or social criteria for the μαλακοί in the
minds of those observing. Although close to some, particularly to Charles
Brandon, Henry's affections were never as threatening to social order as
were Edward's and Gaveston's. It is also entirely plausible that there were
those who certainly thought as much but feared for their physical safety
should they accuse the king. For whatever reason, be it ignorance or simply
fear of the monarch and subsequent repercussions, Henry never seemed to
face accusation regarding the actions of his life, which echoed some definitions of the μαλακοί. The same could not be said, however, about Henry's
great-nephew and eventual successor, James Stuart.

For quite some time, James VI and I has been historically associated
with sodomy.[90] Although never proven to have been involved with anything untoward, such as buggery, James has frequently been assumed to be

89. Stevenson, "Texts and Textiles," 39–57.

90. Examples of such include Young, *King James VI and I and the History of Homosexuality*; Trumbach, "Renaissance Sodomy, 1500–1700"; and Bergeron, *King James
and Letters of Homoerotic Desire*.

homosexual. Ironically, James was, in a number of ways, something of the opposite of Henry. Whereas Henry had multiple spouses and had problems producing a male heir, James had one spouse and numerous children, the oldest of whom was a boy, Henry. James was certainly engaged in his own courtly extravagances, but one might argue this was essential given the spending of his Tudor predecessors and the need to present himself as truly "English."[91] His undoing, however, was his fascination with two courtly favourites, Robert Carr, Earl of Somerset, and George Villiers, Duke of Buckingham.[92] Courtly favourites were nothing new to the world of early modern England. Henry VIII had such a favourite in Charles Brandon, Duke of Suffolk and Elizabeth I in Robert Dudley, Earl of Leicester.[93] What set James' situation apart were two things: Firstly, James had raised his favourites from lowly status to becoming, arguably, the most powerful men in the court.[94] Secondly, James was highly, although not grossly, affectionate to his favourites in public. He fawned, he feigned, he spoiled, and he wooed, which again was not necessarily unheard of with courtly favourites.[95] Apparently, this was enough to send James' contemporaries into panic mode, never speaking of the English equivalents of μαλακοὶ and ἀρσενοκοῖται, but certainly hinting at the terms associated with them in their polemics. In some ways, James' emotional incontinence, as well as with the lowly birth of his favourites, was what created such a commotion for James.[96] To elevate these men in such a fashion and then to treat them in this way was both frustrating and suspicious for early modern minds. It reeked of "pederasty."[97] It seemed that

91. See Stevenson, "Texts and Textiles," 53.

92. Weldon, *Court and Character of King James*, 89, 94, 102–3, 135–36, 149–50, 178; and Anonymous (Though perhaps Weldon), *Cat May Look Upon a King*, 24, 30–31, 37, 39, 41, 43.

93. Adams, *Leicester and the Court*, 134; and Gunn, "Brandon, Charles, first duke of Suffolk (c.1484–1545)."

94. Much as Edward II was thought to have done, to widespread public censure.

95. Though, in the case of Elizabeth, her favorite was a male and she a female—well within the normal prescribed boundaries of sexual exchange. That James' favorites were male—and thus potential pederasts or sodomites—made for something of a different situation as sodomy could bring the destruction of society. For examples of the gravity of sodomy see Samuel, *Warnyng for the Cittie of London that the Dwellers therein may Repent their Evyll Lyves for Feare of Goddes Plages*, 1; and Adams, *Happines of the Church*, 18.

96. One might wonder whether Charles Brandon's noble birth was the only thing saving Henry from similar accusations.

97. James' contemporaries compared him to Sir Anthony Ashley whose own sodomitic pursuits were thought to be common knowledge. So greatly known were Ashley's sodomitic pursuits that, when he finally married a woman, it was only assumed he could find the match palatable due to the woman's large rump and fondness for anal

there could be few other explanations, as these men were both young and attractive at the time of their elevation and both had little to offer the king other than, perhaps, their bodies. This, in turn, for observers, explained the king's affection towards them and the benefits that they reaped from exploiting it. This also made the king a sodomite, as pederasty was, again, a subset of sodomy in many definitions of the time. It is notable that there were never any legal or direct accusations against the king or his person, but there were numerous allusions, particularly after James' reign and during the English civil war and Interregnum.[98] In some ways, James' situation was similar to that of the Earl of Castlehaven. Both found themselves subject to accusations of sodomy, although both faced accusations that had little real proof.[99] Both found themselves placed under such accusations primarily due to the eschewing of social convention, Castlehaven for "noble-icide" and James for elevating men outside of noble birth or status.

These situations seem telling for the wider usage of the term "sodomy" in early modern England. Sodomy, including pederasty and bestiality, might very well occur and be definable within legal, social, and ecclesiastic realms. It was, however, also possible for the term to be applied in situations that defied or riled the social norm or convention, particularly when social standing, particularly a usurpation of social standing, was involved. It was also, arguably, a highly charged term of abuse levelled at one's political and religious opponents.

These are but some of the examples one might find in common literature and society in early modern England. No doubt, one might well cite works by Donne and others; however, such aspects have been well covered in other studies. Nonetheless, this small examination has served the study's

---

sex. See Libel No. 10, "Heaven Bleese King James Our Joy," lines 37–44.

98. Though, these might have been both ways to contrast Charles I's court with James' and perhaps later attempts to blacken James and the Stuarts. See D'Ewes, *Diary of Sir Simonds D'Ewes (1622–1624)*, 92–93; Goodman, *Court of King James the First*, 225–26; Anonymous, *Tom Tell Troath or a free discourse touching the manners of the tyme*, 15, 25–26; and one might look to the writings of Thomas Scott to see sodomy complaints against James during his rule. See Scott, *Belgicke pismire*, 10–12, 37–40. Charles' court has, in some instances, particularly in the writings of Lucy Hutchinson, no friend to the monarchy herself, been noted as having been far less dramatic and debauched than his father's.

99. Young has argued that some of Buckingham's letters to James can be interpreted to show that mutual masturbation was, indeed, happening between the two men. Even if this were the case and even if it were to have been acknowledged by James' detractors, this still would not have been defined as sodomy, per Coke. Thus, short of our authors catching the two involved in coitus or one or the other actors admitting to such actions—they almost certainly were not about to do—there could be no legitimate charge of sodomy against James. See Young, *Reconsideration*, 562–63.

purpose. All of these examples, taken together provide both amplification and frustration. On one hand, many of these examples seem to resonate with and perhaps expand the lexical definitions and legal cases examined previously. On the other hand, the examples raise questions of their own and prevent the attribution of a "clear" or "clean" definition of either the μαλακοì or the ἀρσενοκοῖται in early modern England.

At this point, the study has established something of a strong working definition for both the μαλακοì and ἀρσενοκοῖται in early modern England. The μαλακοì, and particularly those who were thought of as also being ἀρσενοκοῖται, were often associated with acts of sodomy, although not always in similar or literal ways. The μαλακοì were most often, in the definitions, associated with an outward expression of an inward weakness or predisposition towards a lustful lack of self-control; however, this might also be an entirely inward sickness of the mind. In many ways, those who were ill with lust were the customers of the ἀρσενοκοῖται. The ἀρσενοκοῖται were usually associated with the actions of buggery or sodomy. Sodomy was the main and overarching understanding of "unnatural" lusts; lusts that went against what was considered normal and natural action. Sodomy was, in many cases, known as buggery or anal sex. To say, however, that buggery was simply anal sex was, as seen earlier, far too simplistic. Buggery, as seen in both lexical and legal situations, was both anal copulation and was associated with the vice of pederasty. Thus, returning to previous legal examples, Castlehaven, as described by his accusers, was both part of the μαλακοì and ἀρσενοκοῖται by definition, as was Master Stafford. However, there was again no consensus in lexical terms regarding exactly where the μαλακοì ended and ἀρσενοκοῖται began. Therefore, one might also say that, for many, Mr Ivie, as previously examined, was a sodomite by virtue of his buggery, but was not necessarily part of the μαλακοì and was certainly not a pederast.

In practice, the terms synonymous with the μαλακοì and ἀρσενοκοῖται, in early modern England—the terms sodomy, unnatural lust, and pederasty—were often politically charged. They carried with them significant potential for danger or benefit, depending on whether one was the accuser or the accused. They were terms, with attributed concepts which were familiar via the dramas of Marlowe, amongst others, but still occasioned the strictest and harshest penalties in legal circumstances due to their gravity. In the sense of translation, English vernaculars displayed notable reflections of *ad fontes* interpretations for 1 Corinthians 6:9, as well as a considerable number of texts that, even though promoted by reformers, were conservative and more reflective of the Latin Vulgate in their translation. Such understanding and presentation were largely indicative of the highly charged and potentially dangerous religious change that characterized much of early modern English religious life. In summary, the μαλακοὶ and the ἀρσενοκοῖται were quite reminiscent of early modern England itself; twisting, turning, and not easily identified or labelled within a singular proposition. Thus, it is difficult to say whether vernacular translation in early modern England allowed one to understand the original meaning of οὔτε μαλακοὶ οὔτε ἀρσενοκοῖται. England, it seems, was not easily assured of who it was or what it wanted to say.

CHAPTER FOUR

Italy: Hotbed Of Sodomy Or . . . Not?

T he final stop in this study is Italy. The Italian peninsula presents itself as something of an odd feature in this study. On one hand, with
the nation being the central bastion of Roman Catholicism, one may not
expect to find many vernacular texts and thus not much reference to οὔτε
μαλακοὶ οὔτε ἀρσενοκοῖται. On the other hand, the *ad fontes* concept, as
a part of the larger humanist movement, was certainly present in early
modern Italy. In fact, some have noted the way in which even leaders of
the Roman Catholic Church, Cajetan perhaps most of all, were dismissive
of the movement but also greatly indebted to its principles.[1] Nonetheless,
the study should be clear at the outset, the world of Italian biblical production focused largely on other considerations, namely the protection
and continuation of *magisterium* through a *depositum fidei* and a *traditio
apostolica* within the Vulgate.[2]

As Italian territories were close subjects of the Roman Catholic Church
and its preference for the Vulgate, it should therefore not be terribly surprising that there are few early modern Italian vernaculars for this study to
consider. The vernaculars that are available to study were largely produced
prior to the Council of Trent, which officially gave the Vulgate complete primacy over any vernacular text. Moreover, in Italy, the similarities between
Latin and Italian created a situation in which vernacular translation was not
entirely necessary; the significant similarities between the Romance languages allowed for a working understanding of the text. In fact, the Medieval
Latin Vulgate was readily used for most religious purposes and there was
little impetus for change within Italian circles. The average early modern layperson, were he an Italian, would not have "heard" the Vulgate as a foreign
language in quite the same way a Frenchman—let alone a German or an
Englishman—would have done. Therefore, it should be of little surprise that

1. O'Connor, "Neglected Facet of Cardinal Cajetan," 75–93 and Ocker, "Scholastic
Interpretation of the Bible," 266–72.

2. Hobbs, "Hebraica Veritas and Traditio Apostolica," 83–86.

extant vernaculars largely followed the Vulgate rendering of *οὔτε μαλακοὶ οὔτε ἀρσενοκοῖται* as *neque molles, neque masculorum concubitores*.[3] This translation was echoed even within the writings of reform-minded Roman Catholics such as Valla and Pagnini, both of whom reiterated, verbatim, the Vulgate in their subsequent Latin Bibles and annotations thereof.[4] Such a practice might be seen as expressing continuity with the previous iterations of the Latin Vulgate. Italians, even the reform-minded ones, were not interested in creating an entirely new work as much as refining or reiterating that which had existed previously. This lack of explanation, as opposed to full description in the vernacular, could also be seen as both an act of encouraging moral fortitude and of ensuring civil continuity by dissuading divine judgement.[5] *Contra naturam* sins were, quite literally, ranked as the "worst of the worst" sins in late-medieval Italy and, as such, it would be questionable for theologians, even contentious ones, to elucidate upon the topic.[6] Valla and Pagnini, however, were not the only notable Italians to engage with biblical translation in the early modern period.

Antonio Brucioli, a staunch Italian Roman Catholic writing in the mid-sixteenth century, produced a vernacular that translated *μαλακοὶ οὔτε ἀρσενοκοῖται* as *ne queli effeminati, ne quelli che usano con i maschi*.[7] Brucioli's translation was limited with regard to specifics and seemed to assume the colloquial understanding of its readers, particularly as the *effeminati* were exactly as they sounded: effeminates.[8] Nonetheless, given this specific description of *effeminati*, one can perhaps assume that the *μαλακοὶ*, in the mind of this vernacular author, were similar to those seen elsewhere in this study. The effeminate *μαλακοὶ* were those who were often soft, yielding, wanton, needy,

---

3. *Biblia Sacra Veteris et Novi Testamenti*, 121.

4. Laurentii Vallae, *Lavrentii Vallae*, Q2ᴿ; Sante Pagnini, *Biblia*, Fol. 53. Both citations, from Valla and Pagnini were published in Reformation territories. All the same, that they are so oriented to the Vulgate should detail that, with respect to this pericope in 1 Cor 6:9, there was no undue influence exerted by editors.

5. The early fifteenth-century Bernadino de Siena seems to have been one of the few exceptions to this rule. Bernadino was quite vexed by pederasty and preached several denouncements on the topic. His actions, however, were far more the exception than the rule and, by and large, clerical denouncement of pederasty stayed muted. See Crompton, *Homosexuality and Civilization*, 253–55.

6. See *Confessio Generalis Brevis et Utilis*, A6ᴿ. This was, as seen in the previous chapter, not entirely unlike a number of early modern English translations, which guarded their interpretation either out of political or moral fear.

7. See Brucioli, *Il Nuvo Testamento*, 60.

8. See Paravicino, *Choice proverbs and dialogues in Italian and English*, G24ⱽ; Thomas, *Principal rules of the Italian grammer*, X2ⱽ; Blount, *Glossographia*, O44ⱽ; Phillips, *New World of English words*, N3ⱽ; and Howell, *Lexicon Tetraglotton*, Ff2ⱽ.

penetrable, and lustful, or all that was contrary to the strong masculinity of the time.[9] The ἀρσενοκοῖται, however, were far more difficult to define. Brucioli's phrase *ne quelli che usano con i maschi* was less than forthcoming in its intent and was almost certainly a circumlocution of some sort. "Those who abuse themselves with males," the literal reading of Brucioli's translation, is a phrase that seems not unfamiliar and echoes the Vulgate but is also frustratingly broad regardingprecisely what type of "abuse" is implied. *Usare,* the critical verb in this construction, is reminiscent of both basic use and wantonness in early modern Italian dictionaries.[10] Thus, the text refers to some form of male *contra naturam* sexuality, but the specific type cannot be determined. The author seems to have been confident about his audience's ability to understand his intention, concerned about providing too much information to spiritually weak readers or, as seems most likely, simply assumed all forms of "abuse" were included.

Giovanni Diodati provided the foremost Italian vernacular translation of the early modern period but, like his contemporaries, he still echoed the Vulgate with regard to οὔτε μαλακοὶ οὔτε ἀρσενοκοῖται.[11] Diodati rendered οὔτε μαλακοὶ οὔτε ἀρσενοκοῖται in 1 Corinthians 6:9 as *nei molli ne quelli che usano con maschi che i quali perseverano in questi peccati:*"neither the soft, nor those who abuse themselves with males that persist in these sins."[12] This translation was, again, quite similar to that found in the Latin Vulgate, with the final phrase being a small but critical addition as will be discussed below. Once again, as has been previously illustrated, all these authors were vague about οὔτε μαλακοὶ οὔτε ἀρσενοκοῖται. These translations, from the Latin of Valla and Pagnini to the vernaculars of Brucioli and Diodati could, at this point, indicate a myriad of understandings, from moral failures to effeminate men and pederasts, sodomites, and practitioners of non-procreative intercourse of any type.

9. This was perhaps intentionally echoing the understandings of Antiquity, such as Epictetus. See Epictetus, "Epistle," 68. For Florio, the *molli* was a colloquial form of *mollicico*, again, and somewhat simply, the "soft." See Florio, *Queen Anna's New World Of Words,* 319. John Florio is a notable name that will be seen in several other passages within this chapter. Florio was the son of an Italian immigrant who was also notable for his teaching of the Italian language, even offering Italian lessons to Lady Jane Grey. Florio's late sixteenth-century Italian dictionary was the most significant Italian-to-English dictionary of its time. It was later to be expanded in the early seventeenth century to create a truly overarching text. See O'Connor, "Florio, John (1553–1625)."

10. Florio, *Queen Anna's New World Of Words,* 610.

11. Whereas others, such as Valla, Pagnini, and Brucioli, were Roman Catholic Italians providing Italian vernaculars, Diodati was an Italian exile and a firm Protestant. See Grell, *Brethren in Christ,* 211.

12. Diodati, *La Biblia,* 186.

These similarities to the Latin Vulgate, even in the work of a Protestant such as Diodati, are intriguing. Certainly, adhering to the Vulgate translation, even for Protestants, was not unknown. The study has already seen Neo-Latin transcription as a represented format in the works of Francois Bonade in France.[13] Nonetheless, it is difficult for this study to understand what drove translators such as Diodati and Brucioli to adhere to the Vulgate in their vernacular texts and what they meant via their subsequent words. One potential explanation might focus on the intended audience. Valla, Pagnini and Brucioli were all Roman Catholics writing for Catholics. Even Diodati was writing an Italian vernacular that would, ostensibly, be read by Roman Catholic Italians. They would thus want to ensure that their texts were relevant to interested readers and wider society. Accordingly, following the Vulgate made some sense. This point is further emphasized by considering the gravity of *contra naturam* sin in the late medieval and pre-Reformation church. *Contra naturam* sins could literally destroy society; thus few, if any of the reverent, might wish to openly speak of them. Finally, as noted above, discussions of sins, which included οὔτε μαλακοὶ οὔτε ἀρσενοκοῖται, prior to the Protestant Reformation, were not readily encouraged even amongst clerics and academics.[14] This was, again, to prevent both a scandalising and a temptation of those who might be intrigued by a detailed discussion of these topics. Thus, it is highly possible that these translators, skilled though they were, decided the topics associated with οὔτε μαλακοὶ οὔτε ἀρσενοκοῖται were simply too scandalous to discuss via a blunt translation and chose the safety of the Vulgate's vagueness. The laity of the world might truly be seeking a more accessible route to the divine, but that did not mean they could not be swayed from their path by scandalous information. All the same, the vagueness of the Vulgate and these Italian vernaculars does not help this study to understand who or what were implied in the over-proscription of 1 Corinthians 6:9.

Thankfully, the study finds an understanding of these vague translations in the writings of Cardinal Cajetan. Cajetan, in his *Summula Peccatorum*, said that *mollities* were "the opposite of perseverance; effeminateness and masturbation," all three instances being *contra naturam* and thus, echoing 1 Corinthians 6:9, excluded from the *regno dei*. Moreover, Cajetan, in defining sodomy, noted that the sin was also *contra naturam,* again excluding those who commited this sin from the *regno dei,* but also that it was *mares inter se,* "men with one another," quite like the indictments of

13. See Bonadus, *Divi Pauli Apostoli Gentium,* 24.

14. As Tentler identified, there was considerable angst involved in the investigation of a great number of carnal sins in the late medieval world, a world in which the sins of sodomy and *contra naturam*s ins were the worst of the worst. See Tentler, *Sin and Confession on the Eve of the Reformation,* 89.

the Vulgate and Italian vernaculars.[15] Cajetan's descriptions thus provide plausible links for the study to create definitions for οὔτε μαλακοὶ οὔτε ἀρσενοκοῖται in Italian vernaculars. The μαλακοὶ were specific, although potentially tripartite characters: those who lacked perseverance, the effeminate and, perhaps most dangerously, the masturbators.[16] The ἀρσενοκοῖται, on the other hand, were indicative of male sodomy, broadly defined as including all types and subsets of sodomitical practice.

It is at this point, with the boundaries of Cajetan's definitions providing some clarity that the study must pause to address Diodati's small but critical addition to his vernacular text. Diodati's addition of *che i quali perseverano in questi peccati* is an interesting note, which adds to the spectrum of any definition. Taken in conjunction with the *molli*, this clarification presents synergistic categories and was a rather severe indictment of those who were μαλακοὶ. These μαλακοὶ were those who were, as the text states, "soft." What "soft" indicated, however, was something that the author felt his audience might be able to infer on its own. These characters might have been effeminate, lacked perseverance, and/or been masturbators, as Cajetan pointed out, or they might have been something far more nefarious, such as sexually passive males. What is clear, however, is that the μαλακοὶ, however they might have been understood, were those who continuously engaged in a set of sins that were desirable to the ἀρσενοκοῖται. The ἀρσενοκοῖται were those who employed or used such persons. What is less clear is where one sin ended, the other began and how the two might have overlapped. The ἀρσενοκοῖται were clearly those who engaged in the sinful currency of the μαλακοὶ, but the boundaries that contained these characters were unclear in Diodati's verse. Whether these creatures shared traits, such as overindulgence, effeminacy, and other damning descriptors, is difficult to say. The early modern Italian lack of interest in vernacular translation also produced a dearth of lexicographical literature to support or identify words.[17] At the very least, however, one can see that there was a level of transaction between the μαλακοὶ and the ἀρσενοκοῖται in the eyes of Diodati. One sinned, while the other engaged and enticed the sinner to perform in this sin. Thus, while there is little in the way of specifics in Diodati's work, there is evidence that the author saw something of a symbiotic relationship between the μαλακοὶ and the ἀρσενοκοῖται.[18] The ἀρσενοκοῖται were not necessarily μαλακοὶ and

15. Cajetan, *Summula Peccatorum*, 424–25, 519.

16. Cajetan reserves this as the final, and thus perhaps most serious, form of mollity. Cajetan would later argue that male sodomy was worse than sodomy committed between a man and a woman as the later was only committed with the wrong organ, the former with the wrong person. See Jordan, *Silence of Sodom*, 64–65.

17. This lack of literature is why, in this chapter, almost all lexical sources are Italian-to-English translations produced mainly in London.

18. Didodati's work would later be translated into English after his death. The

vice versa, but they were engaged in an economy of sin with one another, which damned them in the eyes of the author. From the previous implications of reformers, such as Luther and Bale, one cannot help but wonder if the author was, less than subtly, hinting at an entirely different understanding of the μαλακοì and ἀρσενοκοῖται than Cajetan was. Whereas Cajetan's descriptions are singular actors, able to sin with or apart from one another, Diodati's definitions seem particularly inclined towards that most Italian -at least for Protestant minds- of vices: pederasty.

At this point, the study is torn between the potential to and difficulty in making definitive statements. Based on the sampled vernacular texts, the study is currently able to make several broad statements about the μαλακοì and ἀρσενοκοῖται in early modern Italy. Both the μαλακοì and the ἀρσενοκοῖται were contra naturam persons and both were excluded from the kingdom of God. The μαλακοì were, quite vaguely, the "soft" characters, which might have been revealed in the effeminateness of the unmasculine, a lack of perseverance or masturbation. The ἀρσενοκοῖται, through circumlocution, were sodomites and indicative of some form of male sexual action, almost certainly with other males, and potentially with those who embodied the characteristics of the μαλακοì. Nonetheless, although this study can generate some understandings from these two vernaculars, it cannot be said that, at present, there is a satisfactory description of those actors who might specifically have been μαλακοì and ἀρσενοκοῖται within early modern Italy. None of the vernaculars have provided singular or descriptive words to describe just who or what they intended the μαλακοì and the ἀρσενοκοῖται to mean.[19] Even Diodati, with the small but critical addition to his text, is somewhat coy regarding just who or what those who persisted in these sins might actually be. Therefore, to begin to add flesh to the bare bones of this understanding, the study must begin by looking outside of the early modern period.

English version of Diodati's rendering of 1 Cor 6:9 was "effeminate—those who endure the unnatural lust." This is a very different type of translation, and one that might cause us to ask significant questions, as it seemingly places a severe onus on those who find themselves having an unnatural lust, not those who would otherwise employ them. In a way, this would seem to accord with the cultural attitudes of English masculinity at the time, when a man who was penetrator may not necessarily be unmasculine, but those who were penetrated would most definitely be unmasculine and thus outside the natural order of God's creation and in a state of sin.

19. This is not to say that there were no words available to name the sins that accompanied contra naturam sins. As will be explained later in this chapter, Florio's dictionary makes it quite clear that the Italian language was extremely capable of naming pederasty, anal sex, and oral sex.

To begin to understand whom the *contra naturam* person or sodomite in early modern Italy might have been, one might begin by progressively sampling the historical writings of the early church. Acknowledging the historical continuation that drove much of Roman Catholic theology and interpretation in the *Traditio Apostolica*, the study now turns to ancient and medieval writings that discussed the *contra naturam* sexuality, effeminateness, and sodomy with which the μαλακοì and the ἀρσενοκοῖται were potentially associated in early modern Italy.[20]

This study, in seeking guidance from the historical texts of the church, immediately encounters problems. As statedpreviously, there was, within the early and medieval church, a specific reticence about discussing and defining sins, such as those who were οὔτε μαλακοì οὔτε ἀρσενοκοῖται, for fear they might provoke such sins in the listener and, ultimately, bring down divine wrath upon their various locales. Thus, the commentaries by numerous authors, including Ambrosius and Jean de Gagny, were quite silent about what or who the μαλακοì and the ἀρσενοκοῖται were within their worlds.[21] Nonetheless, with Cajetan's linking of "men with men" being indicative of *contra naturam* sodomy, his inclusion of the effeminate character as also being *contra naturam*, and the matching of these descriptors with the words of 1 Corinthians 6:9, one can extrapolate a context by searching the history of the church for an understanding of these words and concepts.

The prolific Saint Augustine noted:

> Sins against nature, therefore, like the sin of Sodom, are abominable and deserve punishment whenever and wherever they are committed. If all nations committed them, all alike would be held guilty of the same charge in God's law, for our Maker did not prescribe that we should use each other in this way. In fact, the relationship that we ought to have with God is itself violated when our nature, of which He is Author, is desecrated by perverted lust. Your punishments are for sins which men commit against themselves, because, although they sin against You, they do wrong in their own souls and their malice is self-betrayed. They corrupt and pervert their own nature, which You made and for which You shaped the rules, either by making wrong use of the things which You allow, or by becoming

20. At this point, it is interesting to note that, while Patristic and early medieval sources provide commentaries on the sin of sodomy, later commentaries, particularly the *Glossa Ordinaria*, are silent about both the μαλακοì and the ἀρσενοκοῖται in 1 Cor 6:9. Nicolaus of Lyra, as was explained in a previous chapter, noted the *mollis* to be masturbators, but was otherwise silent on the topic of the μαλακοì and the ἀρσενοκοῖται.

21. Ambrosiaster, "Commentaries on Romans and 1–2 Corinthians," 145 and Gagny, *Brevissima et Facillima In Omnes D. Pavli Epistolas Scholia*, f3[R/V].

inflamed with passion to make unnatural use of things which
You do not allow.[22]

St. Augustine's *Apostolic Constitution* also noted, "Thou shalt not corrupt
boys: for this wickedness is contrary to nature and arose from Sodom."[23]
Based upon Augustine's words one notes that sodomy, or the sin of Sodom as he put it, was highly present within the world of the medieval
church, even from a relatively early period. Moreover, the sins described
at the time were quite similar to the later definitions for μαλακοὶ and
ἀρσενοκοῖται, including perverted lust, masturbation, and so on.[24] These
characters, for Augustine and for those who followed him, were thought
of as having committed an inappropriate act against nature, were associated—though perhaps not entirely synonymous—with the corruption of
boys (pederasty), and were physically dangerous not just to practitioners,
but to the wider society at large.

The emperor Justinian, whose *Institutes* were the basis for Western
Medieval law, noted that "those who commit vile acts of lust with other
men" *qui cum masculis nefandum libidinem exercere audent,* were to be
sentenced to death in an effort to forestall divine judgement like that pro-
nounced upon Sodom.[25] Justinian also noted:

> For, instructed by the Holy Scriptures, we know that God
> brought a just judgment upon those who lived in Sodom, on
> account of this very madness of intercourse, so that to this very
> day that land burns with inextinguishable fire. By this God
> teaches us, in order that by means of this we may avert such an
> untoward fate . . . Wherefore it behooves all who desire to fear
> God to abstain from conduct so bad and criminal that we do not
> find it committed even by brute beasts.[26]

This judgement, coming almost one thousand years prior to the Reformation,
nonetheless appears quite like the proscriptions issued at that later date.[27]
Justinian was concerned not only about the moral implications of sodomy,

22. St. Augustine, *Confessions*, III.8.

23. St. Augustine, *Constitutionum Apostolicarum*, VII.2.

24. It is impossible to tell whether Augustine is referencing Leviticus or Corinthians
in his writing. While there is a reference to the holiness code of Leviticus in Augustine's
chapter, as the chapter begins with a substantial diatribe against Greek "philosophy"
and given the association of sodomy with the Greeks seen elsewhere, one might assume
Corinthians to be included in his writing. See Augustine, *Confessions*, III.8.

25. Justinian, *Institutes of the Corpus Juris Civilis,* IV. XVIII.4.

26. McNeil, *Church*, 79.

27. For instance, Mayer in England. See Mayer, *Commentary,* 184.

but also about its wider civic implications. There was clearly an association with the moral and physical danger occasioned by the sin of sodomy. For Justinian, one almost certainly led to the other.[28] Thus, even from its earliest date, the church was aware (at least to some degree) of what sodomy entailed and how it should be addressed. Although there is no explicit mention of 1 Corinthians 6:9 in Justinian's writing, pertinent context clues do seem to indicate that the writing was in reference to Corinthians. Justinian's declaration in the *Institutes* on the penalties for sodomy appear in a list of sins that bears a striking similarity to the malefactors mentioned in 1 Corinthians 6:9. The adulterer, the sodomite, the swindler, and the poisoner, all present in the wider Corinthian passage, are also readily found in the similar section of Justinian's *Institute*. Perhaps most interesting is Justinian's description of sodomy as *qui cum masculis nefandum*, which was not particularly different from the later Italian *cheusano con maschi*. Thus, it seems likely that the sin Justinian railed against, sodomy, might, on paper, be the same thing that authors such as Brucioli and Diodati vilified.

One might note, again, that the previous citations occur almost a millennium before the time of the Reformation. It is both entirely plausible and possible that the church changed its outlook and engagement with both proper nature and sexuality in the intervening centuries, and thus changed its definitions. The writings of church leaders in the intervening medieval period seem, however, to point toward a continuation and refinement of previous understandings, not a deviation from them. Peter Damian's much later *Book of Gomorrah* (eleventh century) might be thought of as the most descriptive work denouncing sodomy and *contra naturam* persona within the medieval church. The book seems to suggest that there was evidence

28. One cannot help but wonder if Justinian was not trying to put a good face on things, particularly in his claim that sodomy was so alien that it was not even practiced amongst the animals (much as Luther would later do in Germany). Sodomy might have genuinely been alien to the emperor, but it was notable and common enough to occasion both mention in legal code and the harshest of penalties. One cannot help but wonder if this was perhaps in response to the ability of Roman males to penetrate—but not be penetrated by—other males, particularly slaves. Following its absorption into the Roman Empire, the sexual normative of the Hellenist world remained relatively unchanged. Although same-sex interactions were somewhat frowned upon within the Roman world, they were nonetheless quite prominent amongst various sections of society. Similar to the Greco world, the Romans held specific norms for those who engaged in same-sex interaction. Foremost, within the Roman world, it was forbidden for a male of free birth to be sexually penetrated by another male. This stipulation removed the "grey area" of youthful sodomy and the questions about masculinity, or the lack thereof, which plagued Hellenistic pederasty. These same questions also haunted later situations concerning sodomy, such as those in late medieval and early modern Italy. See Low, *Manhood*, 71–75.

of sodomites and *contra naturam* personalities infiltrating the ranks of the priesthood and wider church leadership. Damian wrote:

> Just as Saint Basil establishes that those who incur sins [against nature] . . . should be subjected not only to a hard penance but a public one, and Pope Siricius prohibits penitents from entering clerical orders, one can clearly deduce that he who corrupts himself with a man through the ignominious squalor of a filthy union does not deserve to exercise ecclesiastical functions, since those who were formerly given to vices . . . become unfit to administer the Sacraments.[29]

Certainly, Damian's was not the first pronouncement to acknowledge the existence of sodomy, pederasty and those who engaged in such actions. Damian, however, makes particular note of the offending actions amongst the clergy of the time. This was, as seen previously, an issue that was raised by the First Lateran Council. The council, convening in 1123, made it clear that members of priestly and clerical orders who were convicted of sodomy should either be expelled or sent to a monastery for penance.[30] From this stipulation, together with that of Damian, one might easily speculate that the μαλακοὶ and the ἀρσενοκοῖται were personified in the aberrant priests of the time, much as they would later be in the writings of Martin Luther. However, as Damian does not actually use the words μαλακοὶ and ἀρσενοκοῖται, one can only speculate.

Returning to Damian, who was perhaps expanding upon Augustine, the author explained his understanding of the debilitating and pernicious nature of sodomy:

29. Damian, *Liber Gomorrhianus*, in PL 145 cols. 174f.

30. The Third Lateran Council included a stipulation that clerics who were caught in *peccatum contra naturam* be forced into penance at a monastery (*Quicumque incontinentia illa, quad contra naturam est, propter quam venit ira Dei in filios diffident et quince civitates igne consumpsit, deprehensi furring laborare, si cleric furring eiciantur a clerk vel ad poenitentiam agendum in monasteriis detrudantur*). In a great many ways, this served to encourage Protestant notions that monasteries were full of sodomites. See *Decrees of the Ecumenical Councils*, 217. This stipulation is made even more interesting by the later pederastic actions of Popes Julius II and Julius III. Certainly, one must allow that the accusations against Julius II were quite "grey" and were most definitely politically or confessional motivated (see, for example, Erasmus' implication in *Julius Exclusus de Caelis*). Nonetheless, the actions of Julius III, his adopted "nephew" and the elevation of the nephew were far more scandalous. There is little doubt that the accusations stemming from Julius' actions might easily have been re-cast as pernicious Protestant rumors. Regardless, these actions, rumors and lack of censure would have emphasized the fact that Lateran Council stipulation was enforced only on paper.

This vice strives to destroy the walls of one's heavenly motherland and rebuild those of devastated Sodom. Indeed, it violates
temperance, kills purity, stifles chastity and annihilates virginity
. . . with the sword of a most infamous union. It infects, stains
and pollutes everything; it leaves nothing pure, there is nothing
but filth . . . This vice expels one from the choir of the ecclesiasti-
cal host and obliges one to join the energumens and those who
work in league with the devil; it separates the soul from God
and links it with the demons. This most pestiferous queen of the
Sodomites makes those who obey her tyrannical laws repugnant
to men and hateful to God . . . It humiliates at church, condemns
at court, defiles in secret, dishonours in public, gnaws at the
person'sconscience like a worm and burns his flesh like fire. . .

Damian was undoubtedly concerned about the ill effects of sodomy. As did
those who had written previously, he identified the sodomite in ways that
could certainly have been imitated by later authors who defined the μαλακοί
and ἀρσενοκοῖται. Damian, however, went further than his predecessors
with the following condemnations:

The miserable flesh burns with the fire of lust, the cold intelli-
gence trembles under the rancour of suspicion, and the unfortunate man'sheart is possessed by hellish chaos, and his pains
of conscience are as great as the tortures in punishment he
will suffer . . . Indeed, this scourge destroys the foundations of
faith, weakens the force of hope, dissipates the bonds of char-
ity, annihilates justice, undermines fortitude, . . . and dulls the
edge of prudence.

Damian, again, does not specifically mention the μαλακοί, but one might
speculate, given the later understandings that have been examined, that he
was alluding to the character of the μαλακοί. This description of a sodomite
was, in a great many ways, identical to the descriptions seen elsewhere of the
μαλακοί.[31] Moreover, Damian proceeded to describe both those who might
be μαλακοί and those who might potentially be ἀρσενοκοῖται:

What else shall I say? It expels all the forces of virtue from the
temple of the human heart and, pulling the door from its hinges,
introduces into it all the barbarity of vice . . . In effect, the one
whom . . . this atrocious beast has swallowed down its bloody
throat is prevented, by the weight of his chains, from practicing

31. It seems that Damian is borrowing quite heavily from earlier definitions of the
μαλακοί that were present within the world of the Hellenist. See Martin, *Sex and the
Single Saviour*, 42–43.

all good works and is precipitated into the very abysses of its uttermost wickedness. Thus, as soon as someone has fallen into this chasm of extreme perdition, he is exiled from the heavenly motherland, separated from the Body of Christ, confounded by the authority of the whole Church, condemned by the judgment of all the Holy Fathers, despised by men on earth, and reproved by the society of heavenly citizens. He creates for himself an earth of iron and a sky of bronze . . . He cannot be happy while he lives nor have hope when he dies, because in life he is obliged to suffer the ignominy of men's derision and later, the torment of eternal condemnation.[32]

Damian's writings were, to say the least, descriptive. Although his writings did not reference 1 Corinthians 6:9 or the *μαλακοὶ* or *ἀρσενοκοῖται*, he certainly provided considerable information about who or what the *contra naturam* sinner, associated via Cajetan with 1 Corinthians 6:9, might be. One may certainly gather that Damian's admonishments—being separated from the body of Christ, burning with lust and so on—could have been drawn from Corinthians or were meant to reference it indirectly. In fact, Damian's writings indicate a church that was aware of and meant to be prohibitive of improper comportment, pederasty, and sodomy. Moreover, Damian's sodomite shares a distinct number of characteristics with descriptions of the *μαλακοὶ* and *ἀρσενοκοῖται* that were issued later.[33]

Texts, such as those examined previously, describe a church that was, from its earliest times, quite aware of the existence and gravity of the ills commonly produced by the *μαλακοὶ* and the *ἀρσενοκοῖται*. The *contra naturam* sinner, for these authors, was very much a broad and over-arching character—a trope for the ills of the unnatural. Although the authors expressed their understanding of the gravity of such sins, with the exception of Damian, they were less than forthcoming regarding what actually constituted a fully *contra naturam* person in their eyes. Certainly, one may note that the church seems to have only refined its opinion and opposition as it moved into the medieval period. Nonetheless, despite their verbosity—and

32. Damian, *Liber Gomorrhianus*, in PL 145, col. 159–78.

33. For example, Marlorat's understandings seem to echo both Calvin and the much earlier writings of Damian. "What, on the other hand, differs the fornicator (whoremonger) from the adulterer? The soft are well known and understood, who, although they are not prostitutes, are commonly known as having the wantonness and allurement of a prostitute, effeminate gestures and clothing, and other ornaments of sexual impurity which betray them. The fourth species is the most grievous, certainly the monstrous foulness, which in Greece was very much common. And all these are the precepts that forbid this one, Do not commit adultery . . . " See Marlorat, *Novi Testamenti Catholica Expositio Ecclesiastica*, 689.

although they certainly seemed to hint at the terms—none of the authors examined provided their specific understandings of the μαλακοì, the ἀρσενοκοῖται, the cinadeus, the catamite or any of the other specific titles this study has seen being later associated with those who were identified as οὔτε μαλακοì οὔτε ἀρσενοκοῖται.

This lack of definition changed with the writings of Saint Thomas Aquinas. Aquinas, who was perhaps one of the first theologians to describe the terms in detail, or at the very least the μαλακοì, offered the following from his commentary on the Pauline Epistles:

> Mollices—properly refers to a weakness towards amusements/ pleasures. But pleasures look back to the hindering reason for them, that is work, or some other thing. Therefore, pleasures are kinds of weaknesses. He is called "mollis" who turns back from good, with the excuse of unhappiness caused by lack of pleasures, as if yielding to a weak movement, though he does not, however, yield to a strong one. Softness is a vice opposed to perseverance, and two things, that is, cause it from habit, and from a natural tendency. Those who use feminine things/ suffer the feminine role in intercourse are called "molles," as if made into women.[34]

This definition is both similar to and different from those seen previously in other chapters in this study.[35] On one hand, Aquinas suggested that the

---

34. *Mollices—proprie respicit defectum delectationum. Sed deliciae respiciunt causam impeditiuam earum, scilicet laborem vel aliquid tale. Ideo deliciae sunt quaedam mollities. Mollis dicitur, qui recedit a bono, propter tristitias causatas ex defecto delectationum, quasi cedens debili moventi, non autem si gravi moventi cedat. Mollities est vitium oppositum perseverantiae. Et causatur dupliciter, scilicet ex consuetudinis et ex naturali dispositione. Qui patiuntur muliebra, dicuntur molles, quasi mulieres effecti.* See Thomas Aquinas, *Ordinis predicatorum vire et vite*, 179.

35. This is in comparison to, say, Altensteig, who wrote: *peccatum contra naturam: Et communiter peccati contra naturam quatuor species seu modi assignantur. Primus est quando absq; omni concubitu causa delectationis venereae pollutio procuratur, et vocatur proprie mollities, pertinetque ad peccatum immunditiae venere seu lubricosae. Secundus modus est si fiat per concubitum ad rem non eiusdem speciei et vocatur proprie bestialitas. Tertius modus est si fiat concubitus ad rem eiusdem speciei, sed non ad debitum sexum, ut puta, masculi ad masculum, vel foeminae ad foeminam. Et vocatur proprie sodomiticum. Quartus modus est si fiat concubitus ad rem eiusdem speciei et debiti sexus, sed non fiat in debito instrumento, vel alias fiat monstrosa quaedam deordinatio et vilitas in modis concubendi. Haec. Gers. P. 2 de sep vitiae capitalibus.* Sin against nature: generally, the sins against nature are assigned to four types or modes. The first is when, without having sex with anyone, but for pleasure, sexual pollution is procured, and this is properly called softness [masturbation], and this belongs to the sin of venereal or self-indulgent filthiness. The second kind is if one uses as a sex-partner (per concubitum) something not of one's own species, and this is properly called bestiality. The third kind is if one

μαλακοί were indicative of unmasculine comportment and a lack of deter-
mination and strong will. These are, by now, relatively familiar definitions.
A great number of authors mentioned in the previous chapters have offered
similar definitions of unmasculine and weak-willed persons being μαλακοί.
At the same time, Aquinas pushed his lexical understanding a bit further
than did many authors who came before or after him. The *mollice*, for Aquinas, could very well be indicative of one who was penetrated in sexual intercourse, but only if they were of the variety of *mollice* that "suffered feminine
things." Most significantly, Aquinas saw the essential sin of the μαλακοί as
one of general failure of the will, not simply as a type of sexual laxity. According to this definition, *all* self-indulgences, whether breaking the Lenten
fast or staying in bed rather than getting up to pray, were *mollities*. Therefore,
for Aquinas, the opposite of *mollities* was perseverance rather than simple
chastity or asceticism. This is of great significance for this study. Aquinas was
one of the first authors within the church to present a working and specific
translation of the μαλακοί. While later definitions certainly recognized the
μαλακοί as being indulgent and weak characters, a number associated them
directly with sexual malaise or incontinence.[36] The inverse seems to have
been true for Aquinas. The μαλακοί, for Aquinas, could certainly have been
sexually incontinent, but they were more than sexually lax, as their sexual
misbehaviour was a symptom of a lack of all types of perseverance.[37] Aquinas
indicated that the μαλακοί should be understood as implying both potentially
intrinsic and learned vice. Applying this to later writers, the effeminate characters described by Valla, Pagnini, and Brucioli, might have little control over
whether they were effeminate or not. Moreover, the *molli* mentioned by Diodati might be persons who learned their vice from the corrupting influence
of others—potentially, one may speculate, from the ἀρσενοκοῖται—or they
simply might have been "born that way." The *mollis*, as a naturally occurring

---

uses as a sex-partner someone of the same species, but not of the proper gender, for
example, of a man with a man, or a woman with a woman. And this is properly called
sodomitic [sex]. The fourth kind is if one uses as a sexual partner someone of the same
species and the proper gender, but it is not done in the appropriate orifice, or in other
ways, some monstrous unnaturalness is performed, or filthiness in the ways of having
sex. In this regard, see Jean Gerson, p. 2 of De septem vitiae capitalibus. See Altensteig,
Lexicon Theologicvm, 670–71.

36. This is in comparison to Andream Placum, who described the μαλακοί as "lascivious, drunk, *cinaedus* and catamite" and made a specific call to silence those who
engaged in such activities or to keep silent about such activities so as not to encourage
others to engage in such actions. See Placum, *Lexicon*, 455.

37. It is no accident that Cajetan's definitions closely mirror those of Aquinas. Cajetan's work with the Thomistic text would have made him intimately familiar with
Aquinas' thoughts and understandings.

phenomenon, poses a significant question with regard to understanding the μαλακοì as *contra naturam*.[38] Were the μαλακοì to be born as they were, there would seem to be a distinct ontological question regarding whether the actions of a *mollis* were simply *peccatum* or *peccatum contra naturam*. The distinction between the two might very well differentiate between a view of the actions of the μαλακοì as venial sins and of the μαλακοì as mortal sinners. Although Aquinas never elucidated whether the μαλακοì were simply sinners or were *contra naturam* sinners, it is quite safe to say that his definition was far broader than was the understanding of the μαλακοì as mainly sexual sinners, as many in Europe would later posit.

While Aquinas was somewhat coy regarding whether his understanding of the μαλακοì always included a *contra naturam* stipulation, he withheld no such distinction concerning the concept of sodomy. Discussing the wider topic of sodomy, Aquinas stated:

> Sodomy, that is, the intercourse of males, is a type of dissipation against nature. Sins: fornication, idolatry, dissipation, and against nature. The same philosopher [Aristotle, *Ethics*, 7.5.1148b28–30] says that this sodomitic vice comes about in two ways: that is, as the consequence of a vicious nature, and through perverse habit. Sodomy and idolatry began together and grow together.[39]

Sodomy, for Aquinas, was much more in line with the later definitions promulgated for οὔτε μαλακοì οὔτε ἀρσενοκοῖται. The sodomite, according to Aquinas, was one whose actions were definitively *contra naturam*. While it is unsurprising that sodomites were understood as those men who had sex with men, it is interesting to note Aquinas' association of the actions of the sodomite as being on a par with other sins such as idolatry; thus, pursuing inappropriate sexual partners was similar topursuing false

---

38. The explanation for how μαλακοì may be naturally occurring while still against nature would, ostensibly, focus on concepts of inherited sin and the biblical fall of humanity inserting sinful realities into the natural order. Aquinas explained that sin itself, in its very essence, was in fact a *contra naturam* status. See Aquinas, *Bible*, 203. *Peccatum est contra naturem [naturam] mentis rationalis integrae licet sit quasi naturale postquam peccauit.* "Sin is contrary to the nature of a rational virtuous mind, though it seems natural after sinning." In this way, Aquinas defined the very concept of sin as *contra naturam* and thus all actions that violated the Christian mandate were *contra naturam*. Thus, by these standards, any reference to *contra naturam* was a broad indictment of the μαλακοì and the ἀρσενοκοῖται.

39. *Sodomia idest coitus masculorum est species luxuriae contra naturam. Culpa fornicatio, idolatria, luxuria, et contra naturam. Hoc vitium sodomiticum ipse philosophus dicit accidere dupliciter. Scilicet propter vitiosam naturam et perversam consuetudinem sodomia et idolatria simul incoeperunt et simul creuerunt.* See Aquinas, *Bible*, 256.

gods. Notably, later writers were much keener to label sodomites—ostensibly the ἀρσενοκοῖται, at least according to Cajetan's definitions—as "the worst of the worst" or "the most hideous" of actions. For Aquinas, however, although the sodomite was a serious offender, his actions were no worse than were other grave sins.

These definitions provided by Aquinas and Peter Damian, together with the early writings of Justinian and Augustine and the decree about sodomitical penance from the First Lateran Council, provide this study with significant information. Conveying a continuity of message, these writings provide a significant amount of detail concerning sodomy, *contra naturam* sexuality and thus, through Cajetan's definitions, those implied by οὔτε μαλακοὶ οὔτε ἀρσενοκοῖται. These creatures were anti-normative, engaged in excessive and unexplainable lust and, particularly for Damian, were the antithesis of that which was heavenly and holy. All these definitions and descriptions match the elucidation given by Cajetan quite closely, as well as labels given to these οὔτε μαλακοὶ οὔτε ἀρσενοκοῖται in Valla, Pagnini, Brucioli and Diodati. However, although these definitions seem to provide considerable detail regarding who or what later vernacular authors might have been describing, they do not necessarily detail precisely to whom these descriptions referred. For these descriptions to be associated with a character requires a return to the early modern period and a search for similar beings within its boundaries. It is to this period that this study now turns.

With the background provided by patristic and medieval sources, one can again posit that the μαλακοὶ were the anti-normative, unmasculine or effeminate members of the early modern world. The ἀρσενοκοῖται were the sodomites, although not fully elucidated in some areas. What is needed to further these hypotheses is the acknowledgment of these definitions by actors within the early modern Italian world.

The criticisms of Luther and others might cause one to suspect that sodomy and unmasculine practice were normalized practices within the world of the Roman Church. Luther himself issued more than a few diatribes that seemed to indict both the Pope and the Roman Curia as sodomites.[40] Moreover, that sexual mores, or a lack thereof, were an occasion to mock the early modern Roman Catholic Church is difficult to dispute. The

---

40. Luther was far from the only Protestant of the time to do such. As we have seen in an earlier chapter Florence also appeared in early modern French accusations. In 1534 it was detailed that "In this year and in the month of January, a merchant from Florence named Antoine Mellin was brought from Lyon before the parliament, appealing the death sentence of the lay justice of Lyon for having been found a bugger and having committed this sin unnaturally on a girl and on a young boy." The emphasis is on the assailant's Florentine background despite residency in Lyon, illuminating of the French mindset. See Lalanne, *Journal*, 435–36.

council of Trent did much to re-establish a concept of proper "Catholic" sexuality for both the clergy and the laity.[41] How sodomy and other illicit sexuality fit, outside of traditional condemnation, into this Tridentine re-establishment is less than clear.[42] Discussion of sodomy in the late medieval and early modern period was, as seen in numerous other places, often quite restricted. Whereas writers such as Damian and Augustine were quite forthcoming regarding what they understood the sin of Sodom to be, these descriptive writings were tempered by the actual practice of not describing the "sin that should not be named" in public.[43]

Although limited in its discussion, sodomy and concepts associated with it did still manage to find expression, outside of ecclesiastic circles, in some late medieval and early modern Italian authors. In 1531, Niccolo Leonico Tomeo commented on "the abuse of masculine love," saying:

> Whence the abuse of masculine love (masculaeabusus veneris) arose: As to where the loves of boys and the abusive practice of sex between men first started, the explanation is doubtful, to such a degree various people have recorded various things concerning this matter. For some relate that Thamyris the Thracian, the eighth before Homer to win renown as a bard, who took Hymenaeus, son of Calliope and Magnes as his sweetheart was the first. Others say that Rhadamantus first loved the boy Talon of Crete. Some assert that Laius carried off Chrysippus, son of Pelops, to use after this fashion. Others allege that the Itali, driven by necessity during their protracted military campaigns, abused males. All seem to agree that Cretan Jove, captivated by the beauty of the boy Ganymede, was the very first originator of masculine love.[44]

Tomeo seems to have been somewhat conflicted in his writings, speaking of both the abuse of male love, masculine love, pederasty and forced sodomy in the same breath. While little is surprising regarding the author's Hellenistic origins for sodomy within this passage, what is most interesting is the relatively non-judgemental way in which "boy-love" is discussed. Tomeo seems to have been suggesting that sexual contact between men was a practice with ancient antecedents and, by implication, was therefore sanctioned

41. See Wiesner-Hanks, *Christianity*, 103–4.

42. Sodomy was certainly spoken against in the Catechism of the Council of Trent, however, as will be detailed later in this chapter, what was said on paper did not always translate to reality in early modern Italy.

43. Crompton, *Homosexuality and Civilization*, 253.

44. Tomeo, "De varia historia libri tres," 208.

by custom. This may well just have been a sexual "aesthetic," which was Italian, deriving from a classical tradition that was symptomatic of a divergence from that found elsewhere in Western Europe. All this seems to point towards the concept of a sodomite, at least in the eyes of Tomeo, which was quite well known in the early modern Italian world.

Other early modern authors, such as Francesco Berni, were not as direct in their discussions of sodomy, although they still had quite a lot to say. Berni, employing a popular trend of equating sodomy with sensuous fruits, noted "Oh fruit most blessed / Good before the meal, in the middle and behind. But especially good in front and perfect from behind!"[45] Berni's lyric was a very lightly veiled euphemism using the "fruits" to refer, quite literally, to the berry-like testicles and the peach-smooth bottoms of young boys. This euphemistic description was also echoed in Agnolo Firenzuolo, who wrote that figs, a euphemism for the vagina, belonged to the commons, but apples and peaches, again, euphemisms for the bottoms of young boys, belonged to the great masters.[46] In both these denunciations, there seems to be an inherent association with pederasty. The representative fruits were best consumed when young and fresh, not old and weathered or withered. Thus, one cannot help but readily assume that the authors were lampooning, within their verse, pederastic sodomy and not simply sodomy between adults. This, combined with the writings of Tomeo, seems to point towards a conversational knowledge of pederastic sodomy within early modern Italy. These writings do not necessarily refute the thought of adult sodomy being in existence but point again towards a level of realistic acknowledgment of who or what pederasty entailed in early modern Italy.

Extant early modern Italian lexicons also make it clear that there were, in fact, vocabulary words with which one might readily associate pederasty, sodomy and other types of *contra naturam* sexual sin. As described in previous chapters, words for the passive persons in pederasty, particularly "bardache," were drawn from Italian root words.[47] Moreover, words for ac-

45. Berni, *Rime*, 49, vv. 10–12. See also Ruggerio, *Fruit*, 31–52.

46. Crompton, *Homosexuality and Civilization*, 257.

47. Florio, *Queen*, 55, 71 and della Crusca, *Vocabolario degli Accademici della Crusca*, 105. This first edition of the Vocabolario was largely put together with the guidance of Agnolo Monosini. Monosini's work, particularly with linking the Italian to ancient Greek, and vice versa, was something that makes his involvement particularly notable for the current study. That there existed both wording that was rooted in the classics of Greece and also considerably descriptive towards the pederasty, which was then so common in both Florence and Venice, seems to say much. Certainly, either Brucioli, Didodati, and the rest were reticent to comment on the situation, or it seems probable that they were referencing something else distinct from sodomy. See Pignatti and Monosini, *Etimologia e proverbio nell'Italia del XVII secolo*. Interestingly,

tive pederasty and general anal sex such as buggery were also drawn from
Italian roots.[48] Of particular note is the word *bertone*. Florio identified this
term as the lover of a married man or woman. Della Crusca, however, linked
the term to pederastic lovers, which, as will be seen below, were extremely
common in certain early modern Italian locales.[49] In summary, the early
modern Italian vernacular was well acquainted with words that might describe someone who was a practitioner of anal sex, sodomy and, especially,
of pederasty. Thus, it is significant and interesting that such words were not
utilized to describe the μαλακοὶ and the ἀρσενοκοῖται within early modern
Italian Bibles. This might cause one to suspect that Italian understandings of
the μαλακοὶ and ἀρσενοκοῖται were far broader than were those of a number
of their contemporaries. To obtain a full picture of who might be popularly
referenced within the sodomy and *contra naturam* sexuality associated with
μαλακοὶ and ἀρσενοκοῖται in early modern Italian vernaculars, the study
needs to understand how such things functioned—or did not function—
within their two supposed prime locales: Florence and Venice.

The study now turns to the city that Luther (and perhaps other reformers) considered the most sexually notorious: Florence. Florence was, by Re-
formist standards, so commonly associated with sodomy that "to Florence"
was a colloquialism for engaging in sodomy across Europe.[50] This, however,
does not mean that Florentine sodomy was indicative of practices between
adult males. Florentine sodomy was almost entirely pederastic with few
examples of adult same-sex activity.[51] Within these pederastic unions, the
active partner, who was legally at more risk, would be over the age of

---

such words do not find much, if any, explanation, and expression within the lexicons
of Paravacino and Thomas.

48. Florio, *Queen*, 51, 71 and Academia della Crusca, *Vocabolario*, 105.

49. Florio, *Queen*, 60 and Academia della Crusca, *Vocabolario*, 120. This concept
of the *bertone* might reflect the more historic understandings of pederasty, which,
undoubtedly were being discovered in the renaissance. Theonis seems to note the
relations between married men and young boys by saying "Boy, your form is lovely,
but upon your head Lies a great crown of ignorance. Your habit of mind resembles
the swift-turning kite; You believe the words of other men. You, Boy, who repaid my
attentions with evil deeds, Ungrateful for the good you received, Have never brought
me benefit. Although many a time I served you well, you lack respect. The minds of
a boy and a horse are alike. The horse Weeps not for his rider in the dust, But takes
his fill of barley, then carries another man. A boy loves the man beside him." See
Theognis, *Elegies*, 1259–70.

50. See Puff, *Sodomy*, 25.

51. Same-sex adult interactions were something else entirely as we shall see. Rocke
has been clear that sodomy in Florence was centered on men and boys, not men with
other men. See Rocke, *Friendships*, 19.

eighteen and show signs of adult masculinity, such as facial hair.[52] The passive partner, however, would generally be between twelve and eighteen. This age bracket would prevent the active partner from engaging in child-rape at one end of the spectrum and in "adult" sodomy at the other. Concerning this last point, it should again be emphasized that adult sodomy was very much frowned upon and was uncommon in Florence.[53] Pederasty was seen as a means of mutual enjoyment, a type of youthful abrogation of social norms, but engagement between adults in a similar manner was thoroughly unacceptable and unappealing to virtually all people at that time.[54] Youths, by their very status as "non-males," made penetration a socially tolerable action; thus, it is plausible that they could be thought of as *moli*, or in Diodati's phrase, "those who persisted in such sin." Although they were anatomically male, they were not yet men in the eyes of society. They were, one might say, effeminate, the very opposite of how an adult male could be defined. This possible personification and social preference were further illustrated in the average age of passive partners who were caught in acts of sodomy in early modern Florence. From legal prosecutions between 1478 and 1502, the average age for a passive partner was fifteen, while the average age for an active partner was thirty-four. This, however, should not necessarily be confused with a unanimous blanket of acceptance of pederastic sodomy on the part of youthful actors. Certainly, the non-masculine status of youths who engaged in pederasty was something that might be overlooked in some instances; however, their actions were still troubling to more than a few. The reforms of Girolamo Savonarola brought many changes, both culturally and politically, to late fifteenth century Florence. That Savonarola's powerbase was concentrated within the Florentine youth also created a great change in the status and engagement of sodomy at the time. Savonarola's puritanical bent included an attempt to end the allure and practice of pederasty. However, these reforms actually only succeeded in driving the median age of passive partners upwards to approximately eighteen years of age.[55] It is interesting, however, that even with the quite

52. Rocke, *Friendships*, 100–101.

53. Chojnacki, *Women*, 35–36.

54. This is, again, reminiscent of the practices of Imperial Rome and its Hellenistic predecessors. Masculinity, in Italian city-states, often was not firmly and thoroughly conferred until the time where a male was able to partake in local civic governments. This engagement was not—as shall be discussed a bit later in the chapter—readily available to most men until much later ages. Thus, in a way, engaging in youthful pederastic sodomy was not a huge concern as it was not "men" who were engaging in it, but "pseudo-men."

55. Rocke, *Friendships*, 210. This is rather interesting in it seems that Savonarola's reform disenfranchised a younger part of a generation from engaging in the practices of

strict moral indoctrination that Savonarola and others presented to prevent youths from engaging in sodomy, an adult market for sodomy did not seem to come into existence within early modern Florence.[56] Savonarola's reforms might have driven the age range of pederastic sodomy upwards, but they still did not make adult sodomy an attractive or acceptable option. This would seem to indicate that *contra naturam* activity, even in the days of Savonarola, as encountered in Florentine society, was almost entirely pederastic. Such a reality, in conjunction with the lexical words available to translators, would make it very odd for writers to be referencing pederasty alone in their translations of the μαλακοὶ and ἀρσενοκοῖται. Were Italian vernacular translators exceedingly concerned about pederasty, they had more than enough of a social epidemic and lexical realities at their ready to address the situation. This lack of redress, however, does not necessarily mean there was a blanket acceptance of pederasty in Florence.

Savonarola's reforms aside, by the end of the fifteenth century and through the sixteenth century, pederasty was a well-noted vice within the city of Florence, primarily amongst lower-class youth and, for some, was a problematic occurrence that required a strong response. The period just prior to the early modern period (1494) saw the introduction of harsh anti-sodomy laws, essentially instituting a "three-strike" policy for Florentine offenders. For an individual's first offence, he was to be pilloried and temporarily deprived of offices and honour; for the second, public humiliation, branding and, again, deprivation; for the third conviction, death at the stake.[57] It is interesting that, although these laws were meant to discourage and prevent sodomy, they only seem to have applied to the active partner in the sodomitical act. Honour and offices were not something that a youth could hold because, as they were effeminate, these standards did not apply to them. Instead, the fate of passive partners was often left to an arbitrary decision of the presiding court, often the equivalent of a stern warning. Although these rules for active partners might seem extreme, they were relatively lenient. To be convicted of sodomy in most other areas of early modern Europe was to commit *lèse-majesté*, treason against the sovereign and, in fact, was against God's sovereign order for creation.[58] Thus, to be

---

pederastic sodomy, but it certainly did not seem dissuade those who had already been engaged in the practice. "Newer" passive partners may not have been available, but that did not mean that there still were not others willing to take such roles.

56. Rocke, *Friendships*, 210–14.

57. Rocke, *Friendships*, 205–9.

58. See, for instance, the Earl of Castlehaven in early modern England. As has been seen, this is place where the paper polemics of the church did not match with the relevant realities of civic life. Florentine civic leaders might have been well aware of what

condemned of sodomy was an almost certain death sentence—or at least economic death through banishment—in most locales.[59] Florence was much more concerned with public recidivism.[60]

Based on the laws of the Medici, late medieval Florence experienced a somewhat notable upswing of prosecutions for sodomy, or pederasty defined as sodomy, within the city. Michael Rocke noted that, from 1478 to 1502, 3,364 Florentines were implicated in sodomitical activities.[61] This was a relatively large number of individuals, approximately 140 per year, who were accused of some degree of sodomy. By contrast, most other European locales only prosecuted a fraction of this number in a similar period.[62] All this does, to some extent, seem to support the accusations of Luther and others that sodomy was an extremely rampant Florentine vice, so much so that officials knew the problem existed and, more importantly, acknowledged its existence.[63] Rather than advocating the tolerance of such actions, however, contra to the indications of some reformers, the lawmakers of Florence responded to sodomy with proscription and penalty. For the purposes of this study, such action indicates that the rulers of Florentine society were quite aware of just whom the "sodomite" might be and what actions might be undertaken to earn such a moniker. This is further evidenced in a brief history of the legal stratifications of sodomy within Florence.

From 1325, the Podesta, the ruling body in Florentine society, established a penal code to punish the actions of sodomy, broadly defined. These laws encompassed those men who sodomized males, boys who wilfully allowed themselves to be sodomised, and even women who were sodomized by men.[64] In this instance, one should note that there were far higher penal-

---

was called for from them in the punishment of sodomy and *contra naturam peccatum*, but that did not mean they could reasonably execute those actions without imposing grave civic harm. The church might have been the moral compass of the city, but it wasn't going to put coins in the coffer or bread on the tables.

59. For example, Herr Krafft of Frankfurt, previously examined.

60. As seen in places such as England, even for a bishop of the church, sodomy was almost a guaranteed execution.

61. Rocke, *Friendships*, 247. This is, again, in opposition to approximately 100 Genevan cases in a comparable time frame and ten percent of such in early modern France. See Naphy, *Sex Crimes*, 95.

62. See Naphy, *Sex Crimes*, 90.

63. This is in contrast to regions such as England, Geneva and Germany, where sodomy existed, but was very much an undiscussed or unacknowledged affair. In fact, as Naphy has illustrated, Geneva saw virtually no trials in the seventeenth century and a limited amount in the sixteenth; yet, when trials were conducted, they seemed to illustrate a network of sodomitical activities within the city. See Naphy, *Sex Crimes*, 90, 95.

64. This code is interesting as it notes that only women over the age of 14 can be

ties—including the burning at the stake—for non-Florentines committing crimes of sodomy.[65] Moreover, boys, as the "passive" partners, were, again, generally not punished; or, at the very least not punished as severely as those who penetrated them.[66] In their own way, these proscriptions provide a plausible context to Florentine sodomy and perhaps an understanding of those being popularly referenced within the *contra naturam* actions of the μαλακοὶ and ἀρσενοκοῖται in 1 Corinthians 6:9. Those who sodomized males were easily associated with the ἀρσενοκοῖται, the passive boy sodomized by an older male, the μαλακοὶ, particularly in the definitions by Diodati. However, the inclusion of women who were sodomized by men points towards a definition of sodomy that was much broader than that of simple pederasty. This potential definition is also further complicated by the concepts of masculinity and femininity in pederastic relationships in late medieval and early modern Florence. While those who penetrated a boy could be executed, those who were penetrated, even given the later punishments of the Medici, if under eighteen, could not legally be executed. Instead, their punishment was at the discretion of the court and was often far less severe than were the penalties for those who had penetrated them.[67] This is interesting in that, while not unheard of in later Reformation Europe, it was somewhat different from several instances outside of Italy. In a number of previously sampled areas, the penetrated were often viewed as seducers, prime perpetrators of sodomy and deserving of greater punishment than those who had penetrated them.[68] In this understanding, the sodomiser was the masculine party who had been dragged down into unnatural lusts by the emasculated wiles of the sodomised. While other locations focused on the emasculation of those who were penetrated, the Florentine emphasis was on the active party as both the instigator and, perhaps, the party emasculated.[69]

---

prosecuted for sodomy. This would seem to indicate a certain age of accountability that was exclusive to women. Boys of the time, as we will see later, were generally somewhat acceptable as sodomy partners until they grew facial hair, which might only occur by the age of 18. See Rocke, *Forbidden*, 21.

65. Ironically, just as sodomy in the rest of Europe would often be attributed to Florentines, so too did Florentines attribute sodomitical actions to those who were not Florentine.

66. This was not unheard of within early modern Europe. Naphy has described that there were similar instances in early modern Geneva. See Naphy, *Sex Crimes*, 96.

67. See Chojnacki, *Women*, 33–34.

68. This seems to be supported in the writings of authors such as Garth and Frisius in early modern Germany. See Garth, *M. Balthasaris*, 106; and Frisius, *Novum*, 106.

69. This was, in fact, an interesting understanding of masculinity at the time. The male who sodomized another was giving up his masculine obligation to procreate or the natural function of the man as being drawn to the female. Certainly, the actions of

Therefore, one might speculate that there was, to some extent, an inversion of concepts of masculinity within early modern Italy, and in Florence in particular.[70] Accordingly, one might question whether, in Florence, the μαλακοί were those who were penetrated or were those who were penetrating. While the rest of Europe in the early modern age understood masculinity and propriety to have something to do with penetration and the act of penetrating, to the point of sometimes denouncing the penetrated but not the penetrator, the opposite seems true, in some sense, for Italy.[71] Thus, while it is likely that reference to the μαλακοί and ἀρσενοκοῖται in early modern Florence would have been largely indicative of pederasty, it is impossible to deny that it might have included other actions (such as men with women) and indicate an inversion of the gender roles seen previously. Moreover, the fact that Florentine prosecutions for sodomy were not usually lethal seems to indicate several possibilities. It is possible that, in the eyes of Florentines, true sodomy, the variety to be punished severely and not to be elucidated, was between two adult males. Thus, pederasty was "sodomy-ish," but was really simply a youthful vice and not worth severe proscription. Nonetheless, it is possible that Florentine authorities, late to the realisation that there was a significant culture of sodomy pervading the city, were unable to punish all offenders capitally without doing significant damage to city-wide logistics.[72] Whatever the reason, it seems likely, although not definite, that *contra naturam* sexuality in Florence was often -if not always- indicative of pederasty.

Florence, however, was not alone in its situation regarding rampant sodomy. Venice, another powerful city-state in late medieval and early modern Italy, was highly engaged with the concept of sodomy through the actions of its citizens and the prosecution of them. Sex and sexuality, within Venice was, much like Florence, something of a muddled picture.

---

those whom they sodomized might have led them to commit such actions, but they themselves were ultimately the guilty parties in such cases.

70. This inversion, in and of itself, could possibly explain the level of disconnect that existed between Italian lands and the rest of early modern Europe. Masculinity in one was not necessarily the precise equal of masculinity within the other and was thus confounding or astounding. Quite frankly, the two might not have been comparing like for like. As described below, the early modern Venetian male seems to have been considerably similar and yet notably different from his Florentine counterpart.

71. This was, in fact, the reason that pederasty could function at all within parts of early modern Europe. Those who were "men" could penetrate those who were not men and not lose honor. Those who were not yet men, however, could be slighted were it known that they were penetrated regularly. See Low, *Manhood*, 71–75.

72. This seems quite unlikely given the significant time frame in which ruling figures were enacting proscriptions regarding sodomy.

There was what could be termed the "traditional" picture of sexuality of the time, namely hetero-normative actions. From the fourteenth century onwards, however, Venice provided a vibrant and growing environment for sodomy.[73] Venetian sodomy, at this time, was seen largely as encompassing bestiality, non-copulative anal or intercrural sex acts and, most commonly, pederastic acts between members of the same sex.[74] In Venice, as in Florence, sodomy, at least by its prosecution record, was often, though not always, an action on the part of youthful males, those who had not necessarily achieved status as fully masculine males.[75] Similarly to the situation in Florence, this Venetian pederasty could very well indicate an understanding of the μαλακοί and the ἀρσενοκοῖται, with penetrated youths being seen as the effeminate μαλακοί and penetrating ἀρσενοκοῖται being their older partners. As such, there was an aversion, though not necessarily revulsion, to pederasty within the city.

In the early years of the fourteenth century, the chief legislative group within Venice, the Council of Ten, perhaps fearing divine judgement or perhaps fearing the rise of a wide and acknowledged pederastic subculture, created legislation meant to dissuade and prevent sodomy within the city.[76] For the council, sodomy was a destroyer of the social fabric; it tampered with and circumvented the natural order that was God's intended plan for humanity and, more pressingly, for Venice.[77] As such, actions of sodomy, along with their toleration, echoing the writings of Justinian, were seen as potential causes for divine judgment. Thus, seeking to discourage sodomy via costly penalties, the Council of Ten passed stringent laws, as had the officials in Florence. It is interesting that officials in Venice, much as in Florence, were more concerned with "active" partners than they were with "passive" partners. Active partners could, and often did, face being burned at

73. Ruggiero, *Boundaries of Eros*, 3, 121–36. To call this situation a "public subculture" would be a stretch. Certainly, in the minds of Luther and others, there was a public subculture at work, but the reality is that there simply were lax or unapplied rules concerning sodomy. There was certainly a sect of active sodomites, but to call such persons a dedicated and public subculture would be going too far.

74. Ruggiero, *Boundaries of Eros*, 140. As Crompton pointed out, there was a great emphasis on "companions of unequal age," seemingly indicating a strong association between pederasty and sodomy. See Crompton, *Homosexuality and Civilization*, 250.

75. See Davidson, "Sodomy in Early Modern Venice," 69–70.

76. Crompton, *Homosexuality and Civilization*, 247.

77. This was, of course, how the council presented its views on paper. As we have seen in other chapters, there was a tendency to present things on paper in one manner and apply them in real life in an entirely different way. It is not outside of the realm of possibility to speculate that members of the council had engaged in pederastic sodomy when they were Venetian youths.

the stake.[78] Passive partners, however, could be acquitted based on their age or when the circumstance implied some measure of coercion. This focus on the active partner was again perhaps due to an understanding of the time, according to which the active partner was the initiator or instigator, and the passive partner was the submissive partner, or sometimes the victim. These persons could have been those persons who, as Diodati put it, used "those who continue in these sins," thus creating a synergy of pederasty between the μαλακοὶ and ἀρσενοκοῖται. Aiding this perception is the general ages of those who were engaged in sodomy.[79] In most situations, the active partner within the sodomitical relationships in early modern Venice was an older male and often a full member of civic communities.[80] The passive partner was almost always a younger person who had not yet risen to "masculinity" and manhood, thus making their penetration both possible and somewhat tolerable. This again potentially marked the penetrated as the "effeminate" characters associated with the μαλακοὶ, thus opening a potential link with the synergistic understandings of Diodati.

In a way, this popular pederasty was almost to be expected. Italian culture, much like its Hellenist predecessors, gave considerable attention to the beauty of both the female form and to that of the youthful male.[81] Nonetheless, somewhat expected or not, sodomy, as seen within pederasty, was not a theological proscription authorities were comfortable flouting. Sodomy carried with it a very plausible and possible reaction of divine judgement similar to that, which had been visited upon its eponymous cities. This potential judgement might well explain why, in the mid-fifteenth century, Venetian officials removed the legal protections of youth and made them equally accountable as adult men in their actions.[82] Nonetheless, there was a notable amount of adult sodomy within Venice; so much so that it is impossible to say that sodomy, in Venice, was almost entirely with youths.[83] Thus, although sodomy via pederasty was something of a known vice, it was not alone in being the sodomitical concern of officials. Adult sodomy, as opposed to pederasty, was unequivocally unacceptable and thus had to be dealt with at civic and jurisdictional levels to pre-empt divine retribution. As such, Venetians set up quite thorough methods for

78. Chojnacki, *Women and Men in Renaissance Venice*, 33–36.

79. This was, again, a concern about the older male being a fully "masculine" male and a member of civic society. The penetrated youthful male was biologically male, but not yet entirely a male in the eyes of wider society.

80. See Davidson, "Sodomy in Early Modern Venice," 69.

81. See Crompton, *Homosexuality and Civilization*, 245.

82. See Crompton, *Homosexuality and Civilization*, 249–50.

83. See Crompton, *Homosexuality and Civilization*, 247–49.

determining guilt in sodomy cases. For guilt to be declared in a case of sodomy, there had to be evidence of or testimony regarding both penetration
and ejaculation.[84] To help decide whether these two factors had taken place,
the council required barbers and surgeons of the city to report any damage
they encountered that could have arisen from anal or other illicit sex. All
this displayed a sort of juridical thoroughness regarding sodomy within
early modern Venice. Ironically, it is this thoroughness, much as was the
case in Florence, which might have been detrimental to Venice's reputation.
With its stipulations for evidence of both penetration and ejaculation, Venetian courts essentially assured a lower rate of conviction than did some of
their contemporaries.[85] Short of being caught *en flagrante*, this evidence was
difficult to produce in court. Moreover, as Crompton noted, some of those
employed to verify sodomy were themselves accused of and condemned for
committing sodomy.[86] During this period, engaging surgeons, and barbers
to examine and report suspected sodomitical activities moved the policing
of sodomy from a civic institution to a sort of early modern private-public
enterprise. Venice, in its quest to prevent sodomy thoroughly and judicially,
moved the subject from hushed back-room dialogue to an almost public
conversation. This was, much as was the case in Florence, an example of
Italian stringency that only served to excoriate in the eyes of wider European society and the writings of Protestant reformers.

   Within this early modern Venetian world, one might readily suspect
that the denunciations of Italian vernaculars, particularly Diodati's, might
have found considerable association with appropriate, or inappropriate, as it
were, persons. It seems quite likely that there was a thriving sodomy trade
in the city, most often pederastic in nature, but not entirely so. Within this
economy, youthful boys were enticed to act in an effeminate manner by older
men who were interested in their sexual conquest. This economy of sin might
have matched the realistic descriptors for the denunciations of the μαλακοì

84. This is, obviously, somewhat different from other locales of the time where penetration was most often the action that would condemn an accused sodomite. Certainly,
other locales had stipulations about ejaculation as a crucial part of deciding the guilt of
an accused sodomite—as in England, for example—but this was often recognized as a
burden of proof, for which it was quite difficult to provide evidence.

85. For example, the case of Master Stafford from England is similar to this. Stafford's accusers presented the court with surgical evidence of their penetration by him,
which seems to have been the definitively damning evidence. At the same time, the case
of Bishop Atherton provides a contrast as little to no evidence was produced, yet the
accused was still found guilty. Granted Atherton admitted a type of guilt, but he did not
necessarily admit to sodomitical activities.

86. See Crompton, *Homosexuality and Civilization*, 250.

and ἀρσενοκοῖται within early modern Italian vernaculars. This association, however, is not nearly as neat and tidy as one might think.

Sodomy could also be more than simple pederasty or even adult actions in early modern Italy; it was also an analogue for gluttony. Food within this period was often perceived as having a strong effect on the constitution, both morally and physically, of a given person. To over-eat or gorge one's self was a sign of a lack of moral fortitude and often indicative of lacking commitment to morality. This was, in many ways, an extrapolation of Aquinas' understanding of the μαλακοί as the antonyms of perseverance. Just as gluttons would over engage their lustful stomachs, they could just as easily overengage their lustful penises; or at least, such was the belief.[87] Marital intercourse was purposive for the begetting of children: Sex with men was, by definition engaged in only for pleasure, and was therefore as excessive and self-indulgent as over-eating. Thus, a male who gorged himself or had a tendency with over-eating could often be suspected of having other problems with indulgence as well. As such persons were quite clearly, due to their girth, not able to keep to the natural use of food for sustenance and not for pleasure, what would keep them from engaging in sexual activities with the same lack of care? So entrenched was this belief that innkeepers and publicans of the city were encouraged not to serve food past a certain hour lest their clients be tempted to over-indulge.[88] In base terms, an unhealthy utilisation of food could lead to an unhealthy utilisation of sex. All this brings a note of distinction to the study thus far. While it would seem highly plausible that the denunciations by Brucioli and Diodati were directed at the pederastic sub-cultures of early modern Italy, particularly those in Florence and Venice, it is impossible to say that they were not also referencing the glutton. Somewhat problematically, one cannot say that all pederasts were gluttons, just as one could not label all sodomites as pederasts. Certainly, one might allow that gluttons were to be suspected of pederasty, but the descriptions of usury found in Brucioli's and Diodati's works could just as easily apply to the publican and the glutton as they could the pederast and his lover.

Up to this point, the study has reviewed how locations such as Florence and Venice viewed and responded to sodomy, particularly pederasty. This examination, however useful, has not yet answereda very important question: why? It is apparent that pederastic sodomy occurred with some frequency in Florence and Venice—to the extent that it required highly public engagements to regulate and remove it—but it has not yet been

---

87. See Ruggiero, "Forbidden Fruit," 31–52.

88. See Ruggiero, "Forbidden Fruit," 32.

discussed why it might have occurred at all.[89] Although one might take a
theological approach to this and thus assume that the human corruption
of divine intent would play a significant role in the occurrence of sodomy,
ascribing guilt to the human condition or theological bent is, in its own
way, something of a problem in determining what caused sodomy to be
so prevalent within these locales. Were sin and the human condition the
only causes of sodomy, finding sodomy to be as prevalent within the rest
of late medieval and early modern Europe as it was in Italian lands of the
time might well be expected.[90]

As odd as it might sound, marriage was the strongest cause of pederasty as a viable and tempting outlet for youth and younger adult males.
Specifically, the conditions for engaging in marriage were actually a reason
to avoid marriage in many areas in early modern Italy. This situation thus
made sodomy and pederastic relationships attractive and expedient alternatives. As was the case in many other European countries of the time, marriage within early modern Italian lands could be an overly complex process.
Ideally, the suitability of a marriage was to be based on the worldly maturity
of the male, the chaste youth of the female, and the societal compatibility
of both parties.[91] While these factors could be significantly challenging in
and of themselves, particularly with regard to social standing, over all of
this stood the issue of monetary payment in the form of dowries and bride
prices. While the concept of paying and being paid for marriage is far from

89. Certainly, modernity might make the argument of such relationships simply being an expression of human nature and need. There is something to this rationale, but,
at the same time, this does not fully account for sodomy in the early modern period,
when the concept of need and natural urge were rather—though not entirely—absent
from the conversation.

90. This was, in fact, the argument presented by many Protestant reformers of the
time within their respective cultures and countries. Sodomy, for the reformers, and
particularly for Luther, was an endemic and chronic aspect of Catholicism, as was evidenced in Italian cities such as Florence and Venice. Such reformers would argue that
the lax penalties in these areas would seem to confirm their suspicions that sodomy
was simply part of the Roman Catholic matrix. It was only through the acceptance
of Protestant ideals, specifically that of the conjugal household, that such ills might
be alleviated. Even with reforms to the liturgies, the Protestants would argue, one
would still find sodomy, particularly within the Roman priesthood, and would thus be
plagued with its ills forever. Moreover, together with personal affliction with sodomy
and pederasty, failure to accept the "proper" actions of the Protestant household and
the perpetuation of Roman sodomy would anger God and thus cause a serious rebuke
or case of divine vengeance, with Sodom and Gomorrah being the prime examples.

91. Dean and Lowe, *Marriage in Italy 1300–1650*, 130–51. In Florentine patrician
families, 28 percent of daughters entered a convent in the sixteenth century, and 50
percent in the seventeenth: similarly, half of the daughters of the Venetian patriciate in
the seventeenth century were nuns.

exclusive to the realm of late medieval and early modern Italy, a process of inflation in city-states such as Florence and Venice made the cost of marriage prohibitive.[92] In addition, they occasionally reduced bride prices and raised dowries to attract particular suitors at any given time. These practices made marriage, regardless of social compatibility, highly problematic. The market for marriage within these Italian city-states was both incredibly competitive and unbelievably costly. Men often had to work for a significant amount of time to even consider marriage as an affordable option. This extra period of labor that was required in order to afford marriage effectively extended a male's "youth" and thus kept him from being recognized as a fully masculine male. As discussed, not being "fully masculine" in the eyes of society could be a significant factor in instances of early modern Italian sodomy. Moreover, when marriage did occur, there was a question regarding whether the man would continue in the labors that helped to confirm his status as a man. As discussed previously, women in early modern Italy, most notably in Venice, had significant economic rights with regard to the income from their dowries. As such, men could be tempted to rely on this income and find themselves dependent on their wives and their income in short order.[93] This situation regarding inflated bride prices and dowries helped to create a situation in which not only was the act of taking a wife prohibitive for all but the most prosperous of young males, but also a situation in which males might well fall into unmasculine behaviour—such as sensuality, vanity and other effeminate traits—with the profits of their wives' dowries sustaining them in a comfortable lifestyle. All these factors were seen, at the time, as encouraging sodomy. As young men were kept from the marriage bed, they might find themselves inclined to engage in the youthful venture of sodomy, possibly becoming the licentious ἀρσενοκοῖται described in Diodati's text. Similarly, the male who eschewed his masculine role and lived off his wife's income set a standard that might be enviable within the city and thus create an entire class of weak, subservient and unmasculine men. These men

92. See Dean and Lowe, *Marriage*, 148.

93. This was something of a significant concern, particularly with regard to proper male comportment and station within the marriage union. Although we have examined ways in which masculinity in late medieval and early modern Italy might be understood slightly differently from the rest of Europe, men were still expected to be the providers and sustainers of a marital relationship. For a man to become dependent on the income of his wife via profits from her dowry would essentially reverse the balance of power within the marriage by making the male potentially subservient to the female. As masculinity was, again, very much a limited attribute that was essential to both claim and maintain for life at this time, this would clearly upset the social balance and prescriptions of the period. See Dean and Lowe, *Marriage*, 148.

could, perhaps, have been indicative of the *molli* against whom Brucioli, Diodati and others warned.

This point is where the study finds itself both ready to summarize its findings and pressed against a wall. On one hand, the lack of specific wording in vernacular literature, together with the sample and selection, and reticence in public discourse makes it virtually impossible to define precisely who and what the μαλακοὶ and the ἀρσενοκοῖται were within early modern Italy. In fact, it is at times difficult to understand how such terms might have related to the wider realms of sodomy and *contra naturam* sexuality. Certainly, these examples seem to appear, although not often by name, in the ancient and medieval writings of the church. Moreover, there can be little doubt concerning the presence of sodomites or those who practiced "unnatural" sexuality in early modern Italy. In fact, one might easily say that the region, particularly Florence and Venice, appeared—at first glance—to be veritable hotbeds of pederasty in comparison to the rest of their European counterparts. It is very difficult, however, to say where and how the μαλακοὶ and the ἀρσενοκοῖται would have (literally) fit within this spectrum. Both an adherence to Vulgate interpretation, even within vernacular texts, and a lack of those vernacular texts created a dearth of references to the μαλακοὶ and ἀρσενοκοῖται in early modern Italy.

Nonetheless, extant vernaculars, particularly the texts by Brucioli and Diodati, provide some insight into the Italian vernacular understanding of the μαλακοὶ and the ἀρσενοκοῖται. Certainly, these vernaculars, as corroborated by Cajetan's definitions, seem to refer to specific characters. Given this study's examination of relevant characteristics and situations, one might speculate that the *molli* were those who were unmasculine within society, or those effeminate males who were unmarried and unconstrained in their sexual liaisons and roles. At the same time, in some instances, such as Florence, the "soft" or *molli* characters could have been those who penetrated others and thus cast off their own masculinity in so doing.[94] In addition, one might speculate that the effeminate μαλακοὶ were the gluttons, those who were not sufficiently virtuous to rein in their passions and who were often seen as over-indulgent with regard to both food and sexuality.

The ἀρσενοκοῖται in early modern Italy seem much more likely, according to both Brucioli and Diodati, to have been the active partners in sodomy. From the associations of Cajetan and the supporting references in church literature, it is almost impossible to say that the ἀρσενοκοῖται, for these authors, did not indicate the sodomites. Whether the active partners

---

94. This creates an interesting inversion whereby the active males were μαλακοὶ and the passive ones were ἀρσενοκοῖται.

were those who penetrated or those who were penetrated seems to be dependent on location for early modern Italy. Although they cannot speak in a fully authoritative sense, it would seem highly probable that, due to its popularity as a type of sodomy, when Brucioli and Diodati referenced sodomy they really meant "pedastery." However, one might just as easily attribute the denunciations by Brucioli and Diodati to indulgent publicans kowtowing towards and encouraging their gluttonous patrons.

There is, in the early modern Italian world, simply too much potential association and too little solid corroboration to define the μαλακοὶ and the ἀρσενοκοῖται in early modern Italian vernacular Bibles and society with absolute certainty. This instability, however, does not mean that Italians were not familiar with those denounced by 1 Corinthians 6:9. Where there might have been shock and fear on the part of the rest of their European neighbours, by the time of the early modern, Italian authorities were well acquainted with and aware of sodomy, pederasty and other sexually deviant practices that might be associated with οὔτε μαλακοὶ οὔτε ἀρσενοκοῖται.[95] One might venture that this acquaintance was due to the region's centrality and importance to the councils and workings of the Roman church, as well as familiarity with classical literature that discussed such topics.[96] At the same time, however, one might venture that Luther and others could have been correct: Perhaps sodomy, particularly pederasty, really was an epidemic within early modern Italy. In summary, the average early modern layperson, were he to reside in Italy, would most certainly be aware that sodomy with another adult male was against the law. The strong hints and outright condemnations by those such as Cajetan would have ensured that such knowledge was instilled. Nonetheless, the social and religious exigencies of early modern Italy meant the exact actions of the μαλακοὶ and ἀρσενοκοῖται, which would keep one from heaven, would have been left vague. A Florentine layman could probably have curtly articulated that sodomy was bad and *contra naturam*. Whether he could have said the same about the pederasty he would most likely have practiced is impossible to say.

95. See Naphy, *Sex Crimes*, 90.

96. Crompton seems to argue for this. See Crompton, *Homosexuality and Civilization*, 245.

Conclusion

I t is at this point in the examination that the study finds itself brought to a point at which it might begin to summarize the interactions, understandings, or lack thereof, which broadly characterized vernacular Bible translation and specifically those thought to be implied by οὔτε μαλακοὶ οὔτε ἀρσενοκοῖται within the Protestant Reformation. To review the introduction, one must certainly say that the Protestant Reformation did, in fact, produce a great number of Bibles "in the language of the people." This has been roundly proven in each chapter of the study. From Luther, to Olivetan, Cranmer and Valla, the enterprise of vernacular interpretation was certainly robust during the sixteenth and seventeenth centuries. Moreover, the necessity of creating supporting works for these new Bibles- lexicons, dictionaries, commentaries and more- was quite prominent during this time.[1] Even early modern Italy, where the enterprise of biblical translation was more centred on adherence to tradition, saw the importation or production of a small number of vernacular texts. In almost all these instances, the concept of *ad fontes* translation, returning to the sources of biblical literature, held a position of dominance in the authors' interpretive frameworks.[2] There was, for many of these authors, a distinct goal of bringing an "original" biblical witness to their specific locale, providing original and understandable interpretations. However, as the study has described in detail, this does not mean that specific translations, such

1. Certainly, one might note that Luther's translation was singularly predominant, although not absolutely so, in early modern Germany. Nonetheless, Luther's work was, together with that of LeFevre, the obvious prototype when taking the Bible to the masses and his was thus a predominant movement within Germany, unlike other locales, making his text the representative of its time.

2. As discussed, Italy was something of an oddity in this instance, preferring its vernaculars to maintain continuity with the Latin Vulgate, at least as far as 1 Cor 6:9 was concerned. However, even Cajetan himself was somewhat obligated to the *ad fontes* system in a number of ways. See O'Connor, "Neglected Facet Of Cardinal Cajetan," 71–94.

as that of οὔτε μαλακοὶ οὔτε ἀρσενοκοῖται, could not be bent or altered to suit a translator's presiding worldview and exigencies. As has been shown in a macro and micro spectrum, οὔτε μαλακοὶ οὔτε ἀρσενοκοῖται constituted a significant challenge for lexical understanding, as well as in termsof specific application to a person or type of person.

In the early modern German world, lexical examples suggest that definitions of *weicheling* and *knabenschender*, while malleable, operated within certain lexical parameters. InLuther's Germany, the μαλακοὶ and the ἀρσενοκοῖται were spelled out as the *weicheling* and the *knabenschender*, terms that had accessible everyday meanings, but which seemed to contain considerable innuendo and euphemistic qualities within them. On one hand, the *weiche* simply meant soft or weak.[3] As the study has evidenced, however, the term often meant, euphemistically, unmasculine or emasculated. This weakness could include those who were sexually and/or emotionally incontinent. The *knabenschender*, unlike the *weiche*, was more problematic within the lexicon of early modern German. The *knabenschender* was a term, perhaps created by Luther, which was a straightforward neologism, with all the associated problems this implies for definition.[4] In his wording, Luther was most likely attempting to stay as lexically faithful as possible to the Apostle Paul, matching Paul's neologism with his own. The term, although absent from sixteenth-century lexicons, was found by the mid-seventeenth century to be strongly associated with *contra naturam* sexuality, particularly with pederasty.[5] The terms seem to have been rife with euphemistic intent and, given Luther's emphasis on the topic in other writings, most likely hinted at the sexual practices of the Roman Catholic priests. The rationale for this inference required a close reading of the sexuality and politics of the German Reformation in this study.

Sex and sexuality in early modern Germany experienced continuity and change. The religious and socio-cultural ideal of the (Lutheran) conjugal household, as well as clerical marriage, altered the idea of the "goodness" and "naturalness" of the sex act fundamentally. Nonetheless, concepts of sexual propriety, sexual roles and sexual function remained widely unchanged within the early modern German world despite the Protestant Reformation. Thus, a new and positive view of the sex act inherent in the establishment of the conjugal household, for both the laity and for the clergy, did not usher in

---

3. Grimm and Grimm, *Worterbuch*, 1311–23; Dasypodius, E2 1v; Maaler, *Die Teutsch Spraach*, 488.

4. Lexer, *Mittlehochdeutsches Handworterbuch*, 655–56.

5. Frisius, *Novum Latino-Germanicum Et Germanico Latinum Lexicon*, 455; Grimm and Grimm, *Worterbuch*, Bd. 11, Sp. 1325; Passor, *Lexicon* (1632), 403.

libertinism. Instead, German society, on the whole, was widely conservative regarding sexual propriety. For Luther, Bullinger and others, acts of illicit sex were often understood as being found in the "other," or that which was decidedly non-German and not part of the Protestant Reformation.[6] The most glaring example of this "otherness" could be summed up within the person of the Roman Catholic priest, one who shunned marriage, the conjugal household, and the licit sex lauded by Protestant reformers.

Germans and their reformers were able to accept a range of sexual licence when it involved a person of power or usefulness—or just a well-liked neighbour. Individuals not protected by their necessity, status or power faced the full weight of social disapproval and the severe exactions of the law.[7] This was most evident in the writings by Luther and other reformers in which sexual deviancy was conflated with Italians and the Roman curia. Luther, locked in a struggle he considered of eternal importance, was more than willing to make use of and encourage the prejudices and stereotypes his fellow Germans held for all things Italian. This polemic, however, required a kernel of truth to be effective. Italian cities such as Venice and Florence were notorious for sodomy and pederasty long before the Protestant Reformation. They did little to discourage these views, as shown in this study, by establishing courts and police units specifically designed to control sodomy. Moreover, this polemic was particularly effective against the Papacy, since reports about the sodomitical sinfulness of Rome circulated regularly in Germany.[8] Within this vernacular warning was a fairly astute reading of German prejudices. Luther was explicitly warning his listeners of a vice that Germans associated with Italians while simultaneously castigating the Catholics for their supposed moral laxity and sexual deviance. Luther and others all thus issued writings that connected the actions of the *weicheling* and the *knabenschender*, the *cinadedus* and the catamite, as *contra naturam* and intricately associated with the Roman Catholic Curia. Luther conflated the Roman church's leadership with catamites and male whores while others, such as Zwingli, refused to discuss the specifics of the text, but deemed any offenders to not be children of God. Given the climate of the German Reformation, one must wonder whether this was

6. This is similar to Bale, who considered all Roman Catholics to be synonymous with sodomites. See Betteridge, "Place of Sodomy in the Writings of John Bale and John Foxe," 12.

7. This understanding is seemingly supported in Luther's own writings in which he gives preference to pastoral care and consideration instead of to legal code. See "On Marriage Matters" (1530), LW 46:319; WA 30III: 247.

8. Rubeanus' letter is just one such instance. See "*Crotus Rubeanus and Luther*," in WABR 1:542.

a not-so-veiled indictment of the Roman clergy, the mortal enemy of the Protestant reformers. Locked in a tremendous struggle with the Roman Catholic faith for the very soul of Germany, the reformers were thus not afraid of levelling charges against their spiritual adversaries. Thus, in Germany, one finds 1 Corinthians 6:9 to evidence not only a strong commitment to the *ad fontes* initiative, but also providing an opening to critiques like those later given by More. Luther was certainly concerned with the literal word of the interpretation, but that word might easily be extrapolated into an attack on those who opposed him. This German association of those who were οὔτε μαλακοὶ οὔτε ἀρσενοκοῖται with Roman Catholic clerics, however, was not necessarily true in other early modern locales.

Early modern France, although a geographic neighbour of Germany, was both quite different in its understanding of those who were indicated by οὔτε μαλακοὶ οὔτε ἀρσενοκοῖται, yet also quite similar to its neighbours with regard to general characterisations. In all situations, regardless of the location, ἀρσενοκοῖται seem to have almost always been associated with pederasty. This has been significantly evidenced by the writings of LeFevre, Calvin and those who followed their lead and employed their translations. For the somewhat blunt LeFevre, this was embodied in the person of the *bougre*, a licentious, lustful, and debauched creature who enticed others to engage in sin and folly. Although pederasty was often associated with sodomy, the definitions by Marlorat, Bucanus and van Est indicated that sodomy itself was a much larger category, of which pederasty was only a small subsection. While all pederasts might have been sodomites, not all sodomites were pederasts. Other writings, however, have shown that ἀρσενοκοῖται, although referring to pederasts, could have a much broader connotation. In some instances, who the ἀρσενοκοῖται were has been found to be coded and deliberately opaque; this is a particular frustration for this study, but one that is understandable given the logic of the early modern mind. This was due to the associations of pederasty with sodomy and the destruction of the biblical Sodom and Gomorrah that were equated in the early modern mind. Ultimately, the ἀρσενοκοῖται, while a problematic neologism, was an action that was quite unacceptable and seems almost always to have been associated with sexual activity, specifically with the sin of pederasty that often required colloquialisms, circumlocutions and/or euphemisms to translate it.

While the ἀρσενοκοῖται were singularly defined and despised within the early modern Francophone world, who the μαλακοὶ were was far more dangerous and encompassing. From the writings of LeFevre, Calvin, Marlorat, Miege and others, the term was understood to have signified the unmasculine or atypical males in common society. These males would not have been in keeping with the attributes of *honnetéte* and *bienséance*, the key governors of masculine emotion in the early modern Francophone world. Such men would have been seen to be frivolous, overly passionate, overly decorative or concerned with appearance, and generally ruled by their passions and desires, thus marking them as more feminine than masculine. Moreover, this attribute could affect any male at any level or of any stature of society and could and could not be connected to the sexual misconduct of ἀρσενοκοῖται. Henri III displayed and enacted the attributes of the μαλακοί not only by his indecisive and non-engaged style of rule, but also by his emotional incontinence, displayed via his vanity and through his *mignons*.

Ultimately, both the μαλακοί and ἀρσενοκοῖται were a sort malaise, both mental and physical. This malaise could affect any man in any given time and place and was perhaps just as likely to occur in the common man as in the noble. The *bougres* fulfilled their sinful nature and pederastic desire by the emasculation of the *volupteurs,* while the *volupteurs* indulged their emotional incontinence through submission to warped emasculation by the *bougres.* Thus, while French translators were still quite mindful of the gravity of that on which they commented, there was little of the tepidness that Luther offered in terms of lack of definition. Instead, perhaps due to their commitment to the laity reading the biblical texts, French reformers seemed to have understood the characters to require definition lest ignorance breed destruction. Of particular note is the authors' seeming restraint in employing the given terms, or their analogues, in demeaning one particular class of person. This is contrary to early modern Germany, which seemed to approach οὔτε μαλακοί οὔτε ἀρσενοκοῖται with only slightly veiled reference towards Roman Catholic clerics. Instead, the French Reformation seemed to be more preoccupied with providing a translation of οὔτε μαλακοί οὔτε ἀρσενοκοῖται that was not confessionally but societally driven. Given the cultural context of early modern France, the *volupteurs and bougres*, μαλακοί and ἀρσενοκοῖται, were not only those who could not inherit the kingdom of God, as described in 1 Corinthians 6:9, but were those who threatened the very social fabric of society.

Within early modern England, the μαλακοί and particularly those who were thought of as also being ἀρσενοκοῖται, were often associated with acts of sodomy, although not always in similar or literal ways. The μαλακοί was most often, in definitions, associated with an outward expression of an inward weakness or predisposition towards a lustful lack of self-control; however, it might also refer to an entirely inward sickness of the mind. In many ways, those who were ill with lust were the customers of an ἀρσενοκοῖται. The ἀρσενοκοῖται was most often associated with the actions of buggery, or sodomy. Sodomy was the large and overarching understanding of "unnatural" lusts; lusts that went against that which was considered normal and natural action. Sodomy was, in many cases, known as buggery, or anal sex. To say, however, that buggery was simply anal sex was, as seen earlier, far too simplistic. Buggery, as seen in both lexical and legal situations, was both anal copulation and was associated with the vice of pederasty. Thus, returning to previous legal examples, Castlehaven, as described by his accusers, was both μαλακοὶ and ἀρσενοκοῖται, by definition as was Master Stafford. However, there was no consensus in lexical realms regarding exactly where μαλακοὶ ended and ἀρσενοκοῖται began. Therefore, one might also say that, for many, Mr. Ivie, as mentioned previously, was a sodomite by virtue of his buggery, but was not necessarily μαλακοὶ and was certainly not a pederast.

In practice, the terms synonymous with μαλακοὶ and ἀρσενοκοῖται, within early modern England—terms of sodomy, unnatural lust and pederasty—were often politically charged. They carried with them significant potential for danger or benefit, depending on whether one was the accuser or the accused. They were terms with attributed concepts that were familiar via the dramas of Marlowe, amongst others, but still occasioning the strictest and harshest penalties in legal circumstances due to their gravity. With regard to translation, English vernaculars displayed both notable reflections of *ad fontes* interpretations for 1 Corinthians 6:9 and a considerable number of texts that, even though advanced by reformers, were conservative and better reflective of the Latin Vulgate in their translations. Such understanding and presentation were largely indicative of the highly charged and potentially dangerous religious change that characterized much of early modern English religious life. In summary, the μαλακοὶ and the ἀρσενοκοῖται were quite similar to early modern England itself; twisting, turning, and not easily identified or labelled by a singular proposition.

Italy, as was the case with some of its neighbours, was a locale that was difficult for this study to label succinctly. On one hand, the lack of specific wording in vernacular literature, together with the samples, the selection and reticence in public discourse, makes it virtually impossible to define who and what the μαλακοὶ and the ἀρσενοκοῖται were within early modern Italy. In fact, it is at times difficult to understand how such terms might have related to the wider realms of sodomy and *contra naturam* sexuality. Certainly, these examples seem to appear, although not often by name, in the ancient and medieval writings of the church. Moreover, there can be little doubt regarding the presence of sodomites or those who practiced "unnatural" sexuality in early modern Italy. In fact, one might easily say that the region, particularly Florence and Venice, appeared—at first glance—to be veritable hotbeds of pederasty in comparison to the rest of their European counterparts. It is very difficult, however, to say where and how the μαλακοὶ and the ἀρσενοκοῖται would have (literally) been positioned within this spectrum.

Both an adherence to traditional interpretation, even within vernacular texts, and a lack of these vernacular texts has created a dearth of references to the μαλακοί and ἀρσενοκοῖται within early modern Italy.

Nonetheless, extant vernaculars, particularly the texts by Brucioli and Diodati provide some insight into Italian vernacular understanding of the μαλακοί and ἀρσενοκοῖται. Certainly, these vernaculars, corroborated by Cajetan's definitions, seem to refer to specific characters. Given this study's examination of relevant characteristics and situations, one might speculate that the *molli* were those who were unmasculine within society, the effeminate males who were unmarried and unconstrained in their sexual liaisons and roles. At the same time, in some instances, such as in Florence, the "soft" or *molli* characters could have been those who penetrated others and thus castoff their own masculinity in so doing.[9] In addition, one might speculate that the effeminate μαλακοί were gluttons, those who were not sufficiently virtuous to rein in their passions and were often seen as overindulging in both food and sexuality.

The ἀρσενοκοῖται within early modern Italy seem much more likely, for both Brucioli and Diodati, to have been the active partners in sodomy. From the associations of Cajetan and the supporting references in church literature, it is almost impossible to say that the ἀρσενοκοῖται, for these authors, were not indicative of the sodomite. Whether the active partners were those who penetrated or those who were penetrated seems to be dependent on location in early modern Italy. Although they cannot speak in a completely authoritative sense, it would seem highly likely that, due to its popularity as a type of sodomy, when Brucioli and Diodati referred to sodomy, they really meant pederasty. Similarly, one might just as easily attribute the denunciations by Brucioli and Diodati to indulgent publicans kowtowing to and encouraging their gluttonous patrons.

There is, in the early modern Italian world, simply too much potential association and too little solid corroboration to define the μαλακοί and ἀρσενοκοῖται in early modern Italian vernacular Bibles and society. This instability, however, does not mean that Italians were not familiar with those denounced by 1 Corinthians 6:9. Where there might have been shock and fear in the rest of their European neighbours, by the time of the early modern, Italian authorities were acquainted with and aware of sodomy, pederasty and other sexually deviant practices that might be associated with οὔτε μαλακοὶ οὔτε ἀρσενοκοῖται.[10] One might venture that

9. This creates an interesting inversion whereby the active males were μαλακοί and the passive ones were ἀρσενοκοῖται.

10. See Naphy, *Sex Crimes*, 90.

this acquaintance was due to the region's centrality and importance to the councils and workings of the Roman church, as well as familiarity with classical literature that discussed such topics.[11] At the same time, however, one might venture that Luther and others could have been correct: Perhaps sodomy, particularly pederasty, really was an epidemic within early modern Italy. In summary, the average early modern layperson, were he to reside in Italy, would most certainly have been aware that sodomy with another adult male was wrong. The strong hints and outright condemnations of those such as Cajetan would have ensured that such knowledge was ingrained. All the same, the social and religious exigencies of early modern Italy meant the exact actions of the μαλακοὶ and ἀρσενοκοῖται, which would keep one out of heaven, would have been left vague.

With these regional summations in mind, one notes a number of discordances regarding just who might be indicated by οὔτε μαλακοὶ οὔτε ἀρσενοκοῖται that can be discussed. For the early modern translators, the malefactors in 1 Corinthians 6:9 were unanimously masculine in their physical gender. This assumption of masculine physicality, however, was not always the same as assumed gender. This was particularly true in the often-associated vice of pederasty. Adult males were a critical part of this sodomy, whether their conquests or youthful lovers were considered male or un-male, however, was quite varied.[12] The passage, its two key terms and the actions signified by them were never thought of having any inclusion of or effect on females.[13] Thus, one can rightly posit that any difficulty translators experienced was not regarding how to discuss the oddity of female sins within these texts, but were instead nervous about discussing the sexual incontinence of the early modern male, who was seen as the saviour and agent of social, religious and political society. While it is clear that early modern translators viewed these μαλακοὶ and ἀρσενοκοῖται as being wholly inclusive of masculine sins, just what type of sinful action remains obscure.

When discussing the μαλακοὶ and the ἀρσενοκοῖται, there is more than enough evidence of a more than a casual linkage between the terms

11. Crompton seems to argue for this. See Crompton, *Homosexuality and Civilization*, 245.

12. The youth sodomized by Master Stafford of England received a far different treatment from those found in Reformation Geneva. Similarly, the youths involved in Florentine pederasty received different treatment from those involved in pederasty in Venice. The causative factor in all these instances was the perception of guilt associated with perceived masculinity.

13. This is, again, a point at which it is critical to note Cajetan's linking of female sexuality as being indicative of sodomy and *contra naturam* sexuality. This view would certainly be evidenced in other parts of the Reformation but was quite notable for Cajetan's late medieval commentary on Aquinas. See Jordan, *Silence of Sodom*, 64–65.

and the more general vice of sodomy. Any potential inclusion of general sodomy, however, also includes the possibility of tacit condemnation of non-copulative actions between male and female members of society, such as the accusation of sodomy levelled at Mr. Ivie in early modern England. This association made it more than possible for the μαλακοί and the ἀρσενοκοῖται, by their association with definitions such as sodomy, or buggery in this particular instance, to refer not only to the *contra naturam* sexuality of same-sex practices, but also to what modernity would label as heterosexual practice.

All the same, it certainly seems likely, that the vast majority of references to the μαλακοί and the ἀρσενοκοῖται within early modern society referred to pederasty between adults and youths. This pederasty, however, could take multiple shapes and forms. Pederasty in Germany might very well imply Luther's demeaning of the Roman Catholic priest; in England, it was applied in terms of suspicions about a monarch, while even the rampantly casual pederasty in early modern Italian cities, such as Florence and Venice, was vastly different from that of its neighbours.

Moreover, the difference in types and styles of pederasty lead one to other associations that further muddle yet further defined the μαλακοί and the ἀρσενοκοῖται. Olivetan translated his text in a manner that seemed to indicate a proscription of general sodomy, but also footnoted his translation to focus, specifically on pederasty. These actions raise considerable questions regarding whether, in Olivetan's eyes, the two acts were one and the same, or if the translator saw the passage as referring to general sodomy but functionally indicative of pederasty. Similarly, to Olivetan, early modern Italian translations seemed to indicate a proscription of general sodomy. Nonetheless, in practical applications, the texts seem to find far more potential commonality with the rampant pederasty in locales such as Venice and Florence than with adult sodomy. All these foils, and perhaps others as well, would have been placed quite glaringly and prominently by anyone who undertook an *ad fontes* vernacular translation within the early modern world. These consternations aside, the study can also draw some conclusions regarding those indicated by οὔτε μαλακοὶ οὔτε ἀρσενοκοῖται.

In summarising οὔτε μαλακοὶ οὔτε ἀρσενοκοῖται, one can say that the focus passage certainly implied sexual sin. One is inclined to think that the average reformer, to the extent that one can be imagined, would have associated the μαλακοί mainly with "unmanly" behaviours. On the surface, this Pauline word was the easiest to translate but the most difficult to interpret; "soft" is not particularly helpful. As previously said, however, the two words are clearly associated with males; thus, "soft men" are intended. Paul's second word, ἀρσενοκοῖται, being a neologism, should have been the most problematic for translators but, as has been seen, tended to be summarized with pederasts. While there were some who suggested the wider "sodomite" and others used unhelpful euphemisms, there is a sense that pederasty was understood as a part, even the main part, of the sinful behaviour Paul was condemning. No translator or lexicographer seems to have made a point of linking the Corinthian passage, or that in Timothy, explicitly with Leviticus, but it is fairly obvious that, lurking in the subtext, was the idea that Paul was condemning behaviour that was in some way *contra naturam*. This behaviour, however, clearly encompassed more than mere sexual activity. Overall, the translations are rarely precise, and the translators seem to have spent little time trying to delineate the sinners excluded from heaven by Paul. Nevertheless, they seem to have known "who they meant" in their translations, and probably assumed their readers would as well. This vexation and summarisation allow for an interesting view of vernacular biblical translations in the early modern period.

In some ways, early modern translation of the Bible was something that could, as More alleged, be an action that was engaged for the exigencies of one's early modern life. At the same time, to say that vernacular Bible translation was strictly and entirely motivated by personal situations and desired outcomes would be quite inaccurate. There was instead, as this study has shown, a tension that ran from Germany to France, England and to Italy. In this tension, one could readily find the desire to be textually and lexically authentic to the enterprise of *ad fontes* vernacular interpretation. However, one also need not scratch that lexical surface too deeply to find that interpretation in the vernacular could say similar things but have differing outcomes depending upon the location of the translator. Just to whom οὔτε μαλακοὶ οὔτε ἀρσενοκοῖται referred, be they pederasts, sodomites, emasculated men, male prostitutes, or others, seems to have been specifically dependent upon where a translator resided and the tradition he followed. Thus, one might say that biblical translation in the early modern period seemed to be both *ad fontes* with regard to intention and distinctly local in application.

Bibliography

Academia della Crusca. *Vocabolario degli accademici della crusca: con tre indici delle voci, locuzioni, e proverbi latini, e greci, posti per entro l'opera.* Venice: G. Alberti, 1612.

Adams, Simon. *Leicester and the Court: Essays in Elizabethan Politics.* Manchester: Manchester University Press, 2002.

Adams, Thomas. *The Happines of the Church. Or, a Description of those Spirituall Prerogatiues Vvherewith Christ Hath Endowed Her: Considered in Some Contemplations Upon Part of the 12. Chapter to the Hebrewes. Together with Certain Other Meditations and Discourses . . . Being the Summe of Diuerse Sermons Preached in S. Gregories London: By Thomas Adams, Preacher There.* London: G.P., 1619.

Aland, Barbara, et al., eds. *The Greek New Testament.* 4th ed. Stuttgart: Biblia-Druck, 1994.

Albert, Thomas. D. *Der gemeine mann von dem geistlichen richter. kirchliche rechtsprechungin den diozesen basel, churc, und konstanz vor der reformation.* Stuttgart: Lucius And Lucius, 1998.

Alleine, Richard. *Vindiciae pietatis.* London: S.N., 1665.

Altensteig, Johann. *Lexicon theologicvm qvo tanqvam clave theologiae fores aperivntvr, et omnivm fere terminorvm, et obscvriorvm vocvm; qvae s. theologiae studiosos facile remorantur, etymologiae, ambiguitates, definitiones, vsus, enucleatè ob oculos ponuntur, & dilucide explicantur. post svmmvm laborem joannis altenstaig . . . accommodatum auctum & in meliorem ordinem redactum.* Basil: Petri Henningin, 1619.

Ambrosiaster. "Commentaries on Romans and 1–2 Corinthians." In *Ancient Christian Texts*, edited by Gerald L. Bray, 109. Downers Grove, IL: InterVarsity, 2009.

Anonymous. *A Cat May Look Upon a King.* London: William Roybould, 1652.

———. *Tom Tell Troath or a Free Discourse Touching the Manners of the Tyme: Directed to His Majesty by Way of Humble Advertisement.* London: S.n., 1630.

Aretius, Benedictus. *Commentarii in domini nostri Iesu Christi.* Paris: Le Preux, 1607.

The Arraignment, Judgment, Confession, and Execution of Humphrey Stafford, Gentleman. London: S.n., 1607.

Atersoll, William. *The Badges of Christianity.* London: W. Laggard, 1606.

Augustine, Saint. *Confessions.* Ann Arbor, MI: J. W. Edwards, 1946.

———. *Constitutionum Apostolicarum.* Rome: n.d., 1766.

Bale, John. *The Image of Both Churches.* London: Thomas East, 1570.

———. *The Actes of the Englysh Votaryes.* N.d.: Wessel, 1546.

Bancks, John. *A Critical Review of the Political Life of Oliver Cromwell*. Edinburgh, 1775.

Bauer, Walter. *Griechisch-Deutsches Worterbuch Zu Den Schriften Des Neuen Testaments Und Der Ubrigen Urchristlichen Literatur*. Giessen: Toppelman, 1928.

Bauer, Arndt, et al., eds. *A Greek English Lexicon of the New Testament and Other Early Christian Literature*. 3rd ed. Chicago: University of Chicago Press, 2000.

Baret, John. *An Aluearie Or Triple Dictionarie In Englishe, Latin, And French: Very Profitable For All Such As Be Desirous Of Any Of Those Three Languages. Also By The Twotables In The Ende Of This Booke, They May Contrariwise, Finde The Most Necessary Latin Or French Wordes, Placed After The Order Of An Alphabet, Whatsoeuer Are To Be Founde In Any Other Dictionarie: And So To Turne Thembackwardes Againe Into Englishe When They Reade Any Latin Or Frenchaucthors, & Doubt Of Any Harde Worde Therein*. London: Henry Denham, 1574.

B.E. *A New Dictionary of the Canting Crew in its Several Tribes of Gypsies, Beggers [Sic], Thieves, Cheats &C., with an Addition of Some Proverbs, Phrases, Figurative Speeches &C.: Useful for All Sorts of People (Especially Foreigners) to Secure Their Money and Preserve Their Lives ; Besides Very Diverting and Entertaining Being Wholly New*. N.d.: n.d., 1699.

Beal, Joan C. "Cockeram, Henry (Fl. 1623–1658)." In *Oxford Dictionary of National Biography*, edited by Lawrence Goldman. Oxford: Oxford University Press, 2004. http://www.oxforddnb.com/view/article/5780.

Becanus, Martinus. *Analogia Veteris Ac Novi Testamenti*. Paris: Ex Officina Nivelliana, Sumptibus Sebastiani Cramoisy, 1620.

Benecke, Müller, Zarncke, eds. *Mittelhochdeutsches Wörterbuch*. Leipzig: S. Hirtzel, 1863.

Benedicti, Jean. *Les sommes des peches et le remede d'iceux*. Paris: Guilliaume Noue, 1601.

Bergomatis, Ambrosii. *Calepini Dictionarium Latinae Linguae*. Basel: n.d., 1544.

Bernard, Nicholas. *The Case of John Atherton, Bishop of Waterford in Ireland*. London: E. Curll, and sold by J. Harding, 1707.

Berni, Francesco. *La terze rime*. Venice: Curtio Navo, 1537.

Betteridge, Thomas. "'The Place of Sodomy in the Writings of John Bale and John Foxe." In *Sodomy In Early Modern Europe*, edited by Thomas Betteridge, 12–26. Manchester: Manchester University Press, 2002.

De Bibel. Antwerp: Willem Vorsterman, 1528.

Biblia, dat is, de gantische h. schrifture: vervattende alle de canonijcke boecken des ouden en des Nieuwen Testaments: nu eerst door last der hoogh-mog heeren staten generael vande vereenighde nederlanden, en volgens het besluyt van de synode nationael, gehouden tot dordrecht, inde jaeren 1618. ende 1619: uyt de oorspronckelijcke talen in onse neder-landtsche tale getrouwelijck over-geset: met nieuwe by gevoegde verklaringen op de duystere plaetsen, aenteeckeningen vande ghelijck-luydende texten, ende nieuwe registers over beyde de testamenten. Leiden: Paulus Van Ravesteyn, 1637.

Biblia Polyglotta. Edited by Francisco Jimenez De Cisneros and Diego Lopez De Zuniga. Alcala De Henares: Industria Arnaldi Guillelmi De Brocario in Academia Complutensi, 1514.

Biblia Sacra Veteris Et Novi Testamenti. Lugduni: Apud Ioannem Frellonium, 1568.

Biblia. The Bible, That is the Holy Scripture of the Olde and New Testament, Faithfully and Truly Translated Out of Douche and Latyn in to Englishe. [Translated By Miles Coverdale, Afterwards Bishop Of Exeter. With Woodcut Titlepages, Illustrations, And Map.] N.d.: Marburg: E. Cervicornus & J. Soter, 1535.

La Bible, Qui Est Toute La Saincte Escripture, Contenant Le Vieil & Le Nouveau Testament Ou, La Vieille & Nouvelle Alliance: quant a la traduction du vieil testament reveue en ceste impression, & aux annotations adjoinctes a icelle, lisez ce qui en est dict en l'epistre : quant au nouveau, il a este reveu & corrige sur le grec par l'advis des ministres de geneve. on a aussi adjouste quelques figures de grande consequence, et amende aucunes de celles des precedentes impressions. Geneve: Henri Estienne, 1560.

The Bible and Holy Scriptures Contained in the Old and New Testament. Geneva: Rovland Hall, 1560.

Den Bijbel, met groter neersticheyt ghecorrigeert en op dye canten ghesedt d. ouderdom der werelt, en hoe langhe die gheschiedenissen en historien der bijbelen, elc int sijne voor christus gheboorte gheweest sijn, en daer bi vergadert ut fasciculus temporu, ende ut dye cronike v. alder werelt . . . en dat inhout boue elcken capittel des seluee capittels, soo wel des o.t. als des n.t. met noch sommighe schoone verclaringhen op dye canten, dye op dander noyt gheweest en syn. Antwerp: Jacob Van Liesvelt, 1542.

Biestkens Van Diest, Nicholas. *Den Bybel, Inhoudende Dat Oude Ende Nieuwe Testament* Rotterdam: n.d., 1560.

Black, Antony. *Guilds and Civil Society in European Political Thought from the Twelfth Century to the Present.* London: Methuen, 1984.

Blount, Thomas. *Glosographia.* Cornhill: Thomas Newcomb, 1661.

———. *Glosographia.* Cornhill: Thomas Newcomb, 1674.

Boas, Frederick S. *Christopher Marlowe: A Biographical and Critical Study.* Oxford: Clarendon, 1953.

Boendale, Jan van, and M. de Vries. *Der Leken Spieghel, Leerdicht Van Den Jare 1330* Leiden: D. Du Mortier En Zoon, 1844.

Boes, Maria. *Crime and Punishment in Early Modern Germany: Courts and Adjudicatory Practices in Frankfurt Am Main, 1562–1696.* Surrey: Ashgate, 2013.

———. "On Trial for Sodomy in Early Modern Germany." In *Sodomy in Early Modern Europe,* edited by Tom Betteridge, 27–45. Manchester: Manchester University Press, 2002.

Bonadus, Franciscus. *Divi Pauli Apostoli Gentium . . . Epistole Divine ad Orphica Lyram Traducte Francisco Bonado . . . Paraphraste.* Paris: S. Dubois, 1537.

Borris, Kenneth, and G. S. Rousseau. *The Sciences of Homosexuality in Early Modern Europe.* New York: Routledge, 2008.

Boswell, John *Christianity, Homosexuality, and Social Tolerance.* Chicago: University of Chicago Press, 1980.

Bray, Alan. "Homosexuality and the Signs of Male Friendship in Elizabethan England." *History Workshop* 29 (1990) 1–19.

———. *Homosexuality in Renaissance England.* London: Gay Men's, 1982.

Breitenberg, Mark. *Anxious Masculinity in Early Modern England.* New York: Cambridge University Press, 1996.

Brunet, Gustave, et al., eds. *Memoires-Journaux.* 12 vols. Paris: Lemerre, 1875–1896.

Buchanan, Colin O. *The A To Z Of Anglicanism.* Lanham: Scarecrow, 2009.

"Buggery, n. and adj." OED Online. http://www.oed.com/view/entry/24372?redirecte dfrom=buggery.

Bullinger, Heinrich. *In Priorem D. Pavli Ad Corinthios Epistolam, Heinrychi Bullingeri Commentarius: Quam Uero Ista, Lector, Nostris Conueniat Temporibus: Quam Sit Utilis & Necessaria, Paucissimis Quidem Admonet Cum Argumento Epistolae Operis Praesatio. Iesvs. Hic Est Filius Meus Dilectus, In Quo Placata Est Anima Mea: Ipsum Audite. Matth. 17.* Zurich: Christoph. Froscho, 1534.

Burrows, Mark S. "Jean Gerson on the 'Traditional Sense' of Scripture as an Argument For an Ecclesial Hermeneutic." In *Biblical Hermeneutics in Historical Perspective: Studies in Honour of Karlfried Froehlich on His Sixtieth Birthday*, edited by Mark S. Burrows et al., 154, 159. Grant Rapids: Eerdmans, 1991.

Cajetan, Tommaso de Vio. *Summula Peccatorum*. Venice: Sessae, 1575.

Calvin, John. *Lexicon Iuridicum Iuris Caesarei Simul, Et Canonici: Feudalis Item, Civilis, Criminalis; Theoretici, Ac Practici; Et In Schola & In Foro Usitatarum, Ac Tum Exipso Juris Utriusque Corpore, Tum Ex Doctoribus & Glossis, Tam Veteribus, Quam Recentioribus Collectarum, Vocum Penus . . .* Geneva: Editio Postrema, Prioribus Auctior Et Longe Limatior, 1622.

———. *Opera Omnia Theologica Tomus V.* Geneva: Apud Iohannem Vignon, Petrum & Iacobum Chouet, 1617.

———. *In Omnes Pauli Apostoli Epistolas, Atque Etiam In Epistolam Ad Hebraeos, Item In Canonicas Petri, Johannis, Jacobi, & Judae, Quae Etiam Catholicae Vocantur, Joh. Calvini Commentarii.* Geneva: Robert Estienne: 1557.

The Case of Sodomy in the Trial of Mervin, Lord Audley. London: John Morphew Near Stationer's-Hall, 1707–1708.

Castellio, Sebastien. *Biblia, Interprete Sebastiano Castalione: Una Cum Eiusdem Annotationibus: Totum Opus Recognouit Ipse, & Adiecit Ex Flauio Iosepho Historiae Supplementum Ab Esdrae Temporibus Usq[Ue] Ad Machabaeos, Itemq[Ue] A Machabaeis Usq[Ue] Ad Christum: Accessit Quoq[Ue] Rerum & Uerborum Tam In Ipsis Biblijs, Quam Annotationibus & Historiae Supplemento Praecipue Memorabilium Index.* Basel: n.d., 1555.

"Catamite, N." OED Online. http://www.oed.com/view/entry/28731?redirectedfrom= catamite.

Chojnacki, Stanley. *Women and Men in Renaissance Venice.* Baltimore, MD: Johns Hopkins University Press, 2000.

Cholinus, Peter. *Dictionarium Latino-Germanicum.* Zurich: n.d., 1541.

Cockeram, Henry. *The English Dictionary.* London: A.M. for T.W., 1647.

"Cokayne, George E." In *Complete Baronetage 1611–1800.* Exeter: W. Pollard, 1900.

Cokayne, Thomas. *A Greek-English Lexicon.* London: Lodwick Lloyd, 1658.

Coke, Edward. *The Third Part of the Institutes of the Laws Of England: Concerning High Treason, and Other Pleas of the Crown, and Criminall Causes.* London: M. Flesher, for W. Lee, and D. Pakeman. 1644.

A Complete Collection of State Trials. 4 vols. London: T. Goodwin, 1719–1730.

Confessio Generalis Brevis Et Utilis. Rome: Bartholomaeus Guldinbeck, 1485.

Constitutio Criminalis Bambergis. Bambergische peinliche halszgerichts-ordnung. Bamberg: Hans Pfeil, 1507.

Constitutio Criminalis Carolina. Dess aller durchleuchtigsten, grossmechtigsten, vnüberwindtlichsten keyser karls dess fünfften, vnd dess heyligen römischen reichs peinlich gerichts ordnung, auff den reichsstägen zu augspurg vnd regenspurg, inn jaren dreissig vnd zwey vnd dreissig gehalten, aussgericht vnd beschlossen. Meyntz: J. Schoffer, 1500.

Coogan, Michael. *A Brief Introduction to the Old Testament.* Oxford: Oxford University Press, 2009.

Corbellini, Sabrina. *Discovering the Riches of the Word.* Boston: Brill, 2015.

Crawford, Katherine B. "Love, Sodomy, and Scandal: Controlling the Sexual Reputation of Henry III." *The Journal of the History of Sexuality* 12 (2003) 513–42.

Crompton, Louis. *Homosexuality and Civilization.* Cambridge, MA: Harvard University Press, 2003.

De La Cuisine, E. *Le parlement de bourgogne depuis son origine jusqu'a sa chute.* 3 vols. N.d.: Dijon and Paris, 1864.

Darlowe, T. H. And Moule, H. F. *Historical Catalogue of the Printed Editions Of Holy Scripture in the Library of the British and Foreign Bible Society.* London: Bible House, 1903.

Dasypodius, Petrus. *Dictionarium Latino-Germanicum.* Strasbourg: n.d., 1535.

———. *Dictionarium Et Vice Versa Germanico-Latinum.* Strasbourg: n.d., 1539.

Davidson, N. S. "Sodomy in Early Modern Venice." In *Sodomy In Early Modern Europe* edited by Tom Betteridge, 65–81. New York: Manchester University Press, 2002.

Deacy, Susan, and Pierce, Karen. *Rape in Antiquity: Sexual Violence in the Greek and Roman Worlds.* London: Duckworth, 1997.

Dean, Trevor, and Lowe, K. J. P. *Marriage in Italy 1300–1650.* Cambridge: Cambridge University Press, 1998.

Decrees of the Ecumenical Councils. Vol. 1. Edited by Norman P. Tanner, SJ. Washington, DC: Georgetown University Press, 1990.

Desainliens, Claude. *A Dictionarie French and English: Published for the Benefite of the Studious in that Language: Gathered and Set Forth By Claudius Hollyband. For the Better Vnderstanding of the Order of this Dictionarie, Peruse the Preface to the Reader.* London: Thomas Woodcock, 1593.

Διδαχη Των Δωδεκα Αποστολων: *The Teaching of the Twelve Apostoles.* In *The Apostolic Fathers,* edited by J. B. Lightfoot, 5:1–2. Grand Rapids: Baker, 1970.

De'hoefer, M. *Nouvelle biographie universelle depuis les temps les plus reculés jusqu'a nos jours, avec les renseignements bibliographiques et l'indication des sources a consulter.* Vol. 38. Paris: Firmin Didot Freres, 1852.

———. *Nouvelle biographie universelle depuis les temps les plus reculés jusqu'a nos jours, avec les renseignements bibliographiques et l'indication des sources a consulter.* Vol. 6. Paris: Firmin Didot Freres, 1852.

Digangi, Mario. *The Homoerotics of Early Modern Drama.* New York: Cambridge University Press, 1997.

Diodati, Giovanni. *La Biblia.* Lucchese: n.d., 1607.

Duerden, Richard. "Equivalence Or Power? Authority And Reformation Bible Translation." In *The Bible as Book: The Reformation,* 9–13. New Castle, DE: Oak Knoll, 2000.

Dyrkinus, Johannes, and Van Wingen. *Godfried Biblia: dat is, de gantsche heylighe schrift, grondelick ende trouvvelick verduydtschet, met verklaringhe duysterer woorden, redenen ende spreuken, ende verscheyden lectien . . . aen de kant: met noch rijcke aenwijsinghen, der ghelijck ofte onghelijck stemmende plaetsen. . .* N.d.: Willem Galliart, 1562.

D'ewes, Simonds. *The Diary of Sir Simonds D'ewes (1622–1624): Journal D'Un Etudiant Londonien Sous Le Regne De Jacques Ler / Text Etabli Et Annote Par Elisabeth Boucier*. Paris: Didier, 1974.

Dierauer, Johannes. *Chronik der stadt zurich*. Basel: A. Geering, 1900.

Emser, Hieronymus. *Das New Testament, so durch den hochgelerten hieronymum emser seligen verteutscht, etc*. Friburg Im Breyssgaw: Durch S. Graff, 1551.

Emser, Hieronymus, et al. *Das Naw Testament nach lawt der christliche kirchen bewerte text, corrigirt, vu widerumb zu recht gebracht*. Dresden: Wolfgang Stockel, 1527.

Erasmus, Desiderius. *Novum Instrumentum Omne*. Basil: Johan Froben, 1516.

———. *Novum Testamentum Totum*. Antwerp: Hillenius, 1520.

"Epistle of Crates." In *The Cynic Epistles: A Study Edition*, edited by Abraham J. Malherbe, 69–83. Missoula, MT: Scholars, 1977.

Est, William van. *In Omni Beati Pauli*. Paris: S.I., 1640.

Estienne, Robert. *Dictionnaire Francois Latin Contenant Les Motz Et Manières De Parler Francois, Tournez En Latin*. Paris: R. Estienne, 1539.

———. *Dictionnaire Francois-Latin*. Paris: S.I., 1539.

Farr, James R. *Authority and Sexuality in Early Modern Burgundy, 1550–1730*. New York: Oxford University Press, 1995.

Fasciculi Zizaniorum Magistri Johannis Wyclif Cum Tritico Ascribed To Thomas Netter Of Walden. London: Longman, 1858.

Ferguson, Gary *Queer (Re)Readings in the French Renaissance: Homosexuality, Gender, Culture*. Aldershot: Ashgate, 1988.

Ferrarius, Johannes *A Work of Ioannes Ferrarius*. London: John Kingson, 1559.

"Flesh, N." OED Online. http://www.oed.com/view/entry/71460?rskey=lcwtpy&result =1&isadvanced=false.

Florio, John. *Queen Anna's New World of Words, or Dictionarie of the Italian and English Tongues, Collected, and Newly Much Augmented by Iohn Florio, Reader of the Italian Vnto the Soueraigne Maiestie of Anna, Crowned Queene of England, Scotland, France and Ireland, &C. And One of the Gentlemen of Hir Royall Priuie Chamber. Whereunto Are Added Certaine Necessarie Rules and Short Obseruations for the Italian Tongue*. London: Edward Blount and William Barret, 1611.

Flood, John J. "Martin Luther's Bible in its German and European Context." In *The Bible in the Renaissance*, edited by Richard Griffith, 45–70. Burlington, VT: Ashgate, 2001.

Fradenburg, L. O. Aranye, and Carla Freccero. *Premodern Sexualities*. New York: Routledge, 1995.

Freer, Martha. *Henry III King Of France: His Court and Times Volume 2*. London: Hurst and Blackett, 1858.

Fries, Johann. *Novum Latinogermanicum Et Germanicumlatinum Lexicon*. Zurich: Johannes Wolph, 1596.

Frisius, Johann. *Novum Latino-Germanicum Et Germanico Latinum Lexicon*. Zurich: H. Rodmerie, 1616.

Gagny, Jean de. *Brevissima Et Facillima In Omnes D. Pavli Epistolas Scholia: Vltra Priores Editiones, Ex Antiquißimis Graecorum Authoribus Abunde Locupletata: Itidem In Septem Canonicas Epistolas, & D. Ioannis Apocalypsim, Breuissima Scholia Recens Edita*. Antwerp: Steelsius, 1564.

Garde, Noel. *Jonathan To Gide: The Homosexual in History*. New York: Vantage, 1964.

Garth, Balthasar. *M. Balthasaris Garthii Theologi Lexicon Latinograecum. Kekalligrafeme "Non, Linguae Graece Tyronibus Facilimum, Utilissimum, & Certissimum, & Probatissimis Theologis, Oratoribus, Philosophis, Historicis, & Medicis, Magno*

Labore Sumoque Studio Serie Alphabetica Continnatum. Frankfurt: Prodit Typis Hartmanni Palthenii, Sumptibus Hæredum D. Zachariæ Palthenij, 1620.

———. *Theologogicum Lexicon Latino-Germanicum.* Frankfurt: n.d., 1609.

"Garth, Balthasar." *General German Bibliography* 8 (1878) 372.

Goodman, Godfrey. *The Court of King James the First, to Which are Added Letters Illustrative of the Personal History of the Most Distinguished Characters in the Court of that Monarch and His Predecessors.* London: Bentley, 1839.

Grant, W. Leonard "Neo-Latin Verse-Translations of the Bible." *Harvard Theological Review* 52 (1959) 205–11.

Graf, H. *Geschichte der mathermatic und der naturwissenschaften in bernischen landen.* Bern: n.d., 1888.

Great Britain Public Record Office. *Letters and Papers, Foreign and Domestic, of the Reign of Henry VIII, Preserved in the Public Record Office, the British Museum, and Elsewhere in England Arranged and Catalogued by J.s. Brewer Under the Direction of the Master of the Rolls, and with the Sanction of Her Majesties Secretaries of State.* Vol. 6 Part 1. London: Longman, Green, Longman, Roberts & Green, 1862–1932.

Greenham, Richard. *The Works Of The Reverend Richard Greenham.* London: Felix Kingston, 1612.

Greenslade, S. L. *The Cambridge History of the Bible: Volume 3, the West from the Reformation to Present Day.* Cambridge: Cambridge University Press, 1975.

Grell, Ole Peter. *Brethren in Christ: A Calvinist Network in Reformation Europe.* Cambridge: Cambridge University Press, 2011.

Griffiths, Richard. "Introduction." In *The Bible in the Renaissance,* edited by Richard Griffiths, 1–8. Aldershot: Ashgate, 2001.

Grimm, Jacob, and Wilhelm Grimm. *Deutsches Worterbuch.* Leipzig: Hirzel, 1971.

Gritsch, Eric W. "Luther's Humor as a Tool for Interpreting Scripture." In *Biblical Hermeneutics in Historical Perspective: Studies in Honour of Karlfried Froehlich on His Sixtieth Birthday,* edited by Mark S. Burrows et al., 196. Grant Rapids: Eerdmans, 1991.

Gunn, S. J. "Brandon, Charles, First Duke of Suffolk (C. 1484–1545)." *Oxford Dictionary of National Biography,* 2021.

Haliczer, Stephen. *Sexuality in the Confessional: A Sacrament Profaned.* Oxford: Oxford University Press, 1996.

Harrington, Joel F. *Reordering Marriage and Society in Reformation Germany.* Cambridge: Cambridge University Press, 1995.

"Heaven Bleese King James Our Joy." Libel No. 10. http://www.earlystuartlibels.net/htdocs/king_and_favorite_section/L10.html.

Heckford, William. *Characteristics Or Historical Anecdotes Of All The Kings And Queens Of England.* London: n.d., 1787.

Hemmingsen, Niels. *Commentaria In Omnes Epistolas Apostolorum, Pauli, Petri, Iudae, Iohannis, Iacobi, Et In Eam Quae Ad Hebraeos Inscribitur.* Strassbourg: Theodosius Rihelius, 1586.

Hendrix, Scott H. "Masculinity and Patriarchy in Reformation Germany." In *Masculinity in the Reformation Era,* edited by Scott Hendrix and Susan Karant-Nunn, 71–89. Kirksville, MO: Truman State University Press, 2008.

———. "The Use of Scripture in Establishing Protestantism." In *The Bible in the Sixteenth Century,* edited by David Steinmetz, 37–69. Durham, NC: Duke University Press, 1990.

Henry VIII. *Assertio Septem Sacramentorum Aduersus Martin. Lutheru[M], Aedita Ab Inuictissimo Angliae Et Franciae Rege, Et Do. Hyberniae Henrico Eius Nominis Octauo.* London: Pynsonianis, 1521.

Henson, Marie C. "Osborne, Francis (1593–1659)." http://www.oxforddnb.com/view/article/20875.

Herrup, Cynthia B. *A House in Gross Disorder: Sex, Law, and the 2nd Earl of Castlehaven* New York: Oxford University Press, 1999.

Higman, Francis. "Without Great Effort and with Pleasure: Sixteenth Century Genevan Bibles and Reading Practices." In *The Bible as Book: The Reformation,* edited by Orlaith O' Sullivan, 115, 120. New Castle, DE: Oak Knoll, 2000.

Hildersam, Arthur. *Lectures Upon Psalme.* London: S. N., 1635.

The. Holie. Bible. Conteynyng the Olde Testament and the Newe. London: In Povvles Churchyarde By Richarde Iugge, Printer To The Queenes Maiestie, 1568.

Hobbs, R. Gerald. "Hebraica Veritas and Traditio Apostolica: Saint Paul and the Interpretation of the Psalms in the Sixteenth Century." In *The Bible in the Sixteenth Century,* edited by Richard Griffiths, 83–99. Burlington, VT: Ashgate, 2001.

Hollander, August den, et al. *Religious Minorities and Cultural Diversity in the Dutch Republic: Studies Presented to Piet Visser on His 65th Birthday.* Leiden: Brill, 2014.

Hollyband, Claude. *A Dictionary French and English: Published for the Benefite of the Studious in that Language.* London: Thomas Woodcock, 1593.

"Homosexuality, n." OED Online. http://www.oed.com/view/entry/88111?redirectedfrom=homosexuality.

Howell, James. *Lexicon Tetraglotton: An English-French-Italian-Spanish Dictionary: Whereunto is Adjoined a Large Nomenclature of the Proper Terms (in all the Four) Belonging to Several Arts And Sciences, to Recreations, to Professions Both Liberal and Mechanick, &C. . . . : With Another Volume of the Choicest Proverbs in All the Said Toungs . . . and the English Translated into the Other Three . . . : Moreover, There Are Sundry Familiar Letters and Verses Running All in Proverbs with a Particular Tome of the British or Old Cambrian Sayed Sawes and Adages . . . : Lastly, There Are Five Centuries of New Sayings . . .* London: J. G., 1660.

Huloet, Richard *Abcedarium Anglico Latinum.* London: William Riddel, 1552.

Hume, Alexander. *A Treatise of the Felicitie.* Edinburgh: Robert Walde-Graue, 1594.

Hus, G. de. *Dictionnaire Francois-Latin.* Paris: n.d., 1573.

Ivie, Thomas. *Alimony Arraignd.* London: S. N., 1654.

Jackson, Clare. "Symson, Andrew (C. 1638–1712)." http://www.oxforddnb.com/view/article/25602.

Jewel, John. *An Exposition Upon the Two Epistles.* London: Newberie, 1584.

Jordan, Mark. *The Silence of Sodom.* Chicago: Chicago University Press, 2000.

Karant-Nunn, Susan. *The Reformation of Ritual: An Interpretation of Early Modern Germany.* New York: Routledge, 1997.

Karant-Nunn, Susan C., and Merry E. Wiesner-Hanks. *Luther On Women: A Sourcebook.* Cambridge: Cambridge University Press, 2003.

Keach, Benjamin. *The Display of Glorious Grace.* London: S. Bridge, 1698.

Keene, Nicholas. "Mayer, John (Bap. 1583, D. 1664)." http://www.oxforddnb.com/view/article/18427.

Kettler, W. "Johannes Fries—'günstling' zwinglis, lexikograph und pädagoge." In *Reformiertes Erbe,* edited by H. A. Obermann et al., 1:207–21. Oxford: Oxford Dictionary of National Biography, 1992.

Key, Newton E. "Littleton, Adam (1627–1694)." http://www.oxforddnb.com/view/article/16780.

Kiel, Cornelis van. *Etymologicvm Tevtonicae Lingvae: Sive Dictionarivm Teutonico-Latinum Praecipvae Tevtonicae Lingvae Dictiones Et Latine Interpretatas, & Cum Aliis Nonnullis Linguis Obiter Collatas Complectens.* Antwerp: Plantini, 1599.

King, John. *The Case of John Atherton, Bishop of Waterford in Ireland: Fairly Represented. Against a Late Partial Edition of Dr. Barnard's Relation, and Sermon at His Funeral.* London: Luke Stokoe, At the Golden Key and Bible, 1710.

Knecht, R. J. *Catherine De" Medici.* New York: Longman, 1998.

Kritzman, Lawrence D. *The Rhetoric of Sexuality and the Literature of the French Renaissance.* New York: Cambridge University Press, 1991.

La Bible. Geneva: Imprinted Matthieu Berjan, 1605.

La Bible. Geneva: S.I., 1637.

La Nouveau Testament. Paris: S.I., 1655.

Ladurie, Emmanuel Le Roy. *L'etat Royal: De Louis Xi A Henri IV 1460–1610.* Paris: Hachette, 1987.

Lalanne, Ludovic, ed. *Journal d'un bourgeois de paris sous le regne de francois premier (1515–1536).* New York: Johnson Reprint, 1965.

Lampe, G. W. H. *A Patristic Greek Lexicon.* Oxford: Clarendon, 1968.

Laurentii Vallae. *Lavrentii Vallae, viri tam graecae quam latinae linguae doctissimi, in nouum testamentu annotationes: apprime utiles.* Basel: 1526.

Laurents, Henri. *La Bible, qui est toute la saincte escriture du vieil et novveau testament.* Amsterdam: Chez Henri Laurents, 1635.

"Lechery, n." OED Online. http://www.oed.com/view/entry/106833?redirectedfrom=l echery.

Lefevre D'etaples, Jacques. *Epistolae Divi Pauli Apostoli Cum Commentariis Preclarissimi Viri Jacobi Fabri . . .* Paris: Venundantur Parrihisiis In Edibus F. Regnault: Et J. De La Porte, 1517.

———. *La Nouveau Testament.* Paris: Impr. En La Maison Simon De Colines, 1523.

Leigh, Edward. *Critica Sacra.* London: A Miller For T. Underhill, 1650.

"Lèse-majesté, n." *OED Online,* September 2021. https://www.oed.com/view/Entry/107 459?redirectedFrom=lese+majeste&.

Leonis, Bulla Decimi. *Contra Errores Martini Lutheri Et Sequacium.* Strassburg: Johann Schott, 1520.

L'estoile, Pierre. *Journal Pour le Règne de Henri III (1574–1589).* Edited by L.-R. Lefèvre. Paris: Gallimard, 1943.

Levins, Peter. *Manipulus Vocabulorvm. A Dictionarie of English and Latine Wordes, Set Forthe in Suche Order, as None Heretofore Hath Ben, the Englishe Going Before the Latine, Necessary Not Onely For Scholers that Want Varietie Of Words, But Also for Such as Vse to Write in English Meetre. Gathered and Set Forth by P. Leuins. Anno 1570. For the Better Vnderstanding of the Order of this Present Dictionarie, Read Ouer the Preface to the Reader, and the Epistle Dedicatorie, and Thou Shalt Finde It Easie and Plaine, and Further Thereof Thou Shalt Gather Great Profite.* London: John Waley, 1570.

Lexer, Matthias. *Mittlehochdeutsches handworterbuch.* Leipzig: n.d., 1872.

Lexicon Sive Dictionarium Graecolatinum G. Budaei, J. Tusani, R. Constantini. Omniumque Aliorum: De Quibus in Postremi Authoris, et Typographi Epistles . . . Volume 2. Contributors: Constantin, Robert; Portus, Franciscus; Crespin, Jean; Pseudo-Cyrille D'Alexandrie; Tryphon D'Alexandrie; Chérobosque, Georges; Philopon, Jean; Corinthe, Grégoire Pardos De; Plutarque; Hérodien; Orbicius; Amerot, Adrien; Melanchthon, Philipp. Geneva: Jean Crespin, 1562.

Liddell, Henry George, et al., eds. *A Greek-English Lexicon.* Oxford: Clarendon, 1925–1940.

Liddell, Henry George, and Scott, Robert. *A Greek-English Lexicon American Edition.* Edited by Henry Drisler. New York: Harper, 1853.

Life, Page. "Cokayne, Thomas (1587–1638)." In *Oxford Dictionary of National Biography,* edited by Lawrence Goldman. Oxford: Oxford University Press, 2004. http://www.oxforddnb.com/view/article/5823.

Littleton, Adam *Linguae Latinae Liber Dictionarius.* London: W. Rawlins, 1678.

Low, Jennifer. *Manhood and the Duel: Masculinity in Early Modern Drama and Culture* New York: Palgrave Macmillan, 2003.

Luther, Martin. *D. Martin Luther's Werke. Kritische Gesamtausgabe.* 73 vols. Weimar: H. Böhlaus Nachfolger, 1883–2009.

———. *D. Martin Luther's Werke. Kritische Gesamtausgabe. Briefwechsel.* 18 vols. Weimar, 1930–1985.

———. *D. Martin Luther's Werke. Kritische Gesamtausgabe. Tischreden.* 6 vols. Weimar, 1912–1921.

———. *Das Gantz Neüw Testamet Recht Grüntlich Teutscht: . . . Die Auszlendigen Wörtter Auff Unser Teutsch Angezeigt: [Übers. Von Martin Luther].* Strassburg: Johan Knoblouch, 1525.

———. *Luther: Letters Of Spiritual Counsel.* Translated Theodore G. Tappert. Louisville, KY: Westminster, 1955.

———. *Luther's Works.* Edited by Jaroslav Pelikan et al. 75 vols. Philadelphia And St. Louis, 1955.

———. *Opera Omnia Domini Martini Lutheri.* Wittenberg: Per Iohannem Lufft, 1538.

Lyra, Nicholas. *Biblia Sacra.* Paris: n.d., 1589.

Maaler, Josua. *Die Teutsch Spraach.* Zurich: Christopher Froschauer, 1541.

Macculloch, Diarmaid. *The Reformation.* New York: Penguin, 2003.

———. *Thomas Cranmer: A Life.* Cambridge, MA: Yale University Press, 1996.

"Mankind, n. and adj. 1." OED Online. http://www.oed.com/view/entry/113548?rskey=dnxzey&result=1&isadvanced=false.

Margolin, Jean-Claude. *The Bible in the Sixteenth Century,* edited by David Steinmetz. Raleigh, NC: Duke University Press, 1990.

Marlorat, Augustin. *Novi Testamenti Catholica Expositio Ecclesiastica.* . . Geneva: Petrus Sanctandreanus, 1605.

———. *Thesaurus S. Scripturae.* Geneva: P&J Chouet, 1613.

Marlowe, Christopher. *Edward II.* Oxford: Oxford University Press, 1967.

Marot, Clement. *La Nouveau Testament.* Amsterdam: Chez La Veuve De Schippers, 1692.

Martin, Dale. *Sex and the Single Saviour.* Louisville, KY: Westminster John Knox, 2006.

Martin, H.-J. "Le Temps De Robert Estienne." In *Histoire De L'édition Française,* Vol. 1. Paris: Fayard, 1982.

Mayer, John *A Commentary Upon the New Testament.* London: Robert and William Leyburn, 1631.

McConchie, R. W. "Howlet, Richard (Fl. 1552)." *Oxford Dictionary of National Biography.* http://www.oxforddnb.com/view/article/14119.

McNeil, John J. *The Church and the Homosexual.* Boston, MA: Beacon, 1993.

Mentzer, Raymond. "Masculinity and the Reformed Tradition in France." In *Masculinity in the Reformation Era*, edited by Scott Hendrix and Susan Karant-Nunn, 120–39. Kirksville, MO: Truman State University Press, 2008.

Metzger, Bruce M. *The Oxford Guide to Ideas and Issues in the Bible*. Oxford: Oxford University Press, 2001.

Miege, Guy. *A Dictionary of Barbarous French, Or, a Collection, by Way of Alphabet, of Obsolete, Provincial, Mis-Spelt, and Made Words in French: Taken Out of Cotgrave's Dictionary with Some Additions: A Work Much Desired, and Now Performed, for the Satisfaction of Such as Read Old French*. London: J.C., 1679.

———. *A New Dictionary French and English*. Paris: S.I., 1600.

Monosini, A., and F. Pignatti. *Etimologia E Proverbio Nell'italia Del XVII Secolo—Floris Italicae Linguae Libri Novem*. Rome: Vecchiarelli Editore, 2011.

Monter, E. William. "Sodomy and Heresy in Early Modern Switzerland." *Journal of Homosexuality* 6 (1981) 1–2, 41–55.

Mortimer, Ian. "Blount, Thomas (1618–1679)." In *Oxford Dictionary of National Biography*, edited by H. C. G. Matthew and Brian Harrison. Oxford: Oxford University Press, 2004. http://www.oxforddnb.com/view/article/2697.

Moynahan, Brian. *William Tyndale: If God Spare My Life*. London: Abacus, 2003.

Muller, Richard A. "The View from the Middle Ages." In *Biblical Interpretation in the Era of the Reformation*, edited by David C. Steinmetz et al., 9. Grand Rapids: Eerdmans, 1996.

Naphy, William G. *Sex Crimes: From Renaissance to Enlightenment*. Stroud: Tempus, 2003.

Neus Testament Deutsch. Zurich: Froschauer, 1528.

The New Testamen [Sic] *Both In Latin And English After the Vulgare Texte: Which is Red in the Churche*. Paris: Fraunces Regnault . . . , Prynted For Richard Grafton And Edward Whitchurch Cytezens Of London, In Nouembre, 1538.

The Newe Testamet as It Was Written, and Caused to Be Writte, by Them Which Herde Yt. To Whom Also Oure Saveoure Christ Jesus Commanded that They Shulde Preache It Unto Al Creatures. [Translated Into English by William Tyndale, Assisted by His Amanuensis William Roy.]. Worms: Peter Schoffer, 1526.

Nicot, Jean. *Le Grand Dictionnaire Francois-Latin*. Geneva: De L'Imprimerie De Iacob Stoer, 1599.

Nissinen, Martti. *Homoeroticism in the Biblical World: A Historical Perspective*. Minneapolis: Fortress, 1998.

Normand, Lawrence. "What Passions Call You These? Edward II and James VI." In *Christopher Marlowe and English Renaissance Culture*, edited by Darryll Grantley and Peter Roberts, 172–97. Hants, England: Scholar; Brookfield, VT: Ashgate, 1996.

O'Connor, Desmond. "Florio, John (1553–1625)." http://www.oxforddnb.com/view/article/9758.

O'Connor, Michael. "A Neglected Facet of Cardinal Cajetan: Biblical Reform in High Renaissance Rome." In *The Bible in the Sixteenth Century*, edited by Richard Griffiths, 75–93. Burlington, Vt: Ashgate, 2001.

Ocker, Christopher. "Scholastic Interpretation of the Bible." In *A History of Biblical Interpretation: The Medieval Through the Reformation Periods*, edited by Alan F. Hauser and Duane F. Watson, 254–78. Grand Rapids: Eerdmans, 2009.

Oliver, Mary Anne Mcpherson. *Conjugal Spirituality: The Primacy of Mutual Love in Christian Tradition.* Kansas City, MO: Sheed and Ward, 1994.

Olivetan, Pierre Robert. *La Bible Qui Est Toute La Saincte Escripture: En Laquelle Sont Contenus, Le Vieil Testament & Le Nouueau, Translatez En Francoys. Le Vieil, De Lebrieu: & Le Nouueau, Du Grec. Aussi Deux Amples Tables, Lune Pour Linterpretation Des Propres Nome: Lautre En Forme Dindice, Pour Trouuer Plusieurs Sentences Et Matieres. Dieu En Tout. Isaiah I. Escoutez Cieulx, Et Toy Terre Preste Laureille: Car Leternel Parle* . . . Neuchtal: Pierre De Wingle, 1535.

Oresko, Robert. "Homosexuality and the Court Elites of Early Modern France." *The Journal Of Homosexuality* 16 (1989) 105–28.

O'Sullivan, Orlaith. "Introduction." In *The Bible as Book: The Reformation,* edited by Orlaith O' Sullivan, 2–3. New Castle, DE: Oak Knoll, 2000.

The Oxford Duden German Dictionary. Oxford: Clarendon, 1990.

"Paedophilia | Pedophilia, n." OED Online. http://www.oed.com/view/entry/135968?r edirectedfrom=pedophilia.

Pagnini, Sante. *Biblia: Habes In Hoc Libro Prudens Lector Vtriusq[Ue] Instrumenti Nouam Translatione[M] Aeditam A . . . Sancte Pagnino Luce[N]Si . . . , Necnon Librum De Interpretamentis Hebraicorum, Arameoru[M], Graecorumq[Ue] Nominum, Sacris In Literis Contentoru[M]. . . . Habes . . . Duas Ioannis Francisci Pici Mirandulae . . . Egregias Epistolas Ad Eundem, Epistolam Translatoris Ad Clementem Septimum Pontificem Maximum.* Lugundi: n.d., 1528.

Papon, Jean. *Arrestz notables des covrts sovveraines de france: ordonnez par tiltres, en vingtquatre liures.* Paris: Gourbin, 1563.

Paravicino, Pietro. *Choice Proverbs and Dialogues in Italian and English: Also Delightfull Stories and Apophthegms Taken Out of Famous Guicciardini: Together With the History of the Warres of Hannibal Against the Romans: And . . . a Short Dictionary of all the Words of the Two Genders, Which has the Termination in the Vowel E. . .* London: Thomas Clark, 1666.

Pareus, Johann Philipp. *Lexicon Plautinum: In Quo Elegantiae Omnium Simplicium Vocabulorum Antiquae Linguæ Romanæ, Velut Indice Quodam Absolutissimo, Accuratè Eruuntur & Explicantur. Passim Quoque Variorum Authorum Latinorum Iuxta Ac Graecorum Loca Enodantur & Illustrantur.* Frankfurt: Nicolaum Hoffmannum, Sumptibus Ionae Rosae, 1614.

Parish, Helen. *Clerical Celibacy in the West C. 1100–1700.* Burlington, VT: Ashgate, 2010.

Passor, George. *Lexicon Graeco-Latinum.* Herborn: n.d., 1619.

———. *Lexicon Græco-Latinum, In Novum . . . Testamentum . . . Editio Quarta, Prioribus Plenior.* Neisse: Nassoviorium, 1632.

Paulson, Michael G. *Catherine De Medici.* New York: P. Lang, 2002.

Peter Damian, Saint. *Liber Gomorrhianus.* In Pl 145 Cols. Flanders: Francesco Petrarca, 1400.

Petersen, William L. "Can Apsenokoitai be Translated by 'Homosexuals'? (I Cor. 6.9; I Tim. 1.10)." *Vigiliae Christianae* 40 (1986) 187–91.

Peyton, Edward, Sir. *The Divine Catastrophe of the Kingly Family of the House of Stuarts.* London: T. Warner, 1652.

Pflachero, Moses. *Analysis Typica Omnium Cum Veteris, Tum Novi Testamenti Librorum Historicorum: Ad Intelligendam Rerum Seriem, & Memoriam Iuvandam Accomodata.* Basel: L. Regem, 1621.

Phillips, Edward. *The New World Of English Words, or, a General Dictionary Containing the Interpretations of Such Hard Words as Are Derived from Other Languages. . . : Together with All Those Terms that Relate to the Arts and Sciences . . . : To Which Are Added the Significations of Proper Names, Mythology, and Poetical Fictions, Historical Relations, Geographical Descriptions of Most Countries and Cities of the World. . .* London: E. Tyler, 1658.

Placum, Andream. *Lexicon Biblicum Sacrae.* Cologne: Novesianus, 1536.

Plummer, Marjorie Elizabeth. "The Much Married Michael Kramer: Evangelical Clergy and Bigamy in Ernestine Saxony, 1522–1524." In *Ideas and Cultural Margins In Early Modern Germany: Essays in Honour of H.c. Erik Midelfort,* edited by Marjorie Elizabeth Plummer and Robin B. Barnes, 99–115. Aldershot: Ashgate, 2009.

Keene, Nicholas. "Poole, Matthew (1624–1679)." http://www.oxforddnb.com/view/article/22518.

Poole, Matthew. *Annotations Upon the Holy Bible Volume Two.* Edinburgh: Andrew Anderson, 1700.

Les Proces Civil Et Criminal Divise In Cinq Livres. 2 vols. Lyon: Dare, 1618.

Puff, Helmut. "Localizing Sodomy: The 'Priest and Sodomite' in Pre-Reformation Germany and Switzerland." *The Journal of the History of Sexuality* 8 (1997) 165–95.

———. *Sodomy in Reformation Germany and Switzerland, 1400–1600.* Chicago: Chicago University Press, 2003.

Reyheri, Andrae *Thesaurus Latinitatis Universae Reherianus Recognitus Et Auctos.* Frankfurt: n.d., 1696.

Richelet, Cesar Pierre. *French Dictionary.* Paris: Chez Lovis Bilaine, Dans La Grand Salle Du Palais Au Second Pillier, À La Palme & Au Grand Cesar, 1680.

Rochette, Claude Lebrun de la. *Les proces civil et criminel divise en cinq livres.* 2 vols. Lyon: Roven, 1611.

Rocke, Michael. *Forbidden Friendships.* New York: Oxford University Press, 1996.

Rockwell, William. *Die doppelehe des landgrafen Philipp Von Hessen.* Marburg: Elwert, 1904.

Römer, L. S. A. M. von. "Der uranismus in den Niederlanden bis zum 19. Jahrhundert, mit besonderer berücksichtigung der grossen uranierverfolgung im jahre 1730." *Jahrbuch Für Sexuelle Zwischenstufen* 8 (1906) 365–512.

Roper, Lyndal. *The Holy Household: Women and Morals in Reformation Augsburg.* Oxford: Oxford University Press, 1989.

———. *Oedipus and the Devil.* New York, New York: Routledge, 1994.

Ruggiero, Guido. *The Boundaries of Eros.* Oxford: Oxford University Press, 1985.

Ruggiero, Laura Giannetti. "The Forbidden Fruit." *Quaderni D"Italianistica* 27 (2006) 31–52.

Rummel, Erika. "The Renaissance Humanists." In *A History of Biblical Interpretation,* edited by Alan J. Hauser and Duane F. Watson, 280–98. Grand Rapids: Eerdmans, 2009.

Salisbury, Joyce. *Sex and the Middle Ages.* New York: Garland, 1991.

Samuel, William. *A Warnyng for the Cittie of London that the Dwellers Therein May Repent Their Evyll Lyves for Feare of Goddes Plages.* London: By Me Humfrey Powell, Dewellinge [Sic] Aboue Holburne Conduit, and Are to Be Soulde by Hugh Syngleton at the Signe of Saint Augustine in Polles Churcharde, 1550.

Schneemelcher, Wilhelm, ed. *New Testament Apocrypha.* Rev. ed. Translated by Ed. R. Mcl. Wilson. Philadelphia: Westminster, 1991.

Schueren, Gert van der. *Teuthonista of Duytschlender*. Leiden: Herdingh En Du Mortier, 1804.

Scott, Thomas. *The Belgicke Pismire: Stinging the Slothfull Sleeper, and Auuaking the Diligent to Fast, Watch, Pray, and Worke Out Their Owne Temporall and Eternall Salvation with Feare and Trembling*. London: S. I., 1622.

Scroggs, Robin. *The New Testament and Homosexuality*. Philadelphia: Augsburg Fortress, 1983.

Skinner, Marilyn. *Sexuality in Greek and Roman Culture*. Malden, MA: Blackwell, 2005.

"Sodomy, N." OED Online. http://www.oed.com/view/entry/183887?redirectedfrom= sodomy.

Souter, Alexander. *A Pocket Lexicon to the Greek New Testament*. Oxford: Clarendon, 1917.

Spreitzer, Brigitte. *Die stumme stunde: homosexualitat in mittelalter mit einem textanbang*. Goppingen: Kummerle, 1988.

Stegemann, Victor. "Altenstaig, John." *New German Biography* 1 (1953).

Stephenson, Barry M. *Performing the Reformation: Public Ritual in the City of Luther*. Oxford: Oxford University Press, 2010.

Stevenson, Jane. "'Texts and Textiles: Self-Presentation Among the Elite in Renaissance England." *Journal of the Northern Renaissance* 3 (2011) 39–57.

Stoer, Jacob. *Le Grand Dictionnaire François-Latin, augmenté outre les precedentes impressions d'infinies dictions françoises, specialement des mots de marine, venerie, et faulconnerie. recuelli des observations de plusieurs hommes doctes: entre autres de M. Nicod Conseiller du Roy et Maistre des Requestes de L'hostel, et reduit à la forme et perfection des Dictionnaires Grecs et Latins*. Geneva: Jacob Stoer, 1593.

Stuart, James. *Basilkon Doron or His Majesties Instructions to his Dearest Sonne Henry the Prince*. London, 1603.

Suicer, Johan. *Lexicon Lexicon Graeco-Latinum Et Latino-Graecum*. Zurich: Gessnerus, 1683.

Sutton, John. "Leigh, Edward (1603–1671)." http://www.oxforddnb.com/view/article/16378.

Symson, Andrew. *Lexicon Anglo-Graeco Latinum Novi Testamenti*. London: W. Godbid, 1658.

Teasley, David. "'The Charge of Sodomy as a Political Weapon in Early Modern France: The Case of Henry III in Catholic League Polemic (1585–1589)." *Maryland Historian* 18 (1987) 17–30.

Tentler, Thomas. *Sin and Confessionn on the Eve of the Reformation*. Princeton: Princeton University Press, 1977.

Thesavrvs Thevtonicæ Lingvæ. schat der neder-duytscher spraken. inhoudende niet alleene de nederduytsche woorden. Antwerp: Ex Officina Christopheri Plantini, 1573.

Thierry, Jean, ed. *La Dictionnaire Francois-Latin*. Paris: J. Mace, 1564.

Thomas Aquinas, Saint. *Bible 4NTe Epistoles*. Venice: Peter of Bergamo, 1529.

———. *Ordinis Predicatorum Vire Et Vite Sanctimonia Et Sacarum Literarum Peritia Preclari, In Beati Pauli Apostoli Epistolas, Commentaria, A Mendis Repugatiora Ex Variarum Editionum Ac Betustissimorum Codicium Collatione. Additus Est Index Copiosissimus Rerum Scitu Diginarum*. Paris: Girault, 1529.

———. *Summa Theologia II–II*. Chicago: Encyclopaedia Britannica, 1980.

Thomas, William. *Principal Rules of the Italian Grammer: With a Dictionarie for the Better Vnderstandyng of Boccace, Petrarcha, and Dante: Gathered into this Tongue by William Thomas*. London: Thomas Berthelete, 1550.

Tomeo, Niccolo Leonico. "De Varia Historia Libri Tres." In *Same-Sex Desire in the English Renaissance*, edited by Kenneth Borris, 207–9. London: Routledge, 2004.

Tracy, James D. "Ad Fontes: The Humanist Understanding of Scripture as Nourishment for the Soul." In *Christian Spirituality II: High Middles Ages and Reformation*, edited by Jill Raitt, 252. New York: Crossroad, 1987.

Ulrich, Karl Friedrich. "Georg Pasor." In *Biographic-Bibliographic Church Encyclopedia*, 17:1358. Bautz: Herzberg, 2000.

Vallae, Laurentii. *Lavrentii Vallae, Viri Tam Graece Quam Latinae Linguae Doctissimi, In Nouum Testamentu Annotationes: Apprime Utiles*. Basel: n.d., 1526.

"Vorsterman, Willem." In *Digitale Bibliografe Nederlandse Geschiedenis*. https://www.kb.nl/en/nieuws/2016/studiemiddag-en-studieochtend-maken-of-breken-500-jaar-reformatie.

"Weakling, n." OED Online. http://www.oed.com/view/entry/226554?redirectedfrom=weaklings.

"Weldon, Sir Anthony (*Bap*. 1583, *D*. 1648)." http://www.oxforddnb.com/view/article/28988.

Weldon, Anthony. *The Court and Character of King James*. London: R.I., 1650.

Wenneker, Erich. "Olivetan, Pierre Robert." In *Biographisch-Bibliographisches Kirchenlexicon*, 12007–1209. Herzberg: Traugott Bautz, 1993.

Werner, Tschacher. "Nider, John." In *Encyclopedia of the History of Witch Hunts*, edited by V. Gudrun Gersmann et al. https://www.historicum.net/purl/jezsm/.

The Whole Volume of Statutes at Large, 2 Parts in 1 Volume. London: H. Denham and H. Middleton, 1587.

The Whole Volume of Statutes at Large, 2 Parts in 1 Volume. London: H. Denham and H. Middleton, 1587.

Wibbing, S. *Die dualistische struktur der paulinischen teugend und lasterkataloge en die teugend und laskterkataloge im Neuen Testament*. Berlin: A. Topelmann, 1959.

Wiesner-Hanks, Merry. *Christianity and Sexuality in the Early Modern World: Regulating Desire, Reforming Practice*. New York: Routledge, 2005.

Wilson, Thomas. *A Complete Christian Dictionary*. London: Thomas Wilson and Mary Clark, 1678.

Wood, Anthony. *Athenae Oxonienses*. 4 vols. Edited by P. Bliss. New End. 1813–1820 Hildesheim: n.d., 1969.

Wormald, Jenny. "James VI and I: Two Kings or One?" *History* 68 (1983) 187–209.

Wright, David F. "Homosexuals or Prostitutes? The Meaning of Ἀρσενοκοῖται (1 Cor. 6:9, 1 Tim. 1:10)." *Vigiliae Christianae* 38 (1984) 125–53

Wright, Stephen. "Wilson, Thomas (1562/3–1622)." http://www.oxforddnb.com/view/article/29689.

Winghe, Nicholas von. *Den Bibel inhovdende het ovdt ende niev testament: met cort beduytsel voor elck capittel, ende ghetal aen de canten, tot seker bewijsinghe der concordancien*. Antwerp: Christopheri Plantini, 1548.

Young, Michael B. "James VI and I: Time for a Reconsideration?" *The Journal Of British Studies* 51 (2012) 540–67.

Zedler, Johann Heinrich. *Grosses Vollständiges Universal-Lexicon Aller Wissenschafften Und Künste*. Band 26. Leipzig: n.d., 1740.

Zwingli, Huldrych. *Annotatiunculae Per Leonem Judae Ex Ore Zvinglii In Utranque Pauli Ad Corinthios Epistolam Publice Exponentis Conceptae*. Zurich: Christophori Froschouer, 1533.